RECLAIMING

OUR STORY

Also by Ben M. Freeman

Jewish Pride: Rebuilding a People

BEN M. FREEMAN

RECLAIMING

OUR STORY

The Pursuit of Jewish Pride

First published in 2022 by No Pasaran Media

ISBN 9781915036322

Also available as an ebook
ISBN 9781915036339

Typeset by seagulls.net
Cover design by Emma Ewbank
Project management by whitefox
Printed and bound by CPI Books Ltd

Photography credits

Róisín Jacobson: Andre L., Snappr Photography, San Francisco

Nicky Rawlinson: Emma Reisman Photography,
New York emrphoto@yahoo.com

Shoshana Batya Greenwald: Talya Bendel, CFD-Creative LLC,
Greater New York @carpefashiondiem

Avraham Vofsi: self-portrait, Melbourne @avrahamvofsi

Lyvia Tzamali: PKA Photography, San Diego @pka_photo / pkaphoto.com

Ben M. Freeman: Gary Swart, London @the_refined_fella

This book is dedicated to proud Jews everywhere.

CONTENTS

Thank you to the following people whose patience, love and support has enabled me to write this book, and build this movement:

Gary Swart
Dr Winston Pickett
Jessica Cohen
Eve Barlow
Joanna Mok
Dr Elizabeth Micci
Tracey Allen MBE
No Pasaran Media
All my students

And to my mother, Sarah, and my late father, Malcolm, thank you for building me a strong Jewish anchor.

PROLOGUE

My first boyfriend had a problem with Jews.

He didn't admit to this. But he did. He obsessively demonised Israel and would try to convince me that it was the worst country in the world, even as he disregarded the terrible records of other states. He even went as far as telling me that he could never marry me because he couldn't be connected to Israel, even if it was just through me and my family. He never succeeded in severing my relationship with Israel, but I stayed in this relationship and tolerated his Jew-hate for over a year.

At this point, you might be asking, as I have continuously asked in the decade since our relationship ended, 'How could I, the author of the Jewish Pride manifesto, *Jewish Pride: Rebuilding a People*, have stayed in a relationship with a Jew-hater?'

Sadly, I have come to realise that I was suffering from internalised anti-Jewishness. I accepted that to be in this relationship (which, as my first same-sex relationship, represented an important stage in my journey of self-acceptance) I had to diminish my Jewishness. I was so desperate to be in a relationship which I thought would heal the trauma I had experienced as a young gay teen in a homophobic world that I was willing to tolerate Jew-hate.

Although that was my story, I am not alone in these types of feelings. As I described in *Jewish Pride: Rebuilding a People*, while Jews have consistently defended and fought for our Jewishness, we also, at times, acquiesced to the demands of the non-Jewish world. During the late 18th and 19th centuries, we were coerced by 'enlightened' Western societies into defining ourselves as no more than a religious community, thus shedding the notion of Jewish nationhood which stretches back more than 3,000 years. This demand – rooted in the belief that Jewishness was somehow incompatible with truly belonging to our respective wider societies – led some Jews to diminish, or even totally discard, these central components of our identity.

While some may try to deny it, internalised anti-Jewishness is a global Jewish problem. In the 19th century, the German Jewish community, for instance, grappled with the difficulty of being Jewish in the Diaspora, as do members of the contemporary American Jewish community. And, in a more extreme example of internalised anti-Jewishness, there are Jews today who, through their rejection of Zionism, have discarded their inherent connection to our indigenous homeland, Israel. In so doing, they have accepted, and internalised, non-Jewish negative perceptions of the State of Israel. They, tragically, believe that disavowing Israel, the world's only Jewish state, makes them 'good Jews'. Sadly though, despite our attempts to be 'good Jews', no such thing exists. In truth, there are no 'good Jews' or 'bad Jews'. There are just Jews. These are just categories created by the non-Jewish world's perceptions of Jewish identity.

Suffering from internalised anti-Jewishness does not make you a bad Jew. It simply means you are experiencing a specific manifestation of deeply embedded hate. This is a crucial distinction. We must understand this phenomenon for what it is. It is not an individual failing. It is not a collective Jewish failing. It is a failing of the non-Jewish world that has been unable to overcome its hatred for us.

The effects of internalised anti-Jewishness are far-reaching. It destroys Jewish self-esteem and self-respect and reinforces shame and trauma and causes Jews to diminish or deny our Jewishness in order to be accepted by the non-Jewish majority. It teaches us to keep our heads down and not advocate for the Jewish community. To be embarrassed of being Jewish. So, as a response, we try to qualify our Jewishness with 'we're Jewish, but …' We are told, and sometimes we believe, that our Jewishness is less than, or inferior to, other identities we may have. We may even deploy our Jewishness as a weapon to justify Jew-hate, giving it a kosher seal of approval. And although we continue to suffer from it today, it is not simply a modern phenomenon. The threads of this Jewish response to anti-Jewish racism are visibly woven throughout our people's long history.

But we can fight this virus of hate that infects our peoplehood. Through Jewish Pride, we can bolster our Jewish self-esteem and defend ourselves against this non-Jewish bombardment of negativity.

Healing is a journey. It is both collective *and* personal. We must come together to discuss this phenomenon with empathy and we must support each other while we do our individual work to understand where we may express or embody manifestations of internalised Jew-hatred.

This book is not a polemic against those of us suffering from internalised anti-Jewishness. Instead, it is an attempt to throw open the doors of shame to cast light on this experience so we can begin the process of understanding it, identifying it and guarding against it. Nor is it a polemic against individual non-Jews. When I speak of 'the non-Jewish world', I am specifically referring to Jew-hate as an institutionalised, deeply embedded form of hate – one which impacts upon the system, ideology and culture of society, and shapes the thoughts and feelings of both Jews and non-Jews.

Jewish Pride rejects both the shame of Jew-hate imposed on Jews by the non-Jewish world as well as non-Jewish perceptions of what it means to be a Jew. It is a goal to work towards and a framework that helps us to truly understand ourselves – as both individuals and as a collective – and to recognise and celebrate the joy and beauty of Judaism and Jewishness. It is the future of the Jewish people.

As we embark on this journey, the primary thing to remember is that internalised anti-Jewishness is not our fault. It is the fault of the wider world which has persecuted us, shamed us, and traumatised us for millennia. But while the source of this problem may not be ours, we must be the ones to find a solution.

Quite simply, the continuation of a strong and proud Jewish people depends upon it.

INTRODUCTION

When I was in my late twenties, I received a text message from a friend. The message contained a video of him on vacation chatting to his holiday companion. Along with the video, came one short question: 'Does my voice sound gay?' My friend was an openly gay man who was successful and seemingly happy with his sexuality. But his question revealed to me that he was plagued by internalised homophobia. While, I knew, he was *mostly* comfortable being gay, his comfort clearly depended on him being a specific type of gay man. A 'palatable' gay man, as it were. He had to be masculine and 'straight acting' without any obvious characteristics that could identify him as gay. Any deviation from this self-imposed rule would be perceived as conforming to stereotypes, which were, in his mind, undesirable.

This experience is not unique in the LGBTQ+ community; it is sadly a common phenomenon. Among gay and bisexual men, those who conform to stereotypes, such as being effeminate, are commonly derided. On dating apps, people will state that they are not interested in meeting 'femmes', i.e. feminine men. Of course, for some this could be a simple matter of personal preference. However, it's very difficult to separate the personal from the world in which we live. We are, after all, the product of the environment around us. And what has the world told us about gay and bisexual men? For the most part, it has long told us that we are not 'real men', an idea rooted in misogyny and the notion that somehow femininity is less than masculinity.

Internalised homophobia does not just manifest itself in an attempt to present as masculine or derision of that which is considered feminine. It is rooted in the absorption of shame imposed on LGBTQ+ people by the heterosexual world. My own experiences with internalised homophobia led me to self-harm, investigate conversion therapy and even attempt suicide. Due to the trauma, shame and abuse LGBTQ+ people often receive at the hands of the wider world, we are four times more likely to attempt suicide than our heterosexual counterparts.

When understanding the feelings of isolation, pain and rejection that many LGBTQ+ people experience, we arrive at one of the most fundamental truths regarding internalised hate: it is not the fault of those who experience it. I came to this radical idea in my early twenties, when I was experiencing a particularly serious bout of mental ill health brought on by ongoing internalised homophobia. I realised that I had done nothing wrong. I was being punished by society for a crime I did not commit. It was the world around me that was guilty.

My experiences of internalised homophobia – and that of my friend and the wider gay community – led me to consider this phenomenon in the Jewish world. Just as my experience of working towards LGBTQ+ Pride inspired my first book on Jewish Pride, the manifesto of the modern Jewish Pride movement, the journey of identifying, categorising and ultimately combatting internalised anti-Jewishness also began with a journey I had already taken with regards to my gay identity.

My last book, *Jewish Pride: Rebuilding a People*, was not about fighting Jew-hate. It was about educating, inspiring and empowering Jewish people to stand with me as I build a modern Jewish Pride movement that gives Jews permission to reject the shame of Jew-hate and reject non-Jewish definitions of Jewish identity. However, this book *is* about fighting Jew-hate. But it's specifically about fighting internalised Jew-hate.

In our journey together, we will define internalised Jew-hate. We will explore how and why it occurs as well as the depths to which it exists in our people's long history, and the impact it continues to have on us today. And although this intellectual and emotional voyage may be uncomfortable and even, at times, painful, as with each stop on our exploration of Jewish identity, this is a journey towards healing, towards joy and, ultimately, towards pride.

Lively discussion and debate are an essential part of the Jewish experience. For millennia, Jews have come together to debate challenging ideas. So, in the spirit of *Chavurot* (Jewish discussion groups), to enrich this experience, please make sure you utilise the questions at the end of this book, before the notes; they are designed to facilitate your experience and to support you as you begin your own introspective journey as we heal and come to terms with our experiences. Feel free to get together with loved ones to discuss this book, or, if you prefer, to have an internal dialogue using the questions as your guide.

A UNIVERSAL PHENOMENON

As my friend's WhatsApp demonstrated, internalised prejudice is not a specifically Jewish problem. It is a phenomenon that impacts a variety of different communities. As the Jewish writer Theodor Lessing stated in his seminal work, *Der Jüdischer Selbsthaß* (Jewish Self-Hate), '[Self-hatred] is a phenomenon of the whole human race!'[1]

In our study of internalised hate this must be one of the first truths we accept. However, despite its clear presence in our own as well as other communities, there are Jews today who minimise its existence or who deny it outright. In 2018, for instance, the academic Jacqueline Rose published an article titled 'On the Myth of Jewish Self-Hatred'.[2] It is not a myth. Nor is it rare, as Daniel Levitas suggested in the 2002 article, 'Exploring What is Behind the Rare Phenomenon of Jewish anti-semites'.[3] It is a phenomenon that can, and often does, have a devastating impact on every Jew living in the Diaspora, and even those living in Israel.

In the years following the release of *Jewish Pride: Rebuilding a People*, I conducted hundreds of speaking engagements. In each one, although they took place all over the world, I was asked about internalised anti-Jewishness (a brief study of which featured in Chapter 4 of my first book). I have also received thousands of messages on social media from Jews, again from all over the world, telling me that Jewish Pride has helped them investigate and overcome their internalised anti-Jewishness. Far from being rare, sadly, this seems to be a Jewish pandemic. Minimising the frequency, or even the very existence, of this phenomenon in our community is dangerous. It leads to a situation whereby we suffer from an affliction but refuse to recognise it, which only creates a culture where our suffering is prolonged and we are unable to heal.

Explaining the Jewish reluctance to recognise this phenomenon, there is a notion that suffering from internalised anti-Jewishness makes you a weak Jew, or a bad Jew. However, understanding its prevalence in other communities is crucial as it frees us from these paralysing feelings of shame.

There are a huge number of important academic works that deal with this issue in numerous communities including the LGBTQ+ and Black communities, specifically in the United States. Black Americans have long analysed and documented their own complex relationship with internalised anti-Black racism. In her paper, *Levels of Racism: a Theoretic Framework and a Gardener's Tale*, Camara Phyllis Jones, a Black anti-racism activist, defines internalised anti-Black racism as one of three major manifestations of prejudice and describes it as the 'acceptance by members of the stigmatized races of negative messages about their own abilities and intrinsic worth. It is characterized by their not believing in others who look like them, and not believing in themselves. It involves accepting limitations to one's own full humanity, including one's spectrum of dreams, one's right to self-determination.'[4] Jones's work is significant, not least because it helps us understand that instead of being an individual failing, it is one of *the* major manifestations of prejudice.

James Baldwin, the controversial gay Black American writer, also discussed this issue in the Black community, writing, 'You know, it's not the world that was my oppressor, because what the world does to you, if the world does it to you long enough and effectively enough, you begin to do to yourself.'[5] Baldwin's words encapsulate the roots of internalised hate. If one lives in a hostile environment for long enough, then you can absorb and believe the negative messages, slurs and lies that you receive from the world around you. This results in a situation whereby you see your identity as a source of shame, so you parrot back these negative feelings about your own community. Baldwin's explanation of this in his own community has lessons for us in ours. Jew-hate, in its various manifestations, has plagued the world for literally thousands of years. It is not called 'the oldest hatred' without reason. So, let us create some distance between ourselves and the subject, take a step back and ask if we have been hated, abused, denigrated, oppressed and murdered for thousands of years, do we really think it's possible that we alone, out of all the world's marginalised groups, would not have absorbed negative ideas about our identities?

Baldwin's quote is also strikingly similar to one from Theodor Lessing. In 1929 he wrote, 'In order to change humans into dogs, all that is needed is to shout at them long enough, "You dog!"'[6] This similarity must not be ignored or diminished. The very same issues that Baldwin spoke of in the 1960s, Lessing wrote about in the 1920s.

Similarly, Hussein A. Bulhan, Founder and President of Frantz Fanon University in Hargeisa, Somaliland has written that 'The well-known inferiority complex of the oppressed originates in this process of internalization.' Bulhan argued 'because of this internalization and its attendant but repressed rage, the oppressed may act out, on each other, the very violence imposed on them. They become autopressors as they engage in self-destructive behavior injurious to themselves, their loved ones and their neighbors.'[7]

Bulhan's notion of an 'autopressor' is an interesting but potentially troubling term. While the evidence tells us that it is possible to be an anti-Black Black person, a homophobic gay person or an anti-Jewish Jewish person, the fact of the matter is that these feelings of prejudice did not originate in the specific individual. It was imposed on them, through years of conditioning, by their respective wider world. Moreover, although the same process can be applied to the majority who have been taught to view the minority through specific lenses, the hate the majority espouses is about the other, not the self. This term, much like 'Jewish antisemitism', does not therefore necessarily help us understand the source of this internalised hate.

The connections between Black and Jewish internalised hate are not new and were especially evident from the 1940s to the 1960s when Jewish refugees moved from Europe to the US. In her paper *The Vogue of Jewish Self-Hatred in Post-World War II America,* historian Susan Glenn writes, 'The conceptual vogue of Jewish self-hatred and its analogue "Negro self-hatred" was part of the broader psychological moment in American social science, public policy, and public culture, a development influenced by the arrival of refugee scholars from Nazi Germany.'[8] And in reference to the issue of internalised hatred in both communities, Frantz Fanon, the psychiatrist and political philosopher, referred to Jews and Black people as 'brother[s] in misery.'[9]

Ultimately, although this book focuses specifically on internalised hate in the Jewish community, understanding its presence in numerous other communities is vital in helping us understand its prevalence on our own. In short, if internalised hatred exists in the LGBTQ+ and the Black communities, how could it not exist in the Jewish community?

CONSEQUENCES OF INTERNALISED HATRED

Beyond recognising the fact that internalised hate exists in various communities, we must now consider the consequences of this experience. The minority stress model first used to describe the experiences of LGBTQ+ people 'refers to the additional stress that members of marginalized groups experience because of the prejudice and discrimination they face.'[10] This model specifically examines the issue of internalised hate. It states that, over time, 'negative internal responses for those who experience those events, such as ... [leads to] internalized negative beliefs about their own race, gender or sexual identities.' Given Baldwin's and Lessing's views on how hate becomes internalised, it is important to recognise that this puts an additional mental strain on the individual. To belong to a group that you feel ashamed of can lead to self-esteem and mental health issues. Professors June Tangney of George Mason University and Ronda L. Dearing of the University of Houston have, for instance, found that 'shame-proneness can also increase one's risk for other psychological problems. The link with depression is particularly strong; for instance, one large-scale meta-analysis in which researchers examined 108 studies involving more than 22,000 subjects showed a clear connection.'[11]

Not only does internalised hate harm the mental health of the individual, it is also harmful to the collective. The whole of the Jewish community is compromised by individual Jews diminishing and denying their Jewishness. As we will see later, internalised anti-Jewishness leads entire Jewish communities to warp and change their Jewish identity in an attempt to be accepted by the non-Jewish world. It leads entire Jewish communities to shed Jewish practice in order to be seen as 'good Jews'. Internalised anti-Jewishness leads to the destruction of Jewish self-esteem and can, in the most extreme circumstances, seriously damage Jewish life.

Remarkably, the Jewish people have been sustained in exile for thousands of years. Although our culture and practice evolved in the Diaspora, we remained at our core rooted in our original indigenous culture. This is what sustained us and ensured our survival against all odds. However, internalised anti-Jewishness can lead Jews to see their distinct Jewishness as a source of shame, and not pride. It can lead Jews to see their Jewishness as less important than other identities they may have. It leads Jews to accept watered-down versions of Jewish culture and identity. That's why internalised anti-Jewishness is, quite simply, the single greatest internal threat facing the Jewish people as it leads us to abandon (or at the very least weaken) our commitment to the continuation of Jewish life.

DEFINING THE TERMS

Since the 19th century, there have been different terms proposed to describe this phenomenon. From *Jüdischer Antisemitismus* (Jewish antisemitism) utilised by the Austrian writer, Karl Krauss, to the idea of the 'inauthentic Jew',[12] coined by Jean-Paul Sartre, different Jewish thinkers have attempted to describe this internalised Jew-hate. However, they do not provide us with enough nuance to truly understand this phenomenon.

Although, as we will see, there are those, such as Theodor Lessing, who refer to this phenomenon as 'self-hatred', (or some variation) that is also an imperfect description of this experience that emerged from a specific milieu. Breaking this phrase, my friend who sent the text message did not hate himself, and though he experienced internalised homophobia, there were aspects of his gay identity that he was very proud of. In reality, feelings of internalised prejudice are so much more nuanced than the term 'self-hate' implies.

Self-hate, similarly to autopression (as described by Hussein A. Bulhan), inadvertently implies that the issue begins within the individual. This is not the case. As psychologists recognise, individuals who hate themselves 'assign disproportionate weight to their faults and overlook their strengths.'[13] The most significant part of that description are the words 'their faults'. To describe a Jew as self-hating is to imply that Jewishness *is* a fault or a flaw that one recognises and reacts against. This is not the case. Jew-hate is a non-Jewish problem and although Jews are disadvantaged in the non-Jewish world, this is not because there is anything wrong with being a Jew.

The hatred we experience does not begin within us. And although it targets us, shames us and wounds us, it is a problem that begins outside ourselves. As we will see, anti-Jewish sentiment played a foundational role in building many non-Jewish societies and ideologies. Jew-hate is rooted in a fantasy version of the Jew. It says Jews are unnatural, immoral, perverse, corrupt and are, ultimately, the centre of all evil. These are non-Jewish perspectives on Jews, but by describing Jews, or any other group, as 'self-hating' we imply that the problem is 'ours'.

Instead, some variation of 'internalised anti-Jewishness' or 'internalised anti-Jewish racism' offers a much more empathetic and nuanced understanding of this experience. The Cambridge Dictionary defines the word 'internalised' as: 'to accept or absorb an idea, opinion, belief, etc. so that it becomes part of your character'.[14] This is a more accurate definition of this experience. Their use of the word 'absorb' tells us that that the source of the problem begins outside the individual Jew and then, through a process not dissimilar to osmosis, it passes through the defence membrane and ends up as part of our psychological make-up. By using the term internalised Jew-hate (or another variation of this), we acknowledge that the problem is not a Jewish problem, it is a non-Jewish problem that impacts the psyche and lived experiences of Jews.

A MEANS OF ATTACK?

Because many Jews minimise this phenomenon and pretend it does not exist, discussion around it can be dismissed as simply polemical. It can also be perceived, and used, as a way to attack Jews you disagree with. The historian Todd Endelman, for instance, argues that the idea of internalised anti-Jewishness would be 'foolish to apply ... indiscriminately to any and all Jews who attacked or derided the habits and manners of other Jews'.[15] This is a legitimate concern, so we must then ensure that the idea of internalised anti-Jewish sentiment is not used in such a fashion. It is not acceptable to use this term to attack Jews with whom we simply disagree. Disagreement, debate and dialogue is a much-valued part of Jewish tradition; we cannot disregard that just because differing opinions may make us feel threatened or uncomfortable. Crucially, we must recognise that internalised anti-Jewish sentiment is not the same as Jewish self-criticism. The latter, as we know, can come from a place of love and a desire to see our community progress and better itself. The denial of a *Get* (a Jewish divorce) to Jewish women is an example of misogynistic abuse. To criticise this harshly is not internalised Jew-hate. It is a legitimate and fair criticism aimed at improving the progress of our people.

Nonetheless, it is also the case that, even with a clear and solid definition, the idea of internalised anti-Jewishness can still be dismissed as simply an attack. I myself have been accused of this when I referred on Twitter to the actor Seth Rogen as suffering from internalised anti-Jewish racism. I suggested this after Rogen argued that Israel 'makes no sense whatsoever.'[16] Rogen fits what I define to be the criteria for internalised anti-Jewish sentiment, namely, the absorption of non-Jewish ideas about Jewish experience and history and the discarding of key aspects of Jewish identity, such as nationhood and our indigeneity to the Land of Israel.

However, we must once again reiterate that Jews like Rogen are not the villains in this story. He may possess a huge public platform, meaning he is able to share his perspectives more widely than most people, but he is still a Jew living in the non-Jewish world. He is still experiencing the unequal power dynamic and he has inherited a Jewish identity long warped by his ancestors in order to be accepted by the non-Jewish world and to circumvent anti-Jewish hate. This accusation, however, demonstrates just how difficult these conversations can be (particularly over social media). That is why we must, as a community, come together and have respectful communal discussions about these issues. We cannot ignore them and we certainly cannot attempt to understand them without the relevant history and contextualisation.

It is not the case that internalised anti-Jewishness only impacts one kind of Jew. As my interviews will illuminate, many kinds of Jews experience this phenomenon. When addressing this problem, we must understand that this is not about judgement. We must be empathetic to ourselves and one another. This is not about framing this experience as 'your story', and not mine. As I share my own experiences with internalised anti-Jewishness throughout this book, you will see this is my story too. It is the story of many Jews living in the world. Even those who live in Israel.

To ensure the causes and manifestations of this phenomenon are widely understood, there must be, as Endelman argues, 'ground rules for its usage'.[17] Therefore, we have to establish a very clear definition for utilising the idea of internalised anti-Jewishness. This is only possible, however, through properly understanding how and why it has manifested both historically as well as currently in our community.

Establishing a clear definition is complex. How can we discuss this issue in a community of people already suffering from this phenomenon? Are we as a collective ready to engage in introspection and free ourselves of this manifestation of hate? This work will only be possible if we create a culture of introspection and of support. To embark on this work successfully, we need to have empathy and patience.

Another complexity lies in the diversity of the Jewish people. It is difficult to create rules that all Jews could agree to. The solution is not to create a dogmatic and inflexible rule book that treats Jews as a monolith and destroys diversity, debate and dialogue. Rather, we should work to acknowledge some basic truths about our identity and experience. This is what this book aims to do while providing a framework that will help both individual Jews and Jewish communities to work towards a solution.

A WORKING DEFINITION OF INTERNALISED ANTI-JEWISHNESS: CAUSE IS CRUCIAL

Many great Jewish thinkers have grappled with the notion of internalised anti-Jewishness. Salo Baron, referred to as 'the greatest Jewish historian of the 20th century',[18] wrote of the notion of 'inverted Marranos'.[19] This was in reference to the Crypto-Jews, from pre-Inquisition Spain and Portugal, who were forced to convert to Catholicism but maintained their Jewish identity in secret. The 'inverted Marranos', by contrast, outwardly identified as Jews, but were uncomfortable with this internally. Baron states the inverted Marranos were 'recognized as Jews by themselves and their environment' but sadly, they 'deeply resent this fact.'

Baron's is but one explanation for internalised anti-Jewishness. My offering to the debate on definitions of internalised hatred is rooted in the idea that minority groups absorb the hate that surrounds them. This can present itself in a variety of ways, and, although it is easy to focus on the more extreme manifestations of this phenomenon, there are also more subtle expressions of internalised anti-Jewishness which can impact even those who feel proudly Jewish. Indeed, 20th-century German American psychologist Kurt Lewin said that this issue can be 'indirect' and 'under-cover'.[20] He described a Jew with internal-ised Jew-hatred as a 'marginal man'. This man is caught between two worlds, the Jewish and the non-Jewish, and as a result, belongs fully to neither, he is 'neither here nor there'. Lewin argued that the marginal man 'will dislike everything specifically Jewish, for he will see in it that which keeps him away from the majority for which he is longing. He will show dislike for those Jews who are outspokenly so and will frequently indulge in self-hatred.' Ultimately, these various manifesta-tions of internalised anti-Jewishness, which we will explore further in Chapter 2, can be seen in Jews **diminishing**, **denying** or **deploying** their Jewishness as a weapon.

This understanding then leads us to our working definition of internalised anti-Jewish hate. When seeking a definition, instead of focusing on the varied and distinct manifestations we have briefly mentioned, we should focus instead on the cause. There are mul-tiple ways a Jew can feel and express internalised anti-Jewishness, and by creating a definition that is too specific or narrow, we would fail to grasp the true scale and scope of this phenomenon. It would be very easy, particularly within the modern context, to offer a defin-ition based solely on Jewish antizionism. This is undoubtedly a form of internalised Jew-hate. However, not everyone who experiences internalised anti-Jewishness rejects Israel. There are many Jews who feel pride in their Jewishness and who understand and celebrate our connection to Israel but who also experience elements of internal-ised Jew-hatred. So, an explanation rooted in its varied manifestations does not allow us to connect the dots and spot patterns between seem-ingly disparate experiences of internalised anti-Jewish hate.

Our classification must be both general enough to explain a var-iety of Jewish responses while also being specific enough to allow people to truly understand how this manifests in our community. These various understandings lead us to my definition of internalised anti-Jewishness:

'When Jews absorb non-Jewish perceptions of Jews, Jewishness and Judaism and allow the non-Jewish world to define our narrative.'

This definition is rooted in the erasure of Jewish identity and experience which, as we will learn, has a variety of manifestations. It can explain, for instance, how a Jew could identify as, say, an antizionist. Antizionist Jews have absorbed non-Jewish (and specifically Soviet, Arab and Leftist) ideas about the State of Israel which delegitimise and demonise the Jewish state and hold it to standards to which no other state is held. They have internalised the propaganda that was designed to strip Jews of their indigeneity to the Levant. These Jews, in turn, reject any Jewish connection to our homeland in the Land of Israel. However, this definition can also be used to explain why someone who *is* a Zionist and who feels pride in their Jewishness may also feel shame about their Jewish practice or why they may feel compelled to demonstrate that they are 'just like their non-Jewish friends'. Jewish specificity has been shamed for hundreds of years and many Jews can feel embarrassed about the particularities of our practice and experience. They feel Jewish Pride, but they also want to fit in with the wider world by denying elements of their Jewishness.

Crucially, our journey, which ultimately leads us towards Jewish Pride, requires a huge amount of work and introspection. It requires all Jews, even those who feel proud of their Jewishness, to look inside themselves to see if and where they may have absorbed aspects of anti-Jewishness. If we find elements of this within us, we must not feel ashamed. There is nothing to be ashamed of. Though there are those, such as the early 20th-century writer Martin Englander, who argued that Jews have a special proclivity for internalised prejudice. This is not true. This is a well-established manifestation of hatred, and what's more, while it is our responsibility to combat it, this experience is not our fault. It is the fault of the world around us.

PRIDE OR PREJUDICE?

'"What", one replies, "should the Jews do?" The question is not to be answered. And there is no response, this created an embarrassment of conscience. How can these difficulties be dealt with?"[21] These words, written by Theodor Lessing in 1930, ring shockingly true today. Although this is a disquieting thought, there is very little Jews can do to combat Jew-hatred on a societal level. It is a deeply embedded ideology present all over the world and in every strata of society. History has shown us repeatedly that we cannot make the non-Jewish world accept us; after all, Jew-hatred is not a Jewish problem. For many Jews in the Diaspora, this statement is radical. It is shocking to consider that a world, our world, the world in which we live, the societies to which we contribute, do not really accept us as our authentic selves. The truth is though that, despite moments of apparent acceptance, Jews have never really been truly welcomed by non-Jewish society, not without huge caveats. Indeed, despite the trust many of us put in it after the Shoah – that it would finally learn the lessons of the past – the world has failed to do so.

A joint report commissioned by the World Zionist Organization and the Jewish Agency found that 2021 was the worst year in a decade for global Jew-hate. The report goes on to argue that the situation is in all likelihood much worse than even it suggests as many incidents are not reported.[22] From the surge in Jew-hate in the British Labour party under its former leader, Jeremy Corbyn, to the brutal murder of retired French doctor and school teacher Sarah Halimi and the subsequent miscarriage of justice, to the various terrorist attacks at American synagogues, we are seeing a tsunami of Jew-hate rise up and threaten to engulf us. Despite the instinct we have to fight anti-Jewish hate, there is nothing that Jews can do to truly defeat it; that is the work of the non-Jewish world. All we can (and must) do is fight to reclaim our dignity and to keep it at bay while encouraging the non-Jewish world to set upon its own task.

Regardless of our inability to defeat Jew-hatred, we do have choices. We can choose how we respond to it. Once again, in our people's long history, we are standing at a familiar crossroads. As with all crossroads we are faced with a choice. We can choose between two different paths. A path towards Jewish Pride or a path towards internalised anti-Jewish prejudice.

We must choose between pride or prejudice.

Though the choice we should make is clear, the journey along the road to pride is long and involves real work. We must look inside ourselves, we must investigate how we really feel about our Jewishness and why, and we must decide to heal ourselves in order to utilise, feel and express genuine Jewish Pride.

The path to prejudice does not involve any work. For many of us, it is just a continuation of our journeys to date. Yet, as the road dissects, and the path to prejudice moves further and further away from the road to pride, it becomes harder and harder to find our way back to Jewish Pride. Not necessarily impossible, but certainly much more difficult.

Though we have grappled with this issue for millennia, and thinkers such as early 20th-century philosopher and theologian Josef Prager and psychoanalyst Fritz Wittels have written about it, we have failed to heed their warnings. We have failed to learn the lessons of the past. And now, we must try again.

We must understand how and why this phenomenon exists in our people. We must approach it with empathy and an open mind. And, most importantly, we must create a culture where we, as a people, can heal.

Ultimately, that is what this issue boils down to. Though we have a huge amount to be proud of, we have experienced equal amounts of trauma and pain. We have experienced thousands upon thousands of years of deeply embedded hate. We have inherited the trauma of those who survived multiple genocides, ethnic cleansings, enslavements and legal persecution and segregation. Even without the continuation of anti-Jewish hate, our people experience intergenerational trauma. This trauma can make us afraid to be Jewish to such an extent that we would rather deny or diminish our Jewishness entirely, rather than cope with the reality of being a Jew in the non-Jewish world. The scars and pain we experience are real and tangible, and then, in addition, we also face the continuation of these ancient trends today. We have seen the renormalisation of Jew-hate and it is frightening.

Lessing offers his own solution to the issue of internalised Jew-hate:

'Who are you? Are you the son of Nathan the shifty Jew merchant who accidentally inseminated sluggish Sarah because she brought him a large dowry? No! Your father was Judah the Maccabee, Queen Esther was your mother. The chain continues from you, although some links may be defective, to Saul, David, and Moses. They are in all things present and past and be again in the future'[23]

So, the question today is, do we believe the non-Jewish world when it threatens us and demonises us? Do we believe it when it fails to respect our ancient civilisation and identities? Or do we reject this hate and begin the journey of understanding who we really are? We are the descendants of the Maccabees and the Warsaw Ghetto Up-risers, brave Jews who fought for their rights to live in the world as Jews. We will not warp or change ourselves any longer to be accepted. We will not feel embarrassed to be Jewish.

To be Jewish is to be part of a four-thousand-year-old ancient civilisation that has contributed untold marvels to the world. We have survived and we have thrived. And that is nothing to be ashamed of. We must look to our history and our ancestors with the framework of Jewish Pride and we must understand that the issue of Jew-hate has absolutely nothing to do with Jews. It is a virus that infects the non-Jewish world. But we must vaccinate ourselves and stop it from entering our own minds and bodies.

We must choose the path to pride. We must begin this journey and we must commit ourselves to this work. Otherwise, the continuation of the Jewish people is at risk. And even if we do manage to survive, we will exist as a mere shadow of our once-great civilisation. We must not allow that to happen. We must choose pride.

Chapter 1

BUT WHY?

'To be a Jew in a non-Jewish world has always been and will continue to be a handicap in more ways than one.'[24]

Trude Weiss-Rosmarin, 1947

Internalised anti-Jewishness, with its various manifestations, is a result of several factors, which we will explore in this chapter. All are complex and all stem from deeply embedded societal hate which ultimately harms Jews in very tangible ways. Discussing these deeply ingrained phenomena is not designed to shame or blame individuals. Internalised Jew-hatred (and Jew-hatred itself) is an issue much bigger than individual Jews (or non-Jews). Exploring this issue and its main causes will allow us to let in the light and increase understanding of an important and tragic by-product of the world's oldest hatred.

THE BROKEN MIRROR OF JEWISH IDENTITY: GOOD AND BAD JEWS

Our perceptions of ourselves are rooted in images reflected back to us by the people around us. These reflections are our mirrors. This functions on both an individual and a collective level. However, when understanding this phenomenon, in particular reference to Jews, we must acknowledge two truths. First, that the non-Jewish world simply has no right to define Jewish identity. Only Jews get to do that.

And, secondly, because Jew-hatred is so deeply embedded in society, non-Jewish reflections and definitions of our identity and experience are nearly always harmful.

The Broken Mirror of Jewish identity is the non-Jewish reflection of Jewish identity back to Jews, who then use it to define themselves. Warped by Jew-hate, the image we see of ourselves reflected back at us is broken. It is not a true reflection. It is rooted in the erasure of authentic Jewish identity by a world obsessed with Jews. 'Self-hatred results from outsiders' acceptance of the mirage of themselves generated by their reference group – the group in society that they see as defining them – as reality,'[25] writes historian Sander Gilman in *Jewish Self-Hatred: Anti-Semitism and the Hidden Language of the Jews*. The dynamic by which Jews absorb non-Jewish reflections of Jewish identity is also rooted in the imbalance of power between the minority (Jews) and the majority (non-Jews). Despite all the accusations and myths about all-powerful Jews – which have been propagated for millennia – the reality is, we are a tiny minority which has attempted to interact, and navigate relations, with much greater powers. So, for thousands of years, Jews have constantly negotiated a world defined not only by a majority but a majority rooted in Jew-hatred.

Although the dual identities – British and Jewish, for instance – that many diasporic Jews have can make it difficult and complex to recognise, we must acknowledge that the societies whose eyes we see ourselves reflected in were formed, at least in part, through Jew-hatred. This is exemplified by the 4th-century homily, *Adversus Judaeos* (Against the Jews), which was directed at Christians who were still following certain Jewish traditions. It ultimately utilised accusations of Jewishness and Judaising as a way to demonise and denigrate those considered to be unsavoury by the Christian rulers. This concept was part of the evolution of Christian identity and ideology, which in turn went on to form the roots of our societies in the West. The utilisation of ideas of Jews, Judaism and Jewishness to build non-Jewish identities means that Jew-hate is buried deep in the ideological foundations of the non-Jewish world.

As a result, on some level, parts of the non-Jewish world are at their core inherently hostile to Jews. This, of course, is not the fault of non-Jewish individuals. They are born into this culture, just as Jews are. And just like Jews, they are shaped by the societal constructs and ideologies of the world around them. However, they are (even inadvertently) the ones who spread and, ultimately, help evolve the deeply embedded Jew-hatred present in the world.

In this environment, as Gilman's definition indicates, the minority group becomes unable to distinguish between fantasy and reality. This relates to our working definition of internalised anti-Jewishness and it is crucial. If, as Jews, we recognise that non-Jewish definitions and expectations of our identity (for example, the idea that Jews are simply a religious community or seeing Jewish identity as incompatible with membership of a wider society) are false, then they become easier to reject. Similarly, we need to recognise the lies which underpin the various libels that have been levelled against us for centuries. These include the Economic Libel (the idea that Jews are obsessed with money); the Blood Libel (the notion that Jews are bloodthirsty predators); the Racial Libel (the racialisation of Jews either through ancestry or physical appearance); and the Conspiracy Fantasy (the idea that Jews are locked in a conspiracy to control the world).

By contrast, if we accept the non-Jewish world's false claims, lies and libels about Jews, internalise them (or parts of them) and begin to see ourselves through non-Jewish reflections, we mistake these anti-Jewish ideas to be our reality. This, in turn, impacts how we view ourselves and the rest of our community. It ultimately leads Jews to see our relationship with Jewishness through a warped prism. Our relationship with Jewishness is thus reframed and, if we don't conform to how the non-Jewish world views us, we are made to see it as a source of shame and not pride.

A particularly significant example of when Jews adopted non-Jewish reflections and expectations of their identity occurred in 18th-century France when Jews shed the notion of Jewish nationhood – their connection to the Land of Israel, our indigenous homeland – in order to fully integrate into French society. In 1789 French nobleman and politician Stanislas Marie Adélaïde, Comte de Clermont-Tonnerre, demanded:

'We must refuse everything to the Jews as a nation and accord everything to the Jew as an individual. They must be citizens ... every one of them must individually become a citizen. If they do not want this, they must inform us and we shall then be compelled to expel them. The existence of a nation within a nation is unacceptable in our country.'[26]

French Jews' understandable desire to be accepted led them to acquiesce to the Comte's demand and adopt the French reflection of acceptable Jewishness as their own. In 1791 an anonymous letter to the *La Chronique de Paris* argued that 'France ... is our Palestine, its mountains are our Zion, its rivers our Jordan. Let us drink the water of these sources; it is the water of liberty ...!'[27] Thus, after over 3,000 years of Jewish nationhood, French Jews rejected our connection to the Land of Israel because of the pressures that emanated from French society and their hope and desperation for a future which would enable them to overcome the torments of the past. Ultimately, the acceptance and internalisation of the modern non-Jewish post-Enlightened European idea that Jews must only be a religious group was one of the most damaging changes made to Jewish identity in the last several hundred years.

Through the erasure of Jewish identity and the imposition of non-Jewish perspectives upon us, the Broken Mirror creates categories of 'good Jews'. 'Good Jews' are those who conform to the Broken

Mirror of Jewish identity. The French Jews who proclaimed France as their Palestine are, per the non-Jewish world's perspective, 'good Jews'. This, as famed psychoanalyst Anna Freud argued, is a Jewish attempt to 'identify with the oppressor'[28], i.e. the non-Jewish world.

We may initially assume that a Jew suffering from internalised anti-Jewish hate will simply try to shed their Jewishness and live their life as a non-Jew. However, the complexity of identity means that it is possible for Jews to suffer from internalised anti-Jewishness while still living a Jewish life, or at least a version of Jewish life, particularly if they are able to conform to non-Jewish expectations of 'good Jews'.

Similarly, to the concept of yin and yang, there must be balance. So, the existence of a 'good Jew' necessitates the existence of a 'bad Jew'. 'Bad Jews' are those who refuse to conform to non-Jewish demands and expectations, warp their identities or change themselves to be accepted. Today, Zionist Jews are thought of as 'bad Jews' by antizionist Jews, who see us as complicit in colonialism and the oppression of the Palestinians and not representative of Jewish values. In an attempt to further ingratiate themselves into their respective non-Jewish societies, we repeatedly see a pattern where 'good Jews' feel compelled to demonise 'bad Jews' to prove their worth and to emphasise their palatability. This dynamic of 'good Jew' or 'bad Jew' is a direct result of warped Jewish identities reflected by the Broken Mirror of Jewish identity, which we will explore throughout the rest of this book.

In the 19th century, an idea known as *Wissenschaft des Judentums* ('Science of Judaism') emerged that reflected this 'good Jew'–'bad Jew' dynamic. A result of the *Haskalah* (the Jewish Enlightenment that followed the wider Enlightenment), it was a Jewish academic exercise in understanding Jewish history through, what the Leo Baeck Institute describes as, 'new methods of textual study, especially philology and history, to the study of Jewish texts and the history of Judaism.'[29] The use of the term *Wissenschaft* was an important statement by Jews which effectively declared: this is a scientific approach to the study of Judaism, on par with non-Jewish academic work. It was thus an attempt to further advocate for Jewish emancipation and integration into non-Jewish ideas of identity by arguing that Jewish identity – rooted in Jewish history – is rational and therefore compatible with modernity.

Although *Wissenschaft*, at its core, was an attempt to study Judaism and Jewishness using the same methods as non-Jewish academic study, some of those who participated in it assumed that traditional rabbinic-Judaism was a thing of the past, and was, therefore, an ancient relic. As such, so, too, were Jews who continued to practise rabbinic-Judaism. The proponents of this strand of *Wissenschaft* viewed their Judaism, which rejected Jewishness rooted in religious superstition and rituals, as a modern Judaism. This Jewish denigration of Judaism was, however, a reflection of a non-Jewish perspective, which viewed traditional Jewishness as inferior to, and incompatible with, Christian culture. Georg Wilhelm Friedrich Hegel, the famed German philosopher, even went so far as to state: 'The tragedy of the Jewish people is not a Greek tragedy[;] it cannot evoke fear or compassion, since both of them arise from a necessary false step of a beautiful creature, while that [destiny of the Jews] can only arouse repugnance. The destiny of the Jewish people is the fate of Macbeth, who had to be crushed by his own beliefs.'[30] Thus the long and ancient civilisation built by Jews was deemed to be worthless.

A modern study of Judaism is, of course, not inherently problematic. But the way in which many of those who participated in this movement viewed aspects of traditional (particularly) Ashkenazi Jewish culture was highly questionable. As Ilana Maymind, Lecturer at Chapman University, argued, the aim of *Wissenschaft* 'was to rebuild Judaism for a newly conceived emancipated Jew.'[31] In this world, the emancipated Jews were the 'good Jews' and the traditional Jews were the 'bad Jews'.

As a result, some of those who promoted *Wissenschaft des Juden-tums* even came to believe that this academic pursuit, and their modernity, made them superior to other, more traditional Jews. In 1812 David Friedländer wrote in *Über die Verbesserung der Israeliten im Königreich Pohlen* (About the Improvement of the Israelites in the Kingdom of Poland) that the Polish Jews were 'the most cloddish and unrefined class of human beings. In terms of culture and morality they stand on the lowest level next to wild animals.'[32] Similarly, at the end of the 19th century, the Jewish historian Heinrich Graetz wrote *Geschichte der Juden* (History of the Jews), in which he referred to Yiddish as a 'half-bestial language.'[33]

This denigration of Eastern and Orthodox Jews and Judaism was an expression of the assimilated Jews' desperate attempt to integrate into German society. Instead of standing tall and disagreeing with Hegel and those in the non-Jewish world who saw Jewish culture as inferior and incompatible, they demonised other Jews and Judaism to prove their own worth. Ultimately, such portrayals of *Ost Juden* (Eastern Jews) as 'bad Jews' created distance between them and the *Maskilim* (Jews of the Haskalah), who sought to sever connections which they believed would corrupt the work done by German Jews to integrate.

In *Jewish Self-Hatred*, Sander Gilman draws a parallel between the German Jewish intellectuals of the 19th century and Jewish converts to Christianity in the Middle Ages (which we will explore in detail later). To an extent, both groups felt protected from anti-Jewish hate but couldn't escape their own insecurity and 'nagging sense of self-doubt'[34] regarding their Jewishness (because, as we know, Jewishness is not simply a religion that one can easily shed). To soothe this self-doubt, these Jews had to find a physical manifestation of their Jewishness to react against, like the Eastern Jews.

In *Future Tense: Jews, Judaism, and Israel in the Twenty-First Century*, the late Rabbi Lord Sacks argued: 'At some stage Jews stopped defining themselves by the reflection they saw in the eyes of God and started defining themselves by the reflection they saw in the eyes of their Gentile neighbours.'[35] Attempting to understand who you are, who you really are, through the perceptions of others can never result in an honest reflection. Especially if the mirror is broken.

JEWISH TRAUMA

Jews are not victims. We are survivors. We are a people who, against the odds and through an undying commitment to Jewish life, have survived everything that can be thrown at a people. A major component of Jewish Pride is celebrating Jewish resilience in all its forms. We take as our inspiration the Jews in displaced persons' camps after the Shoah who exclaimed in Yiddish '*Mir sinnen do!*' (We are here!)

However, despite our fortitude, the immense historical and ongoing trauma inflicted by the non-Jewish world upon Jews has often reframed Jewishness in the minds of Jews. In some cases, trauma has led Jews to forget Jewish joy and view Jewishness as something that brings nothing but pain, shame and hurt. At the outset of this discussion, we must therefore acknowledge that internalised anti-Jewishness (as is the case with all internalised prejudice) is a response to trauma.

Though most of us have an understanding of what is meant by 'trauma', it is helpful to establish a definition that will better enable us to understand its impact on our people. In Chapter Five of *Breaking Intergenerational Cycles of Repetition: A Global Dialogue on Historical Trauma and Memory*, Bjorn Krondorfer, the Director of the Martin-Springer Institute and Endowed Professor of Religious Studies at Northern Arizona University, writes that 'trauma is caused by severe violations of integrity (often described as a shattering of self and the world), and it has a lingering, long term-impact.'[36]

With this in mind, most Jews I speak with cannot remember when they first learned of the Shoah. They say that it has always been a part of their understanding of our history, our story. If we take a step back for a moment and gain some distance from our experiences, we can acknowledge that, while incredibly common, this is damaging to our integrity and our place in the world and is therefore traumatising. Although we may be removed from it by several generations, Jews grow up knowing that, within living memory, many of the Western world's governments conspired (either through direct action and the murder or facilitation of the murder of Jews or inaction and standing by) to murder every single Jewish man, woman and child they came into contact with. Our loss is almost incalculable and this loss is still felt keenly by Jews all over the world. This trauma also exists regardless of each Jew's individual connection to the Holocaust. I personally do not know if any of my family members were murdered by the Nazis and their allies, but that does not mean that I do not experience intergenerational trauma because of it. Growing up in the shadow of such a catastrophe has an impact upon one's sense of self, safety and security.

It is also the case that the trauma of the Holocaust is not the only source of collective pain and trauma that Jews have to contend with: Mizrahi and Sephardic Jews living today understand the experiences of their families living under legal segregation and oppression. They understand what it means to be a *dhimmi* (second-class citizen). They know of the Farhud (the 1941 Pogrom against Baghdadi Jews that saw the murder of an estimated 1,000 Jews) and various Pogroms experienced by Jews in the Middle East and North Africa throughout history. They know that, despite their presence in countries like Yemen or Iraq for thousands of years, Jewish communities were ethnically cleansed and were forced to seek refuge in the newly formed State of Israel.

Sephardic Jews also know the pain of multiple ethnic cleansings and genocides. First from our homeland, Israel, and then later their homes in Spain and Portugal in the 15th century. They know the horror of the forced conversion and they understand the cultural genocide that was committed against them while they were, once again, ethnically cleansed from their homes.

Almost all Ashkenazi Jews today are the descendants of 300 Jewish individuals who survived numerous genocides by the crusaders in the Middle Ages. Most Ashkenazi Jews today understand the continuous cycle of violent and often genocidal Jew-hatred faced by their families in Central and Eastern Europe, and why they had to flee this region in the 19th and early 20th centuries even before the Shoah.

Beta-Yisrael Jews know the trauma that their families experienced while living in Ethiopia. They know that their faces were marked with crosses so they could hide their Jewishness and they understand the realities of what being a *Falasha* (outsider) meant. They know anti-Jewish violence that Ethiopian Jews experienced and the horror of their journey from Ethiopia to Sudan before their rescue by Israel in the mid-1980s.

Although there is clearly diversity to the Jewish story, each Jew is part of *Am Echad* (one people) and therefore share a common narrative. We share experiences and these stories – whether taught in schools or just discussed as part of our families' personal histories – can be traumatic.

When discussing Jewish Pride, I have often said that the Jewish community is very good at commemorating our dead, those who have been stolen from us through anti-Jewish violence. But we are not as good at understanding the impact thousands of years of anti-Jewish genocidal violence has on us emotionally and how this is passed on throughout the generations. As author and psychiatrist, Bessel Van Der Kolk wrote in *The Body Keeps Score*: 'Trauma affects not only those who are directly exposed to it, but also those around them.'[37] And not only those around them, but those who descend from them as well. The descendants of Jews who have experienced Jew-hate can also experience psychological manifestations of trauma. Through the continuous retelling of Jewish pain, this trauma can be culturally passed on to future generations, who are far removed from the experience themselves. Many Jews I speak to, who are not known to be the descendants of Holocaust survivors, found themselves having nightmares about Nazis and being afraid of Hitler as someone who was still able to harm them because of how deeply embedded cultural trauma is in the Jewish world. In writer Olga Khazan's 2018 Atlantic article, 'Inherited Trauma Shapes Your Health', she details an exchange she had with her therapist:

'Often when I complain to my therapist about how stressed out I am by a problem I'm having, she says a variation on the same thing: "Well, like all Ashkenazi Jews, you have a lot of intergenerational trauma. You know, because of everything that's ... happened." Of course you're anxious, she seems to say; you're Jewish!'[38]

As I explained, this is not only applicable to Ashkenazi Jews. Nor is it only passed on through the cultural retelling of stories of Jewish death and destruction that can harm generations of Jews. There is also evidence that genes themselves can be altered through epigenetic trauma. As we know, there is an important ancestral element to Jewishness which genetically connects Jews today to our ancient ancestors in the Levant. Thus, many Jews today could have inherited epigenetic trauma caused by events dating back thousands of years.

Recent evidence for this idea comes from the findings of scientists with the University of South Florida Genomics programme and the Center for Global Health and Infectious Disease Research investigating the Rwandan Genocide. They discovered that the 'terror of genocide was associated with chemical modifications to the DNA of genocide-exposed women and their offspring. Many of these modifications occurred in genes previously implicated in risk for mental disorders such as PTSD and depression.'[39] Similar research has been

conducted into the impact of trauma on the descendants of Holocaust survivors, such as the 2019 study, 'Intergenerational consequences of the Holocaust on offspring mental health: a systematic
review of associated factors and mechanisms', which found 'intergenerational effects on offspring cortisol levels'[40] in the children of
Holocaust survivors. It is important to note that much of the research
into epigenetic trauma has only been conducted among the children
of those who experienced the trauma, and more research would need
to be conducted into the impact on later generations. However, it is
clear from research that trauma is, at least, passed on to an extent; the
question would be how far it can be passed on.

Van Der Kolk also notes that trauma can be triggered long after the
event itself. He writes: 'Long after a traumatic experience is over, it may
be reactivated at the slightest hint of danger and mobilize disturbed
brain circuits and secrete massive amounts of stress hormones.'[41] I
have experienced this several times. Whether it's disembarking from
a crowded train and seeing rows of people lining up to embark or
feelings of panic and claustrophobia when the majority of flights out
of Hong Kong were suspended during the Covid-19 pandemic. My
responses are layered, and many people, including non-Jews, experience discomfort in these situations. But I am aware that they have an
impact on me in a different manner because they trigger intergenerational trauma, seemingly out of nowhere. Rows of people waiting to
get off a train forces my mind to remember the images of Jews at the
ramp in Auschwitz. Feelings of being trapped in Hong Kong frighten
me because for Jews having escape routes blocked has had devastating
consequences. Many Jews I have discussed these feelings with have
had similar reactions.

Freud argued that those who experience trauma are suffering
from their 'reminisces'.[42] And Pumla Gobodo-Madikizela, the South
African psychologist who played a pivotal role in South Africa's post-
apartheid Truth and Reconciliation Commission, suggested: 'Trauma is

a memory illness, healing can only be done in the present.'[43] However, this can be incredibly difficult, as the events that we are trying to process feel in some way as if they are still occurring or that they could easily happen again. This is, of course, not to say that our experiences are the same as those in the past, but, because of our past, Jews understandably have a heightened sensitivity to external threats.

Many Jews are indeed not able to process the trauma of our past experiences because we continue to experience new – albeit highly similar – threats and trauma. In the lead up to the 2021 May war between Israel and Hamas, I felt dread at what I knew was coming. I experienced the shocking rise in anti-Jewish racism during the 2014 war between Israel and Hamas and I knew that, based on current levels of Jew-hate, 2021 would be worse. For many Jews, the overt Jew-hatred and fear that we felt in 2014 was traumatic, but how can we ever hope to process that when we experience similar trauma over and over again, as we did in 2021? Sadly, I was proven right, with the war in 2021 being used as an excuse to unleash a global grassroots uprising against Jews. And thus, the cycle of trauma continues.

Because of the lack of Jewish conversations on trauma, many of us lack the knowledge and the language to help us explain how we feel. We also lack awareness of how the trauma has affected us. Following the Shoah, a nameless Holocaust survivor stated:

'Hitler is dead. Still, he may yet achieve his goal of destroying us if we internalise the hate, the mistrust, and pain, all the inhumanity we were exposed to for so many years … I am afraid we might have come out of it lacking the human capacities we had before … to hope to love and to trust. Have we acquired the wisdom to prevent such a terrible outcome?'[44]

Our failures to recognise and discuss our trauma has created a situation whereby those who are suffering are not supported. The process sees our relationship with Jewishness stolen from us and reframed into something traumatic. Jew-hate inflicts long-lasting wounds and trauma can lead Jews to internalise the racist views of the world around them, forcing them to see their Jewishness as the source of their pain and shame and something they wish to distance themselves from, rather than as a source of pride.

Additionally, Jews who are unable to cope with our collective and individual trauma often then turn their attention towards another kind of survival, in the form of being accepted by the wider world as opposed to fighting to stake their right to live in peace as a Jew. This is a powerful factor in the seeming ease in which some Jewish people will warp themselves to be accepted or why they would be willing to accept the conditions the wider world imposes on Jews. They want to survive, and they want to escape what they perceive to be the source of their pain of difficulty: their Jewishness. These factors, as we will see throughout the rest of this book, play a crucial part in the development of internalised anti-Jewishness for Jews across the world.

SELF-BLAME AND SELF-DENIGRATION

As we have discussed, continually facing hate is traumatic. Because trauma reframes our relationship with our Jewishness, our trauma responses can manifest in self-blame and self-denigration. Lessing certainly believed this to be the case, writing in 1930: 'It is one of the deepest and most certain principles of national psychology that the Jewish people are the first – and perhaps only – nation that has only sought solely within themselves the blame for world events.'[45] When attempting to understand why the Jews have judged themselves guilty for supposedly provoking the hatred of the non-Jewish world, Lessing looks to the Jewish concept of *Viddui*, the Jewish prayer of atonement, which includes the following:

'We have transgressed, we have acted perfidiously, we have robbed, we have slandered. We have acted perversely and wickedly, we have wilfully sinned, we have done violence, we have imputed falsely. We have given evil counsel, we have lied, we have scoffed, we have rebelled, we have provoked, we have been disobedient, we have committed iniquity, we have wantonly transgressed, we have oppressed, we have been obstinate. We have committed evil, we have acted perniciously, we have acted abominably, we have gone astray, we have led others astray. We have strayed from Your good precepts and ordinances, and it has not profited us. Indeed, You are just in all that has come upon us, for You have acted truthfully, and it is we who have acted wickedly.'[46]

Viddui is a Jewish prayer traditionally recited at Yom Kippur (the Day of Atonement). This prayer has contributed to a culture whereby Jews accept responsibility for their actions. This is not a bad thing. It is a remarkable, if not unique, aspect of Jewishness that we understand that we hold responsibility for the things we say and do. However, Lessing argues that 'the key to the pathology of our national consciousness lies in this acknowledgement of guilt'.[47] We are predisposed to feel guilty because we acknowledge and understand that we are capable of sin.

Viddui has precedence in *Megillat Eicha* (The Book of Lamentations), where the 'cause' of the destruction of the First Temple is not seen as the result of a brutal imperial occupation, but rather it was our own fault because we had sinned and had made God angry. *Eicha's* first chapter declares: 'Her adversaries have become the head, her enemies are at ease; for the Lord has afflicted her because of the multitude of her sins; her young children went into captivity before the enemy.'[48] These were attempts to understand our experiences, but they developed into an almost theologically ordained predisposition towards self-blame.

Understanding the wider context of the Jewish people helps explain our tendency for self-blame. Although we are extraordinarily resilient, we are not like other groups whose fortunes may have risen and fallen as history progressed. Though the majority of the Jews were expelled from their indigenous land 2,000 years ago, we were consistently colonised since the Assyrian invasion in 721 BCE and since then have been forced to desperately fight for our survival. From 721 BCE until 1948 CE (excluding a brief interlude in the form of the Hasmonean dynasty from 140 BCE to 37 BCE), Jews were without any sovereign power and faced attempted destruction of our land and our civilisation at every turn. Despite our incredible survival and our commitment to Jewish life, our backdrop has so often been one of disaster, genocide, ethnic cleansing and trauma. The calamities we faced were so consistent and continuous that it is not hard to see why a people predisposed to accepting responsibility for their actions would accept guilt, not just for their actions but their experience, as they did in the past. As Lessing writes, 'Many great Jewish thinkers have perceived the central core of Jewish teachings in this formula, "Because we are guilty"'.[49]

Additionally, as the example of *Wissenschaft des Judentums* demonstrated, tension between Jews themselves can develop as we see ourselves reflected in a Broken Mirror and define ourselves against the standards of 'good Jews' and 'bad Jews' imposed by the non-Jewish world. As Donna K. Bivens, an anti-racist trainer, has suggested: 'Continually facing racism … can negatively impact the ability of people of color to maintain healthy and fulfilling relationships with each other'.[50] As Bivens states, self-blame does not necessarily mean blaming yourself as an individual, rather it can be self-blame on the collective level. In other words, the trauma of Jew-hate can lead Jews to blame other Jews for anti-Jewish racism.

This can be a coping mechanism whereby oppressed groups attempt to come to terms with their experiences. This has been evident following the Shoah, where Orthodox Jews, trying to cope with the almost unfathomable catastrophe that had befallen them, sometimes blamed the conduct of other Jews, such as assimilation, for what they perceived to be God's wrath. This trend continues today, with certain anti-Zionist Orthodox communities describing Zionists as 'Amalek's Accomplices'.[51] The Amalekites were the biblical sworn enemies of the Jews, and thus, the anti-Zionist Orthodox Jews are framing Zionism as antithetical to Judaism and responsible for the Holocaust, which they see as a punishment from God.

Such behaviour was also evident in the 19th century when many acculturated German Jews (Jews who had integrated or assimilated into the dominant Christian culture) accepted the narratives imposed on Jews by the wider world. As we know from those who pursued *Wissenschaft des Judentums*, while they defined themselves as 'good Jews', they juxtaposed themselves against the 'bad', uncivilised Eastern European Orthodox Jews. They thus purposefully sought to demonstrate their difference to highlight their own palatability. The apparent need for such distinctions became even more pertinent with the influx of Eastern Jews (including my mother's own family), whose presence and cultural difference only intensified the notion that all Jews, including German Jews, were foreign interlopers. Jewish industrialist Walter Rathenau exemplified this attitude when he encouraged Jews in Germany to shed their 'tribal attributes'[52] and transform into 'Jews of German character and education.'

Nineteenth-century Germany saw the birth in Jewish satirical literature of a Jewish character called the Schlemiel. This derogatory character portrayed traditional, 'unenlightened' Jews who spoke Yiddish. 'Schlemiels are fools branded with the external sign of a damaged language, a language that entraps them,' Gilman writes.[53] The Schlemiel was crucial in forming the identities of the *Maskilim*. Creating this separation was also particularly important because, despite what the *Maskilim* argued, all Jews were inherently connected to the global

Jewish community (including the Eastern Jews they so desperately wanted to distance themselves from). As the 19th-century Austrian philosopher Otto Weininger suggested: 'We only hate others who remind us unpleasantly of ourselves.' Although designed to emphasise their own identities as new 'cultured' Jews, the creation of the Schlemiel was a painful attack on Jews from within their own ranks and is a manifestation of aggressive internalised anti-Jewish sentiment. 'Good Jews' are enlightened, modern and speak German. 'Bad Jews' are ignorant, archaic, traditional and speak Yiddish. Weininger explains the manifestations of self-blame and the projection of anti-Jewish hate on to other Jews:

> 'Thus the fact that the bitterest antisemites are to be found amongst the Jews themselves … This one thing, however, remains nonetheless certain; whoever detests the Jewish disposition detests it first of all in himself; that he should persecute it in others is merely his endeavour to separate himself from Jewishness; he strives to shake it off and localise it in his fellow-creatures, and so for a moment to dream himself free of it. Hatred, like love, is a projected phenomenon; that person alone is hated who reminds one unpleasantly of oneself.'54

A tragic example of the demonisation of the Schlemiels and the *Ost Juden* was the experience of poet Moses Ephraim Kuh from Breslau. Though Kuh was born Orthodox he began to identify with the ideas of the *Haskalah* and began to integrate into the non-Jewish world. However, as we will explore later, Jewish attempts at integration were not necessarily always successful and Kuh found that his efforts to acculturate did not result in him being able to 'overcome' his Jewishness. In a biographical poem of an incident that took place at the Saxon border that exemplified his struggle and failures, he wrote:

The Custom Official in E. and the Travelling Jew

Official: Hey you, Jew, you have to pay three dollars.
Jew: Three Dollars? So much money? Why Sir?
Official: You ask me? Because you're a Jew.
If you were a Turk, a heathen, an atheist,
We wouldn't want anything from you.
But as a Jew we must collect from you.
Jew: Here is the money! Does your Christ teach you this?[55]

This poem was inspired by real events in Kuh's life. In the real story, however, he did not identify himself as a Jew, he was identified by others as a Jew, even though there were no outward symbols of his Jewishness. So, what gave him away? It appears as though Kuh was identified by his accent and by the fact that he most likely learned German later in life. He was identified as a *mauscheln* (a native Yiddish speaker). In a world obsessed with language as an indicator of identity and belonging, the supposed Jewish accent of the *mauscheln* continued to set Jews apart, even when they spoke German fluently and even though Yiddish is itself a kind of Germanic language. Ultimately in this world, as historian Sander Gilman states, 'Being Jewish and sounding Jewish are linked with acting Jewish.'[56]

'These Jews speak the language of the nations in whose midst he dwells from generation to generation, but he speaks it always as an alien,' writes Sander Gilman. As we saw with Kuh, even when they were emancipated and fluently learned the language of the world around them, Jews were still marked as different, seen as foreign and rejected. Gilman argues, 'language was the key to Kuh's unmasking as a counterfeit, as a Jew in intellectual's dress'. Robbed of his money, Kuh had to then rely on his Orthodox family in Breslau for help. This is the never-ending bind Jews are placed in by the world around them. With the promise of acceptance and equality, the world coerces Jews to abandon or downplay their Jewishness. However, it never upholds its end of the bargain.

In another sad example of self-blame and self-denigration, Kuh blamed his rejection by the Christian world on his Jewishness and, as Gilman writes, 'the evils of orthodoxy'. This also represents another bind Jews are placed in: by warping themselves to be accepted, they no longer feel a connection or a kinship with their own Jewish community. However, neither are they permitted to be at home in the Christian world. In attempting to overcome his difficulties, Kuh 'could only fall back onto distinctions between good Jews and bad Jews, between the rational and the Orthodox,' suggests Gilman. It is this tragedy that befalls Jews. We internalise anti-Jewish ideas from the world around us, and then we may try to warp or escape our Jewishness. However, the non-Jewish world refuses to allow us to because they always identify us as Jews. And tragically, instead of holding the real culprit accountable, we blame our catastrophes and failures to integrate on ourselves, other Jews or Jewishness itself.

BELONGING – THE DIFFICULTY OF JEWISH INTEGRATION

Jews are both individuals and part of a distinct collective. This means there are layers to how we interact with the world around us. We can engage as individuals but also as a larger group, both of which play a role in shaping our experience. We may feel as individuals that we are able to integrate into our respective wider societies; however, conversations on the difficulty of Jewish integration are really focused on our ability, as a whole, to integrate with the world around us. The difficulty of our integration is connected to our collective ability to acculturate into a non-Jewish society, but it still obviously impacts the lives of individual Jews. This is especially the case when we as people consider the specifics of our collective identity and what that entails, both in how we see ourselves and in how we are seen.

Even if we were born and live in the Diaspora, Jews are part of a specific and unique civilisation. We have our own indigenous land, calendar, traditions, language, culture, politics and even media. This creates complexity because while I am British, I am also a Jew. I am a Jew via my ancestry, my nationality, my connection to my indigenous homeland and the modern State of Israel, my culture and my religion. This is the exceptional thing about the Jews. Despite the fact that the majority of us were ethnically cleansed from our indigenous land 2,000 years ago, we maintained a connection to it. The beating heart of Jewishness was kept alive inside Jews who then spread all over the world. In the Diaspora, we developed iterations of our indigenous culture. We adopted cultural practices from the lands in which we settled, but the beat of Jewishness that we felt in our chests was never extinguished. It is this constant beat of Jewishness, deep in our hearts, that the non-Jewish societies we find ourselves a part of often try, because of their Jew-hatred, to extinguish if we are to join their ranks.

Following the Enlightenment, Jews were forced to choose between their traditional Jewish identities and membership of the newly formed modern nations of the West. We were forced to be universal, and to give up what we might term our specificity. The notion of specificity is rooted in honouring and celebrating authentic minority identity, while universality is rooted in centring the wider – say, state-level – identity. In this identity tug of war, there must be balance and a healthy tension between specificity and universality. The rope that connects them must be taut. However, due to the pressures and weight of universality, for Jews the rope has become slack, the necessary tensions have disappeared and our specificity has lost the game. However, Jewish specificity is what maintained, nurtured and evolved Jewishness even when we were living in exile. It was our commitment to the continuation of the Jewish people and our resistance to assimilation. Although the rise of nationalism in the 19th century led some – for instance, Napoleon in France – to argue otherwise, Jewish specificity does not pose an inherent problem to our belonging to other societies. Universality and specificity can coexist within one person, one community, but not if the world demands that you choose.

The unwillingness to accept Jewishness for what it is, stems from the historic nature of deeply embedded Jew-hate. The vast majority of diasporic Jews (half the world's Jewish population) live in either Christian or Muslim societies. As Jewish academic David Nirenberg illuminates in *Anti-Judaism: The Western Tradition*, and as referenced earlier in this chapter, both Christian and Muslim ideologies were created in opposition to the ideas of Jews. According to Saint Paul, Jews were seen as old, and Christians as new. If Jews were physical (as exemplified through circumcision), Christians were spiritual. In the process of Christian and Muslim identity forming, Jews were assigned roles that would help, as Nirenberg points out, non-Jewish people 'make sense of … their world'.[57]

The creation of Christian identity, and the role it played in the formation of Western culture, meant that even after the power of the Church had been reduced (after the gilded age of the Enlightenment and Emancipation), we continue to see virulent and aggressive Jew-hatred in the West. The roots of Christian Jew-hate were thus too deep to be swept away by the changes of the Enlightenment. Coupled with the Broken Mirror of Jewish identity, this deeply embedded core of ideological Jew-hatred results in a 2,000-year-old pattern of anti-Jewishness that we repeatedly see emerge, to this very day. It also makes it difficult for Jews to fully integrate into these societies while maintaining their authentic Jewishness.

The 'Cloud of Jew-hatred', which I described in *Jewish Pride: Rebuilding a People*, also helps us understand how Jew-hate is passed on from generation to generation. These clouds cover much of the world. At different times, in different places, they may rain harder or softer, but even the softest of drizzles still wets the people below with anti-Jewish ideas. For some of them, they absorb these drop-lets of hate deep inside their core and they become truly hateful, but those people are the minority. For most people, it simply stays on the surface of their skin or their clothes. Though it is not deeply absorbed, it still shapes their thinking and their perceptions of Jews and Juda-ism, but they could be open to education as their bias has not become full-blown hate, yet. Through critical thinking, education, empathy and dialogue, some people develop umbrellas to keep themselves safe from a soaking of Jew-hatred. The aim is, of course, to help everyone develop an umbrella. But the rains of Jew-hate are the reality of the world and of our place in it.

This constant stream of Jew-hatred then proceeds to warp Jewish perceptions of ourselves. As mentioned, Jews are a Middle Eastern diasporic community, which ultimately means that we are connected to a nation other than the one in which we live. We can, of course, be a British Jew or an American Jew, but our status as a nation and people within other nations has historically posed specific difficulties to how readily and easily we are accepted. Take the charge of dual loyalty that is made against Jews. This is a manifestation of Conspir-acy Fantasy which sees Jews being accused of being more loyal to Israel or the Jewish people than the country of their birth. The fact of the matter is, I *do* have a deep connection to both Israel and Brit-ain. And that is *not* a bad thing. It is the non-Jewish world, through their fantastical perception of Jews as constantly conspiring against the non-Jewish world, who frames that as something nefarious. I am loyal to both the country of my indigenous land *and* the country of my birth. These are not incompatible. Many groups have connections to more than one place, but it is only in the case of Jews that we see this accusation being used to demonise us. This only leads Jews, once again, to desperately pledge their loyalty to a country that is hostile to them while attempting to diminish their specificity in the form of their connection to Israel. Of course, one can be loyal to more than one place. This is not impossible, nor is it out of the ordinary. What do other diasporic communities do? Do they just cease to be connected, or loyal, to the country of their birth or their homeland? No, of course, they do not. But Jews must.

Jews continue to try and integrate, regardless of how much opposition and Jew-hate we experience in the process, because we continue to put our faith in the non-Jewish world.

In Britain, Jews say prayers for the Royal Family in every synagogue on Shabbat. Many toast the Queen, alongside the President and the State of Israel at British Jewish *simchas* (happy events such as weddings or Bar/Bat-Mitzvot). Nonetheless, while British Jews have worked incredibly hard to integrate into British society, their efforts have never been fully appreciated, recognised or accepted by the nation as a whole. Jew-hate has been a prominent feature of the British upper-classes, including the Royal Family (as evidenced by several recent members' support for the Nazis and the policy of appeasement all the while German Jews were being oppressed), and British Jews were never able to achieve even the perception that we had been able to integrate as much as our American cousins. Like Jews around the world, British Jews today face rising Jew-hate (in fact, according to a CST report, 2021 saw a 24% increase from the previous peak of 2019[58]). While traditional forms of anti-Jewish racism persist, in recent years self-proclaimed left-wing anti-racists in the Labour party have been at the forefront of the modern British Jew-hate. It's also worth bearing in mind that – despite the extensive coverage given to the anti-Jewish hate which dominated Labour on his watch – 10 million British people voted for Jeremy Corbyn in the 2019 election. Of course, not everyone who backed Labour was motivated by anti-Jewish racism. However, at a minimum, they weren't sufficiently concerned about the problem of Jew-hate not to vote for a party which would later be officially deemed institutionally antisemitic by Britain's anti-racism watchdog. Additionally, while many non-Jews rejected Corbyn, and some specifically because of his Jew-hate, this experience demonstrated the prevalence of Jew-hate in the UK. Ultimately, what these various examples of British Jew-hate tell us is not necessarily that Britain is unsafe for Jews, but that our repeated efforts to integrate have not been as successful as we would have hoped – not due to our lack of effort, but because the non-Jewish world has not been able to overcome its own Jew-hate.

Jewish efforts to integrate into the non-Jewish world are ultimately rooted in the faith that Jews place in the response of our wider societies. This is perhaps embedded in our own cultural ideas of self-improvement. As we explored with *Viddui*, Jews are instructed to apologise, to self-reflect and to take responsibility for our actions. This idea – that we are capable of change and capable of self-improvement – is a wonderful aspect of Jewish culture and of Judaism. I think though, it also leads us to a rather sad (and also beautiful) perception of our respective non-Jewish societies. Because introspection and self-betterment are ingrained into our Jewish psyche, we believe that this is the same for other groups or nations. However, this has not, yet, seemed to be the case, particularly with regards to their treatment of Jews. Following the Shoah, overt Jew-hate became a taboo for a period. It was driven to the fringes of society, and this is where many Jews believed (and, sadly, some still believe) it would remain. In certain places, the general Jewish attitude towards anti-Jewish hate was that it belonged on the pages of history books. We understood that it had not been erased entirely, our communities were still threatened, but many Jews felt safe in the Diaspora. We thought that for the most part, the world had learned its lesson. The last ten years have demonstrated very clearly that they have not. The renormalisation of overt Jew-hatred has shown us that this problem never really went away. The monster of overt Jew-hate had just, for the briefest of moments, slunk back to the dark shadows of society.

Ultimately, whether as a collective or even as individuals, being Jewish in the non-Jewish world is a disadvantage. As Dara Horn, the

author of *People Love Dead Jews*, argues, 'being a Diaspora community means being vulnerable.'[59] This is not because there is anything
wrong with being Jewish. It is simply because we are trying to integrate into societies which, as David Mamet describes in *The Wicked
Son: Anti-Semitism, Self-hatred, and the Jews*, 'hates Jews … and will
continue to do so.'[60] And the difficulty of Jewish integration, unsurprisingly, creates the perfect breeding ground of internalised anti-
Jewish hate. Jews have a specific history and identity which we are
asked to abandon to gain membership to society. We want so much
to be accepted. This then creates a situation whereby, through the
Broken Mirror of Jewish identity, Jews have to warp their authentic
selves to be accepted or even just to feel safe. But this never works.
This, though, is nothing new. As we will see in Chapter 2, from altering the concept of Jewishness to changing our names and noses, Jews
have been working to make themselves less Jewish for hundreds of
years. The demands of the non-Jewish world and the hate they refuse
to process make integration an almost inherently difficult thing for
Jews. The difficulty of Jewish integration was summed up by Theodor
Lessing when he wrote:

> 'We cannot do right. People say, "you are parasites on others". So
> we have elected to leave our adopted homes. People say, "you are
> always middlemen," so we bring our children up to be gardeners
> or farmers, and people say, "you are degenerate, and have become
> cowardly sissies," so we go out to battle, proving ourselves to be
> the best soldiers. Then people say, "Wherever you are, you are
> really only tolerated". We respond, "we have no greater longing
> than to emerge from mere toleration."'[61]

Lessing is right. We must emerge from mere toleration, but we must
do so with pride and with an understanding that, sadly, being a Jew
in the non-Jewish world is not easy. This does not mean we should

stop trying to integrate, but it does mean that we must understand the terms of our engagement and proceed accordingly. We should not blindly trust and we should not continue to make incredible efforts to integrate if we are not respected and appreciated. We are in a relationship with our respective wider societies, and, as in every relationship, there should be mutual respect and appreciation. With Jewish Pride, we can develop and nurture Jewish self-esteem which supports us in maintaining our proud Jewish identities while also being productive members of these other communities of which we also find ourselves a part.

JEWISH ANCHORS

The Jewish people are a unique example of a group who were able to preserve their distinct culture and identity for thousands of years after being expelled from their indigenous land. Through a belief in God, an observance of Jewish law and tradition and the Jewish calendar as set out in the Torah and the other Jewish holy books and a deep connection to the Jewish indigenous land, Jews were anchored in their Jewishness.

Jewish anchors are how all Jews, whether they were Ashkenazi, Beta-Yisrael, Mizrahi or Sephardic or other, were able to maintain a connection to one another *and* their indigenous culture throughout thousands of years of exile. And although, of course, we see diasporic iterations of our original culture emerge, each Jewish community is anchored to the wider Jewish civilisation through Jewish action and Jewish education. We learned who we were and we lived Jewish lives according to Jewish law and the Jewish calendar.

However, this began to change from the late 18th to the early 20th centuries when emancipation brought about the end of legalised oppression of Jews in Europe. And though this period led to unprecedented Jewish freedom in the Diaspora, the preconditions set as part of Jewish admittance into non-Jewish society, resulted in many Jews weakening or discarding their Jewish anchors altogether. These non-negotiable terms and conditions necessitated the warping of Jewishness in order to bring it in line with non-Jewish values to be accepted. Although they may have diminished or shed their Jewishness, these Jews were not 'bad Jews'. They were people who, for the first time in their lives, were being offered a glimmer of hope. They were going to be able to leave the segregation of the ghettos and join the bright new world. And, for many, the understandable lure of this prospect was simply too great to resist. This dramatic change in circumstances, brought about by the non-Jewish world, would have been life-altering and as historian Michael A. Meyer argues in *Judaism within Modernity*, 'The Jews who were thrown into non-Jewish society by state centralization and Enlightenment ideology, Germans during the Napoleonic era were forced to reorient themselves to a profoundly changed situation.'[62]

This dramatic shift led many Jews to shed or weaken their Jewish anchors. They no longer defined themselves via their Jewishness, and now saw themselves as citizens of the modern world, equal to and, most importantly, the same as their non-Jewish neighbours. The new universalistic Jewish identity created generations of Jews who rejected or diminished their Jewishness and who saw their inherent connection to it as the source of their shame and their torment. And despite their best efforts, the tragedy here is that they were not accepted by non-Jewish German society. And, as we will learn in Chapter 3, Jew-hate continued to haunt them like a spectre. Ultimately, Jewish anchors root us into our Jewish identities, but without them, Jewish identity is defined via the Broken Mirror of Jewish identity. Thus, traditional Judaism and Jews were derided and the ideal Jew, the good Jew, was an assimilated Jew.

Although they are often perceived to be analogous, integration and assimilation are not the same thing. Integration is rooted in cultural fusion while assimilation is 'the decline, and at its endpoint the disappearance of an ethnic/racial distinction and cultural and social differences that express it.'[63] Assimilation was actively promoted by Jew-haters such as Heinrich von Treitschke, the extreme German nationalist, who, in response to Heinrich Graetz's *Geschichte der Juden* (History of the Jews) argued that, for Germans to accept their Jews, assimilation had to be 'complete and unqualified, not [the] creation of a German-Jewish synthesis that would make a mockery of the entire German cultural tradition.'[64] So, the Jews were left with very little room to manoeuvre. Ultimately, through the shedding of their Jewish anchors, these Jews were altered, and they took pride in being 'good Jews'. As Hannah Arendt suggested, they 'feel flattered when an antisemite assures them that he does not mean them, that they are exceptions – exceptional Jews.'[65] Their lost Jewish anchors were their connections not only to their most authentic selves but to the wider Jewish people. Without it, their connection to other, especially non-German, Jews had been severed. As we have seen, this lack of Jewish loyalty was exhibited by those who pursued *Wissenschaft des Judentums* and the creation of the Schlemiel. They could denigrate Eastern European Jews instead of defending them (and traditional Judaism) because they no longer felt an inherent kinship to the wider Jewish community. They were now first and foremost Germans.

The shedding of Jewish anchors also resulted in, as Professor Ilana Maymind, argues in *On the Concept of Self-Hatred: A Misnomer*, the shedding of Jewish nationhood and the adoption of a solely religious identity.[66] But even Jewish religious rituals that had been developed over hundreds, if not thousands, of years were de-Jewified to bring them in line with Christian ideas of religion. Meyer thus describes the establishment of 'modern' Jewish service in Berlin with 'prayers in German, an organ, a choir, and an edifying German sermon.'[67] Crucially, the issue here is not the modernisation or evolution of Jewish practice; these can occur with strong Jewish anchors. Jewish culture has always evolved. Instead, it is the willingness to shed and alter Jewishness in order to be accepted by the wider world that is problematic. Sadly, as we will explore in Chapter 3, for many Jews, it was not enough to maintain a much-weakened Jewish anchor; they had to destroy it completely. And the total shedding of Jewish anchors continued with the mass conversion of German Jews to Christianity.

The events of the 19th century led to the weakening and destruction of Jewish anchors, creating an intergenerational problem, which we are still dealing with today. Adults who abandoned their Jewishness cut the thread that connected them and their descendants to thousands of years of Jewish continuity. At the same time, many of those who remained Jewish brought their children up according to their new Jewish values and identity, which were often rooted in a lack of Jewish action and quality Jewish education. As we will discuss further, Jewish action has often been watered down to bring it in line with the secular or Christian world, and there are Jews who have forgotten the significance of Jewish practice, whether they are religious or not.

Education has been at the core of our Jewishness for thousands of years. It contextualises our own experiences against the wider sweep of Jewish history. This is vital for ensuring a collective Jewish identity. In *Jewish Pride: Rebuilding a People*, I quoted Mordechai Kaplan, the founder of the Reconstructionist movement, who argued, 'Jews should learn Judaism's essential character so that they might know what to do with it in times of stress.'[68] But Jews must be properly educated at all times; it is always important, and especially so anytime we interact with the non-Jewish world. This is particularly crucial because, as we have explored, the worlds in which we live are more often than not inherently hostile to us. They have their own narratives and perceptions of our identity and our experiences, which they then project on to us. We must reject this Broken Mirror of Jewish identity and, through education, understand Jewish experience and history through our own lens.

Despite its centrality to the survival of the Jewish people, there are those who argue that formal Jewish education has failed. In *Positive Jewish Education: A Pathway to Thriving in 21st Century Jewish Education*, Sarah E. Rosenblum, a positive psychology teacher, suggests that Jewish education today often focuses primarily on post-Shoah survival. This has 'created a negative association with Judaism and did not provide a compelling answer to the critical question of why be Jewish in the 21st century.'[69] Others, such as Rose Clubok, a young Jewish leader and writer, argue that Jewish education is overly focused on religion and not inclusive enough of Jewish diversity.[70] Moreover, not every Jew receives Jewish education, depriving them of Jewish knowledge and a Jewish anchor. The questions of whether, and how, we reach these people must be addressed. For the last two years, I have educated Jews and non-Jews all over the world in webinars and short courses on Jewish history. In many of these sessions, Jews ask me, 'Why didn't we know this?' Many Jews are despairing at their own ignorance and do not even know where to start when realising they need to know more.

The failure of Jewish education to create strong and lasting Jewish anchors is not a new problem either. In 1969 Isaac Tobin, the Executive Director of the American Association of Jewish education, stated that Jewish education failed to 'explain the significance of the Jewish existence'.[71] That was over fifty years ago, but anecdotal evidence suggests that Tobin's warning was not heeded.

Jews must understand that Jewish anchors are how we maintain our identities and our specificity. We must learn our Jewishness and we must also live it. It is how we are able to define our own identities and how we actively engage with what it means to be a Jew. Having a strong Jewish anchor isn't incompatible with an active role in a diasporic society, but, as stated, integration must be done in a way that values and respects our Jewishness. Otherwise, without a Jewish anchor, our Jewishness will continue to be defined by the non-Jewish world and imposed on us by the Broken Mirror of Jewish identity.

RECOGNITION

Each of these explanations for internalised Jew-hatred is not alone responsible for this phenomenon. Instead, each contributes to the gradual chipping away at Jewish self-esteem or blocks its development altogether. It forces us to accept an identity defined by the other via the Broken Mirror. It traumatises us, leading us to see our Jewishness as the source of our pain and making us desperate to survive and seek out the acceptance of those around us. It leads us to blame and denigrate ourselves, either as individuals or as a collective, for the hate that we experience. Because of these factors, being Jewish in the non-Jewish world is not easy. In fact, it is very challenging and often has a devastating impact on Jewish identity. Accepting the information contained within this chapter may be challenging for some of you. And, on this, I understand and you have my empathy. Realising that the world around you doesn't accept you, or doesn't accept you in your most authentic form, is difficult. I wish it wasn't the case. However, what history and our own modern experience have taught us is that it *is* the case. Neither this chapter, nor any other chapter in this book, was written to shame those of you who may see yourself identified in some of these scenarios. If that is the case, I first applaud your ability for introspection; that is not easy, nor is it as common as it should be. Secondly, you must understand that if you do begin to see that you may be suffering from aspects of internalised anti-Jewishness, you must not feel guilty or ashamed. This is a by-product of deeply embedded institutional hate. You have done nothing wrong. You have lived your life in a world that is hostile to us, often without us being entirely cognisant of that fact. Our task now lies with understanding this phenomenon on a deeper level so that we can begin the collective and individual task of healing and building a barrier to the barrage of hate that we are forced to experience.

Chapter 2

THE MAJOR MANIFESTATIONS

'I wish I had not been born a Jew, I disown any bond with the long travail of my race, I will outdo the Gentile in mocking at our separateness.'[72]

George Eliot (Mary Anne Evans), 1876

We now have a working definition of internalised anti-Jewish senti-ment and an understanding of the various reasons *why* it manifests itself. We now turn our attention to *how* it manifests. As I stated in the Introduction, the reason our definition was left so broad is that there are several distinct manifestations of this phenomenon. As psychologist Kurt Lewin has suggested, 'The self-hatred of a Jew may be directed against Jews as a group, against a particular fraction of the Jews, against his own family, or against himself. It may be directed against Jewish institutions, Jewish mannerisms, Jewish language, or Jewish ideals.'[73] These various manifestations are what makes it an issue for our whole community. This is not just an experience that impacts one specific kind of Jew or another. This is a global Jewish issue that has the capacity to impact all Jews everywhere.

In my research, I have identified three major manifestations of internalised anti-Jewishness:

1. **Diminishment:** When Jews attempt to diminish their Jewishness in order to better fit in with the non-Jewish world and its ideas of palatable Jewishness.

2. **Denial:** When Jews outright deny their Jewishness in order to shed the handicap that often comes with being a Jew in the non-Jewish world.

3. **Deployment of Jewishness as a Weapon:** When Jews deploy their Jewishness as a weapon to harm other Jews in order to prove their own status as a good Jew.

Understanding the various manifestations of internalised anti-Jewishness is crucial. For us to be able to fight this, for us to be able to build barriers that will guard our community against this, we must all look inwards to investigate our own behaviour and experiences. Once again, this process should not shame us. It should not lead us to feel as if we have failed ourselves or our community. We have experienced a well-documented and well-researched manifestation of deeply embedded hate. And while it is not our fault, it is, as previously suggested, our responsibility to overcome it.

MAIN MANIFESTATIONS: DIMINISHMENT

Though many of us are familiar with the more extreme manifestations of internalised Jew-hatred such as Jewish antizionism, we must also recognise that it does have more subtle expressions that can infect even the proudest of Jews. This is a crucial aspect of understanding this phenomenon. Even Jews who feel genuinely proud of their Jewishness can experience internalised anti-Jewish hate. Importantly, there is also a nuanced difference here between these Jews, who make up the vast majority of the Jewish population and Jews who, while they also consider themselves to be proudly Jewish, in reality, engage with more extreme (and harmful) versions of this phenomenon. These Jews identify themselves as Jews and may claim to feel proud of it but they engage in behaviour that is contradictory to what it means to be proudly Jewish, like advocating for antizionism. These Jews may attack Jewish culture or they may reject a fundamental aspect of Jewish identities, such as our connection to the Land of Israel, all the while thinking their version of Jewishness is correct. They are the ultimate 'good Jews'.

While the Jewish people we are analysing in this specific section of our study are proud of their Jewishness, they have (in a variety of ways) also absorbed perceptions of Jews from the non-Jewish world. This results in them diminishing their Jewishness. This can manifest in Jews identifying as *Jew-ish*. Though, of course, to some Jews, this is just a play on the word 'Jewish' that may reference their specific level of observance, there is also a more sinister meaning to this term. The idea that we are just partly Jewish (in terms of our identity, rather than our ancestry) is rooted in the tension between universality and specificity, as referenced in Chapter 1.

The idea of Jews being coerced into changing themselves to be accepted is clearly different from a natural evolution of the practice. Even today, we can be influenced by the world around us. I am not suggesting that Jews in the Diaspora should segregate themselves. We should integrate, and genuine cultural exchange is a part of that. However, Jews changing themselves to be accepted is a reaction to unequal power dynamics, oppression and the Broken Mirror of Jewish identity. This unequal power dynamic can result in even the proudest of Jews being locked in a situation which results in them seeing their Jewishness as less important than their membership of the wider society. As the Identity Salience Hierarchy states: 'an identity high in the hierarchy would have high salience – it is more relevant to the individual and more likely to be used'.[74] The diminishment of Jewishness and its downgrading in a hierarchy is rooted in a desire to be accepted and an internalisation that overt Jewishness is not compatible with membership to whichever society Jews are trying to join. This can result in a number of different manifestations of internalised anti-Jewishness, but each of them ultimately leads to the creation of categories of 'good Jews' or 'bad Jews'.

QUALIFICATION

The qualification of Jewish identity is rooted in the diminishment of Jewishness, in order to bring it in line with non-Jewish ideas of what constitutes palatable Jewishness. This is rooted in the false dichotomy of 'good' or 'bad' Jews, via the Broken Mirror of Jewish identity and standards of Jewishness created by non-Jewish societies. This is also something I experienced with regards to my identity as a gay man. I was at university when I came out as gay and began my journey towards LGBTQ+ pride. During this period, the phrase 'that's so gay' was still a common, mocking feature of vernacular in society. I remember a specific incident when I was in the third year of my degree. I was at a flat party with my friends (who are still some of my closest friends today). We were in one of my friend's bedrooms and someone, not in my immediate circle, said, 'Oh, that's so gay.' Everyone stopped and looked at me. They were seeing how I would react to what I now understand is a microaggression. I did not want to make a fuss. I didn't want them to see me any differently now that I had come out, so I just nervously laughed and said, 'Oh, don't worry, I am not that kind of gay.' Whatever that means. I have realised since that I was qualifying my sexuality, by trying to assure my friends that I was a palatable kind of gay person that wouldn't rock the boat. That wouldn't make my gayness an issue. It took me many years to understand that I was allowed to make it an issue because it impacts how I experience the world.

My journey to LGBTQ+ pride has provided me with a framework to understand similar experiences in my Jewish self. And I realised that I have qualified my Jewish identity in similar ways. This qualification was to demonstrate that while I may be a Jew, I was a 'good Jew'.

There have, for instance, been times in my life when discussing Zionism, I have immediately followed up with 'but I am for the creation of a Palestinian State'. I am a Zionist, but I wanted the world to know that I am a good Zionist (and a good Jew). Of course, voicing my support for the creation of a Palestinian State doesn't necessarily mean that I am suffering from any kind of internalised anti-Jewishness. However, if we analyse the manner in which I stated my support for a Palestinian State, I was clearly qualifying my Zionism. I wanted whoever I was discussing this with to know that I wasn't an 'extremist'. I also didn't say 'I am a proud Zionist who believes in the right of Jews to self-determine in our indigenous homeland and I also support the creation of a Palestinian State alongside the Jewish state', I used the word, '*but*' not '*and*'. This '*but*' is important. It represents the idea that, on some level, I internalised the notion that being a Zionist was not compatible with supporting the idea of Palestinian State. This is, of course, nonsense, and Zionism at its very core is not, in any way, contradictory to Palestinian nationalism. Since I have engaged in introspection and pursued my own healing journey regarding my Jewish identity, I have stopped caring what non-Jewish people think of my Zionism. Do not mistake me, I will always explain what Zionism means and explain why it is one of *the* central Jewish concepts. And if I am ever questioned on my thoughts on an independent Palestinian State, I respond with, 'I am a Zionist and, in principle, I support the establishment of a Palestinian State alongside the State of Israel'. I will not qualify the Jewish right to self-determination.

We also see this same qualification more broadly with regards to our religiosity. Ask yourself, have you ever said that you are 'Jewish … but'? Again, I know that I have. There were periods of my life when I was proud of my Jewishness, but only to an extent (like during my first relationship, for example). Being Jewish was just as important to me as being seen as the same as everyone else, and perhaps even less important. I did not want my Jewishness to result in my segregation from other communities that I may belong to. I did not realise that were that to happen, then it would be due to the potential hate of the people I was surrounded by. It was not because being openly, fully and completely Jewish in the way that best suits my values, was incompatible with belonging to that specific community.

When I told people that 'I was Jewish, but not that type of Jew', I meant that I wasn't an Orthodox Jew. And by that I really meant, I wasn't specifically Jewish. I was universal. I was *Jew-ish*. Though my statement was not designed to demonise a specific sect of Jews, that is what it did. Because I was not like 'them', I framed myself as a 'good Jew', and them as 'bad Jews'.

The demonisation of Orthodox Jews is something that many people, both Jews and non-Jews, participate in. This specifically stems from a post-Enlightenment world, where Jews were, at least formally, permitted to participate in wider society. This led many Jews to throw off what they perceived to be their cloak of specificity so they could interact with their non-Jewish counterparts as equals. As we saw in Chapter 1, Jewish communities in Germany often used Eastern European Orthodox Jews to define what they perceived to be bad Jews: Jews who stubbornly clung to their traditions instead of embracing the new world of emancipation. Many Jews of the *Haskalah* distinguished themselves from their older, more traditional lives by demonising *Ost Juden* (Eastern Jews), the Jews of the Russian Empire who were overwhelmingly Orthodox and traditional. This is partly because they were still living under the oppressive yoke of the Russians. Unlike their Central or Western counterparts, they had not yet been allowed to integrate into non-Jewish society.

While this is part of a wider problem where overtly religious communities are demonised, the prejudice against Orthodox Jews is highly specific. Orthodox Jews are demonised because their commitment to traditional Jewish life represents 'Jewish obstinance and specificity'. They refuse to abandon their identity and integrate and are therefore perceived as being incompatible with Western values. They cling to their Jewishness while the Western non-Jewish world is trying to eradicate it. Tragically, they also experience this demonisation while being the diasporic Jews most likely to experience violent Jew-hate.

Though Jews are involved in both the Netflix shows, *Unorthodox* and *My Unorthodox Life*, each frames the Orthodox community through a non-Jewish lens. It is portrayed as backward, oppressive, misogynistic and abusive. While there are certainly issues, such as misogyny or LGBTQ+phobia, in the Orthodox community (as there are in multiple communities), to paint it as monolithically bad or evil or oppressive is narrow, prejudiced and, most importantly, anti-Jewish. We can engage in self-criticism and identify issues in all parts of our community that need to be resolved while still understanding our nuance and complexity. Neither *Unorthodox* nor *My Unorthodox Life* addresses the beauty of the Orthodox community. Neither feature strong, feminist Orthodox Jewish women who love their lives. And neither show the important role that Orthodox Jews have played in preserving and building Jewish life, particularly in the post-Shoah world. In response to *My Unorthodox Life*, Kylie Ora Lobell, a Jewish journalist, wrote an op-ed in the *Jewish Journal* that began:

> 'As an Orthodox Jew, I'm always learning something new about myself thanks to the media. I'm a fundamentalist who is insular, backward, stuck in the past and, of course, because I am a woman, I am oppressed. I am so oppressed I don't even know I'm being oppressed. I can't hear all the horrible things these terrible male Orthodox rabbis are saying to me beneath my head covering.'[75]

As we know, because of the difficulty of Jewish integration and the multiple traumas of living in hostile environments, Jews often engage in self-blaming and self-denigration, which as it was in the 19th century, is still routinely directed at Orthodox Jews. They are framed as representing all the negative aspects of non-Jewish perceptions of Jewish identity. However, this representation is created through the Broken Mirror of non-Jewish perception. It is not an accurate portrayal of Jewish people.

A September 2021 article from Religion News Service (RNS) chose to lead a story about Orthodox Jews raising money for the Haitian victims of Hurricane Ida and the Taliban takeover of Afghanistan with the headline: '"Insular" Orthodox Jews mobilize to save lives, from Haiti to Kabul.'[76] Instead of simply celebrating this act of Jewish generosity and the power of shared human experience, RNS chose to report in a way that suggested surprise that Orthodox Jews would care about the experiences of others. This kind of narrative reinforces the same anti-Jewish points: Orthodox Jews are insular, backward and obstinate. And they are those things even when they are helping others. Even when they are showing quite literally that they are not insular. It is this narrative that Jews like me tried so hard to distance themselves from.

The qualification of Jewish identity, whether it is rooted in our Zionism or our religiosity is a subtle and insidious manifestation of internalised anti-Jewish sentiment. We live in a world that rejects our authentic selves and mandates we give up our specificity and conform to universal values. This form of internalised anti-Jewishness is especially dangerous as it is so latent that many people who experience it aren't even aware of it. The subtlety of diminishment is why it is imperative we recognise this specific form of internalised anti-Jewishness.

ALTERATION

For millennia, Jews have engaged with the idea that we must alter ourselves to be accepted by the non-Jewish societies in which we live. The impact of Jews shedding the concept of nationhood discussed earlier in this chapter – a fundamental altering of Jewish identity – can still be felt today. Tragically, based on the enforced rejection of

Jewish nationhood, many Jews have only ever been taught that we are just a religious group. On 24 September 2021, the Twitter account for an organisation calling itself Torah Jews tweeted that:

'There is no racism in the Jewish identity.

Jews are not a race.
Jews are not a nationality.
Jews don't have a "separate" country.

Jews can be white or black. Our religion accepts converts from any ethnicity. Its only our shared religion that is our common denominator. #racism'[77]

It seems that Torah Jews take this position to demonise Israel and Zionism. This is the result of Jews altering our identity to be accepted. It filters into our ways of thinking and through the Broken Mirror, and it fundamentally alters our perceptions of ourselves.

Not only have we altered ourselves conceptually, we have also frequently altered ourselves physically. With regards to the physical altering of Jews, we must refer to the Racial Libel, as I defined in *Jewish Pride: Rebuilding a People*. This libel explains the racialisation of Jew, the demonisation of our physical appearance and ancestry which frames our physicality as representative of our worst perceived character traits and our characteristics as being an inherent part of our identities.

While the non-Jewish world has targeted Jews through religious Jew-hatred, it has also historically, and in modern times, racialised us. In her book, *England and the Jews: How Religion and Violence Created the First Racial State in the West*, Professor Geraldine Heng describes how racial markers were applied to Jewish bodies. Jews were said to have 'special stench, a facial physiognomy, even horns and a tail.

Jewish men were said to bleed congenitally like menstruating women, stigmatized as conspiring with the Antichrist'.[78] This was so systematic that Heng goes on to argue that:

'When the Jewish minority in England were tagged with badges, herded into towns with a surveillance system to monitor their livelihoods, imprisoned for coinage offenses, judicially murdered by the state for the trumped-up lie that they mutilated and crucified Christian children, slaughtered by Christian mobs, targeted for conversion by the state, taxed to the point of penury, subjected to a branch of government specially created for their surveillance, and then finally deported from England in the last exploitation of their usefulness – when so totalizing a racial apparatus is marshalled against a minority group, a label of "premodern prejudice" hardly suffices as a descriptor of the dimensions of horror endured. I've argued that, in fact, England's Jews lived under the conditions of a racial state, the first racial state in the history of the West.'

This racialisation has taken place throughout history (in Medieval England, as explained by Heng, in Spain and Portugal in the period of the Inquisition, Europe in the 19th century, Nazi Germany and the USSR in the 20th century) and it still takes place today. Almost every single time a Jew is depicted, the same stereotypes are utilised. These shame Jews in a very real and tangible way as they are used to reinforce the separateness (and ugliness) of Jews as a collective. As Sander Gilman writes when discussing Jewish rhinoplasty and the need to disguise oneself, 'for visibility means being not seen as an individual, but as an Other, one of the "ugly" race.'[79] This deeply embedded racialisation of Jews, often coupled with the fact that many of us don't conform to Eurocentric beauty standards (due to our indigeneity to the Levant), can lead Jews to alter themselves physically or to feel ashamed of their physicality.

In Chapter 3, we will see how the Jewish men in Greek-ruled Judea attempted to reverse their circumcision to be accepted into Hellenised society. Jewish attitudes to physical alteration were summed up by a poem from writer Jakov Lind's *Counting My Steps: An Autobiography*. He wrote:

> All he needed was a foreskin,
> Otherwise he felt all right.
> He lived it up like a Duke on his castle,
> With pheasant shooting and old paintings.
> All he needed was a little foreskin,
> Otherwise he was all right.[80]

It is the crux of this idea that is still prevalent in our community. All we need to do is alter ourselves and we will be accepted. And this has led generations of Jews to do just that.

Though in recent years, Jewish rhinoplasty has decreased, it is still a part of the Jewish narrative. Of course, it goes without saying that people are free to do with their bodies what they want; however, the wider context of internalised anti-Jewish racism (because of the Racial Libel) and Eurocentric beauty standards cannot be ignored. As Mary Douglas, the British anthropologist stated, 'The human body is always treated as an image of society and ... there can be no natural way of considering the body that does not involve at the same time a social dimension.'[81] We are all, each of us, a product of the world around us. And as Jews, as we have learned, our identity is constantly shaped by a hostile world. The Broken Mirror of Jewish identity is constantly reflecting a warped and unrealistic version of Jewish identity which creates standards by which we, as Jews, must live to be accepted. In short, it tells us that our original and authentic forms are not good enough.

Modern rhinoplasty itself was created specifically to help Jews better integrate into non-Jewish society. This surgical intervention was invented by an assimilated German Jew, Jacques Joseph (born Jakob Joseph). Joseph thought Jews could more easily integrate into non-Jewish society if their noses didn't make them look 'too Jewish'. Joseph's aim was to 'cure them, to make them less visible in their world'.[82] In short, they wanted to pass as gentile Germans. Later in his career, as the Nazis took power, Joseph intended to ease the 'suffering'[83] of Jewish noses by operating even for those who could not afford it.

There is clearly no one way to look Jewish, nor do 'Jewish noses' really exist. However, Jews are indigenous to the Levant, a fact that is reflected in the physical appearance of many of us. This, coupled with the fact that Jews engaged, and still do to an extent, in endogamy, means that there are certain physical features common to Jews. This reality, of course, does not justify the racism we have experienced on account of our bodies.

Another tragic dimension of the altering of Jewish physical appearance is that it does not really work in allowing Jews to escape the wounds of Jew-hate. Rhinoplasty in the 1930s did not save Jews from being murdered en masse by the Nazis and their allies. Jewish attempts, even surgical ones, have not worked in allowing Jews to integrate and overcome anti-Jewish hate. In *The Jew's Body*, Sander Gilman writes, 'The Jew's experience of his or her own body was so deeply impacted by antisemitic rhetoric that even when the body met the expectations for perfection in the community in which the Jew lived, the Jews experienced his or her body as flawed, diseased.'[84]

This notion that Jews can simply alter themselves to be accepted also fundamentally fails to consider the psychological impact of this process on Jews themselves. These attempts do not work because Jews themselves are often wounded by what they have done to themselves. Whether or not we are aware of this, the fact that many Jews felt they had to surgically alter their faces to be accepted into non-Jewish societies is a terrible thing. It wounds Jews and we may ultimately regret our decisions, as author Diana Bletter experienced. In 2007 Bletter wrote an article for *Tablet* magazine titled 'A Bridge Too Far: How one woman lived to regret her nose job'. In it, she described how she regretted her decision because 'I miss my old nose and I regret my decision to alter it.'[85] It also may wound us because on some level we are aware of what we did to be accepted. We are constantly seeking acceptance from a world that doesn't accept us. And if, for a moment it looks like they will accept us, it comes at great personal cost.

This is tragic. It is tragic that Jews have been made to feel that the only way to be accepted is if they alter themselves. This is not acceptable, nor is it any kind of privilege. It is a very clear expression of oppression. This warped and flawed version of Jewish experience was expressed by Recho Omondi, the non-Jewish host of *The Cutting Room Floor* podcast, who, when talking about the false idea of Jewish privilege, stated: 'At the end of the day you guys are going to get your nose jobs and your keratin treatments and change your last name from Ralph Lifshitz to Ralph Lauren and you will be fine.'[86] The idea that Jews altering themselves physically is just 'fine' is abhorrent. This is not a notion that we would accept with regard to any other community. We understand that Asian people pursuing double eyelid surgery or Black people attempting to lighten their skin is a form of internalised prejudice based on standards created by wider society. But is this not the same for Jews? That is a double standard and is indicative of deeply embedded Jew-hatred. It is not indicative of any kind of Jewish privilege.

Another way in which Jewish identity has been altered is the act of changing our names. My mother's original maiden name was Shmulev-itz, but in 1928, her father, my grandfather David, changed it to Samuels. The act of name changing can be seen as a kind of cleansing of our overt Jewishness. Though these names were not originally ours – they were given to us by our oppressors in Eastern Europe – they became synonymous with Jewishness. And in order to be accepted, in order to fit in, we were willing to cast off this mark of overt Jewishness. Even though newer Jewish names, like Freeman, are still associated with Jews, they are not as easily identifiable Jewish as Fredoluvitch (my late father's family's 'original' name). This allowed Jews to integrate more easily without being visibly Jewish. In a 2020 article titled, *What the Jewish Name Changing Narrative Gets Wrong*, historian Kirsten Fermaglich detailed how Jews were encouraged to engage in this practice of self-cleansing. Fermaglich writes, 'Jews described being counselled to change their names by family members, employers, teachers, and mentors; one New York Jewish author remembered that it had been a matter of course for Jewish college students to change their names upon graduation in the 1930s.'[87] The context of this was of course the legalised and societal oppression that Jews faced in America during this period. Given the rise of Jew-hate in America in the 1930s, it is unsurprising that Jews opted to be less identifiably Jewish. However, the act of name changing, like other forms of Jewish alteration, has always been seen for what it was by parts of our community. Just like Jewish rhinoplasty, this was not a universal practice and a '1950 survey of Bronx residents found that about 50 percent of those 181 Jews defined name changing as "a shame" and a reflection of "a lack of pride".'[88]

Like the Jews who recognised the shame in Jewish alteration, we have to ask, what did we lose with our name changes? What does the ease in which we shed our more authentic selves to be accepted say about our Jewish self-esteem? We do not sit in judgement of those that came before us; we must be able to empathise with their experience while also fairly critiquing their actions. We know why they did what they did, but the impact of these actions is something we are less familiar with. It is a form of Jewish alteration which is a subtle manifestation of internalised anti-Jewishness.

Jewish evolution has always been a part of Judaism and Jewishness. We have never stood still. However, any modern iterations of Jewish identity that we create must be rooted in Pride. They must not stem from trying to be more like our non-Jewish neighbours. If we adopt non-Jewish ideas, values or practices, that is perfectly fine (and not out of the ordinary when it comes to Jewish history). But understanding the power dynamic that exists between Jews and non-Jewish societies is vital. We must understand the difficulty of Jewish integration. We must understand the 'good Jew'/'bad Jew' dynamic and we must strive for authentic Jewishness, even as we progress and evolve our nation.

There are countless examples where Jews have altered their identities so they can more easily pass as non-Jewish, or at the very least so they are more like them. This was not in any way designed to be an exhaustive list of every way a Jew has altered themselves. Rather, it was intended to spark a thought in you, my reader. As we must throughout this journey, we should ask ourselves, 'How does this apply to me? Have I changed my identity to be accepted? Did my family? Did my wider Jewish community?' I must reiterate: if the answer is yes, you must not be ashamed. These are my stories, and the stories of most other Jews, as much as they may be your stories too. We are a community that has been shamed, oppressed and traumatised for millennia and though we have survived and flourished, we still bear the scars of our mistreatment.

KEEP YOUR HEAD DOWN

A third manifestation of this more subtle form of internalised Jew-hatred is rooted in the notion that Jews are not permitted to advocate for themselves. Though it emanates from the wider world, rooted in the rejection of Jewish specificity and, more recently, ideas of Jews are privileged and powerful, we see this narrative absorbed into our own community. It is the unofficial policy of 'keep your head down' that was part of the inspiration behind my first book, *Jewish Pride: Rebuilding a People*. When I joined Twitter in 2018 to take part in the fight against Jeremy Corbyn, the former leader of the Labour Party,

I saw many British Jews embody Jewish Pride. They took to the streets and shouted, 'Enough is enough!'. They followed in the footsteps of the great Jewish rebels that came before us to fight against Jew-hate.

There were other Jews, though, who couldn't quite bring themselves to join the fight. There were Jews on the Left, like David Schneider, the British Jewish actor, who seemed unable to fight Corbyn. This is for a variety of factors, including, it seems from my perspective, the perception that issues facing the Jewish community are less important than other issues facing the country more widely. On 17 November 2019 (just one month before the pivotal 2019 General Election, which Corbyn ultimately lost and after years of abuse and racism directed at Jews from Labour), Schneider tweeted 'Labour has great policies which are desperately needed. I want to see them implemented. But do I rejoice at Corbyn as PM? No. His history's too problematic and he's failed to respond appropriately to antisemitism & Brexit. But JC as PM's the only way to implement such policies.'[89]

This trend is also evident in Jews on the Right. Gary Cohn, a Jewish White House economic advisor under Donald Trump, remained in the administration despite his public discomfort with the president's comments following the 2017 Unite the Right rally in Charlottesville where Neo-Nazi protesters chanted 'Jews will not replace us'.[90] Following the riot, Trump stated there were 'very fine people'[91] among the Neo-Nazis at the march. Despite stating that Trump 'must do better'[92] in condemning Jew-hate, neo-Nazism and white supremacy, Cohn stayed in the administration and worked with Trump until 2018 and seemed to only resign when the president planned to impose tariffs on steel and aluminium imports. If we refer back to the Identity Salience Hierarchy model, it seems that both Schneider and Cohn have prioritised their other identities or values over their Jewish ones. We also see this in other circumstances when Jews on the Left are told not to put their experiences at the centre of their conversations about hate and racism. We are told, and we internalise the notion, that our experiences do not matter as much as other people's. Theodor Lessing summed up this notion suggesting:

'When we stand up for our own rights, they respond, Have you not yet learned that dogged self-preservation of a special people is nothing more than a treachery against universal, human, trans-national values.'[93]

When Jews do stand up for ourselves, it is alleged, we are placing our own experiences over the wider experience. We are betraying universalism. We are selfishly focusing on ourselves, while we should be focused on others. It is an illogical idea that the Jews, the most continuously persecuted minority in the history of mankind, are treated this way. To anyone with an iota of historical knowledge, it would be obvious why Jews should stand up for themselves. However, due to the universality of post-Enlightenment values, Jews were perceived to be obstinately Jewish unless they yielded to the pressures of the non-Jewish world. The idea of Jews standing up for themselves is perceived as being a contradiction to being a modern enlightened person. Some Jews have internalised that Jews prioritising Jewish experiences somehow puts us at odds with the rest of humanity. This is a ridiculous and hateful proposition.

This is an act of self-sabotage, and one rooted in shame imposed on Jews by non-Jewish worlds. Jews have only survived because we ensured that we did. For thousands of years, we fought back against the multiple genocides, ethnic cleansings and oppressions we experienced. Jews such as Mordechai Anielewicz and Emanuel Ringelblum fought back in the Warsaw Ghetto by taking up arms or recording the crimes that were being committed against the Jews respectively. Jewish resistance takes many forms, but each of them is rooted in the fight for Jewish life and lives. We have not survived by accident. If we don't fight back, if we don't defend ourselves through Jewish Pride against Jew-hate, against assimilation, then, simply, we cease to exist.

David Schneider's statements have a worrying parallel. In 1934 the Association of German National Jews stated that 'we have always held the well-being of the German people and the fatherland, to which we feel inextricably linked, above our own well-being. Thus we greeted the results of January 1933, even though it has brought hardship for us personally.'[94] There are those who would blame these Jews for not doing enough to stop the Nazis, but we are not here to pass judgement. Instead, with empathy, we must learn from this experience and understand their actions and so we can identify the threads that connect our experience to theirs. Like many Jews that came before and after them, they suffered from internalised anti-Jewishness. They were in a very complex situation, and they inherited a very complicated identity which ultimately taught them that their Jewishness was less important to them than their Germanness.

Like all things, the concept of Jewish diminishment has many manifestations. These are some of the most prevalent examples, but there are doubtless many more. Despite the seeming disparity in their expression, their commonality though lies in the notion that our Jewishness is somehow incompatible with membership to a diasporic society. We therefore want to diminish it, we want to qualify, we want to alter it and we will not defend it. But we must reject this notion and see the value in our Jewishness, even if the world around us does not.

MAIN MANIFESTATIONS: DENIAL

The second major manifestation of internalised Jew-hate that I have identified is denial. Like all aspects of the Jewish experience, this has taken different forms throughout history, although all manifestations are rooted in the outright denial of one's Judaism or Jewishness. Trad-itionally, this would have been exemplified by the conversion of Jewish people to another religious community, such as Christianity or Islam. When we discuss these Jews who converted to other religions, we are specifically *not* referencing the various Jewish communities who were forced to convert as part of cultural genocide. The Sephardic Jews who experienced the genocidal policies of the Catholic monarchs of Spain during the Inquisition were faced with a choice between life and death. These Jews are victims of overt anti-Jewish hate. They are Jewish victims of cultural genocide. They are not Jews who chose will-ingly to deny their own heritage.

The Jews we are discussing at this point in our journey are Jews who made the choice to convert during non-genocidal periods of our history. The motives behind these choices are complex. It is possible that some of the Jews who converted were doing so for 'pull' factors. They could have legitimately favoured the doctrines of Christianity or Islam and felt drawn to those religions. Being born and raised as a Jew does not always – although it usually does – guar-antee an instant and deep connection with Jewishness and Judaism. These pull factors cannot be entirely dismissed. Nor, however, can the strong 'push' factors present when Jews have denied their Jewish-ness. The wider context of Jewish life, and the overt and oppressive nature (even if not genocidal) of historical anti-Jewish hate, cannot be ignored as a push factor.

For the most part, Jews who converted to other religions were doing so to rid themselves of the disadvantage they experienced because of their Jewishness. They were living in times when it was dangerous and difficult to be a Jew, and even in 'better times' Jewish-ness was still defined by the non-Jewish world, which, as we will see, only further warps our relationship with ourselves which can lead us to outright deny our Jewishness. This part of our story is well told by the examples of Johannes Pfefferkorn and Ella Emhoff.

Johannes Pfefferkorn

A 16th-century Jew who denied his Jewishness to free himself of its disadvantage was Johannes Pfefferkorn, born Josef Pfefferkorn. In 1504 Pfefferkorn, along with his wife Anna and their son Laurentius, converted to Christianity. Of his conversion, Pfefferkorn later wrote:

'After I converted together with my wife and children from the Jewish error to the Christian faith, I looked within myself to understand why the Jews continue to hold and disseminate their evil, destructive, perverted ways.'[95]

Following his conversion, Pfefferkorn was employed by the Dominican monks in Cologne. In a clear and tragic effort to prove his membership to the Christian community of the good, though he had denied his Jewishness by converting, Pfefferkorn spent his life demonising Jews. In his 2006 book, *Contemporary Left Antisemitism*, David Hirsh coined the 'community of the good' to describe Leftists' attitudes towards their own high morality in opposition to the immorality of everything opposed by the community of the good. Although Hirsh's focus is modern Left Jew-hate, the concept of the 'community of the good' can be applied, not just to the modern Left, but to communities throughout history. And as certain Jews on the Left will disavow their Jewishness (or parts thereof) to maintain their membership to the community of the good, so did Jews at various points in history by converting to Christianity. Incidentally, the idea of a community of the good is in fact a very Christian notion, whereby one achieves redemption by seeing and following the supposed true path. For some today, it is the Left, and in the Middle Ages, it was the path to Christ.

According to Sander Gilman, Pfefferkorn's writing reflected his 'ardour in his conversion, a conversion that was voluntary to the extent that Pfefferkorn evidently chose Christianity without any overt physical threats having been lodged against him.'[96] Pfefferkorn's writing came in the form of pamphlets whose legitimacy was supposedly based on his 'special status' due to his knowledge of the 'inner workings of the Jewish mind'.[97] Unlike other Jews who had converted to Christianity, Pfefferkorn's work was not focused on convincing Jews to convert, rather it was Pfefferkorn's overt attempt to demonise, not persuade, Jews. Gilman says, 'They were written to be read by those whom Pfefferkorn perceived as fellow Christians, who were then to act based on the knowledge presented to them against the perfidious Jews.' In his first pamphlet, Pfefferkorn advocated for Jews to be converted by force, through compelling them to attend Christian services. In an attempt to prove his own loyalty, he further advocates for the forced conversion of Jews by arguing that converted Jews – like him – make even better Christians than the Christians themselves. As time progressed, we see a radicalisation of Pfefferkorn's attitudes to the Jews. In 1509 he produced yet another pamphlet on the Jews, *Der Judenfeind* (The Enemy of the Jews). In this pamphlet, Pfefferkorn wrote of 'the Jews' daily mocking of Christ'.[98] To justify this, he purposefully mistranslated Hebrew terms and passages attempting to demonstrate the 'demonic language of the Jews'.[99]As we saw in Chapter 1, the languages of the Jews have long been attacked and demonised.

In a striking example of misojewny (misogyny and Jew-hate), Pfefferkorn attacks Jewish women as immoral. Sander Gilman writes that Pfefferkorn 'condemns them as seductresses whose sole interest is in having bastards by Christian men whom they can then raise as Jews. The gross immorality of the Jews seduces and captures the souls of Christians.'[100] And in *Der Judenfeind*, Pfefferkorn wrote:

'Where Jews live there is much heresy. One finds that Christians lie with Jewesses and if a child is produced, it remains with the Jews. This is clearly a remarkable and sinful evil which puts Christian blood in eternal damnation. As I said at the beginning of my booklet, there is no sect nor people that hates the Christian as much as the Jews.'[101]

Pfefferkorn's anti-Jewish campaign was so successful that he was eventually appointed the Keeper of the Jews' Books by Emperor Maximillian I (of the Holy Roman Empire) in 1509. In this role, he confiscated Jewish books, such as the Talmud (the central text of Rabbinic Judaism), which, as we will see in Chapter 3, was so often demonised by Christian societies.

Throughout his career, Pfefferkorn was locked in a long-running feud with Johann Reuchlin, a German Christian humanist. In 1510 Reuchlin wrote a letter that split Jewish books into two separate categories: those perceived to have attacked Christianity and those that did not. In the latter, Reuchlin included the Talmud and advocated that Christians study those books included in the second category to gain a deeper understanding of the Bible. In defending certain Jewish books, Pfefferkorn (among others) accused Reuchlin of defending the Jews. Adding fuel to the fire, Reuchlin's letter also included a direct attack on Pfefferkorn, doubting his expertise despite his former Jewishness, stating: 'in my entire life, no Jew has ever been baptised who has understood the Talmud or has even been able to read it'.[102] In a fascinating response, particularly when we consider the former Jewishness of the accuser, Pfefferkorn attacked Reuchlin as a 'Judaizer' and a 'false Christian' (the common Christian allegation referenced in Chapter 1 that stretches back to John Chrysostom in the 5th century CE) and alleged that he was not a true Christian, but a secret Jew who was surreptitiously spreading Jewishness and Judaism.[103] Despite his attempts to discard his Jewishness and Judaism, the world around Pfefferkorn would not let him forget his roots. This offers us an insight into the fervour with which he attacked Jews. In his response to being called a false Christian, in 1511 Reuchlin wrote, 'The Eye Glasses', in which he consistently referred to Pfefferkorn as 'Pfefferkorn the

Baptized Jew'.[104] Even when a Jew denies their Jewishness the non-Jewish worlds around them never let them forget. The inescapability of Jewishness can then drive such Jews to deny their Jewishness with even greater intensity, as was the case with Pfefferkorn.

Pfefferkorn's effectiveness in demonising Jews was due to his former Jewishness. In this sense, he became a token (former) Jew in Christian society. Had he been born a Christian, his perspectives would have held significantly less weight. He would have been just another run-of-the-mill Christian Jew-hater. His desire to join the Christian majority itself tells us that he had internalised anti-Jewish perspectives on Jews, Jewishness and Judaism. He took the 'good Jew'/'bad Jew' dichotomy to the nth degree, ultimately arguing that the only 'good Jew' was a 'good Christian'. He spent his life attempting to prove just how good he was, and his tireless effort in demonising Jews demonstrates just how insecure he may have felt his position truly was.

Ella Emhoff

The modern secular world is very different from that of Johannes Pfefferkorn. Jews no longer need to convert out of Judaism to renounce their Jewishness. They can simply decide that they are not Jewish. This is the modern manifestation of the Jewish act of denial. As there are differences in context, so are there differences in explanation. Despite growing up as a Jew, Pfefferkorn purposefully denied his Jewishness because he lived in an overtly hateful world that demonised Jews. Today, not every Jew who denies their Jewishness purposefully rejects their identity. Some never feel connected to it in the first place.

At the 2021 inauguration of American President Joe Biden and Vice President Kamala Harris, Harris's family were also in attendance. VP Harris's husband, Doug Emhoff, is Jewish and accompanying her father and stepmother was Doug's daughter, model and artist, Ella. When she walked on to the inauguration stage, tweets celebrating positive representation of Jewish women were written: 'Ella Emhoff's

curls made me tear up. Never have Jewish curls like hers been represented in the White House. During a day of so many firsts, let us not
forget the Jewish girls – and women – that can see themselves in our
nation's Second Family. #InaugurationDay'[105]

For many Jews, this was a moment to celebrate natural Jewish
beauty. A rejection of anti-Jewish racism and the expectation that
Jews must alter their appearance to conform to non-Jewish beauty
standards. However, when *Forward* magazine later requested an interview with Emhoff to mark her inclusion in their Forward 50, a list
of the top influential American Jews, Emhoff's spokesperson politely
declined, stating, 'Ella is not Jewish.'[106]

Using Emhoff as a case study into the modern denial of one's
Jewishness as a form of internalised anti-Jewishness is not meant to
demonise or shame her. Ultimately, she is able to define her own identity. But, for the purposes of our study, her lack of Jewish affiliation
is important. It is a modern manifestation of denial, and we must ask
ourselves why someone whose father is Jewish does not in any way see
themselves as Jewish.

The statement that Emhoff's spokesperson made regarding her
connection to Judaism and Jewishness also read, 'It's not something
she grew up with … Ella truly has no qualms with the faith, but
she does not want to speak on behalf of Judaism, as she does not
celebrate herself.'[107] These statements reveal something very specific
about her understanding of what it means to be a Jew. Based on what
was reported, Emhoff perceives Jewishness to be a solely religious
identity. Therefore, as per her understanding, because she does not
practise, or in her words 'celebrate', Judaism and Jewishness, it does
not apply to her.[108]

To understand why this denial is a manifestation of internalised
anti-Jewishness, we must utilise our working definition of internalised
anti-Jewishness. If we understand that internalised anti-Jewishness is
rooted in the acceptance of non-Jewish narratives by Jewish people,

then we seem to have an answer to the question of why Ella Emhoff declares herself a non-Jew. Importantly, the denial of Ella Emhoff's Jewish ancestry and family does not mean in any way that Emhoff hates Jews. However, it does reveal that her definition of Jewishness is rooted in a post-Enlightenment idea that the Jews must not be a distinct nation, they can be only a religious group. So as Emhoff's spokesperson explained, if you don't believe then you don't belong.

While an important facet of Jewish identity is rooted in religion and faith, we know that is not all we are. We are also bound by many things other than faith, such as land, history, language, traditions, values and ancestry. Although *Hey Alma*, the online Jewish magazine, published an article titled, 'We Were Wrong to Assume Ella Emhoff Is Jewish'[109] the assumption that Emhoff was Jewish is a rational and sensible one, given our understanding that Jews are not only a religious group, but a tribe and a nation bound by many components including ancestry.

From my own experiences, I have found that many Jews are uncomfortable with discussing Jewish ancestry. However, prior to the Holocaust, this was not controversial. It simply meant your ancestors were Jews. It is the Nazis – and others – who warped this idea and stained it with the blood of six million Jews. Tragically, Jews today are so traumatised by the racism we experienced during the Shoah that many have totally rejected the notion of Jewish ancestry and clung even further to the notion that Jews are just a religious community. It is likely this notion also had an impact upon Ella's perception that to be Jewish is to simply be part of a religious community.

The ancestral element of Jewishness means it is not something one can easily shed. Now, of course, if a Jew converts to Christianity or Islam then they (and most people) would view themselves as being Christian or Muslim. However, their new faith does not erase their Jewish ancestry (nor does it erase the *Halacha*'s perspectives on matrilineal Jewishness). We obviously have to respect people's right to identify as they wish, but that doesn't mean basic truths, such as ancestry, are erased. In a later communication to *Forward*, Emhoff's spokesperson stated that Doug Emhoff had been 'celebrating Judaism for a few years now but out of an independent search.'[110] However, it is curious that in her statement regarding her identity, Emhoff's spokesperson didn't even acknowledge her own ancestral connection to Jewishness.

Another interesting component of the denial of Jewishness is that Jew-hate doesn't care whether someone identifies as Jewish or not. As was the case with Pfefferkorn being referred to as the 'baptised Jew' by Reuchlin, the non-Jewish world often targets someone as Jewish even when they themselves don't identify as Jewish. This, of course, does not mean that we allow Jew-haters to define Jewish identity; rather we must recognise the reality that Jew-hatred does impact all Jewish people whether they self-identify as Jewish or not. Although this is complex, it is an aspect of our reality so it must be included in discussions on denying Jewishness. This was Emhoff's experience when she was targeted with racism on Twitter. In an act of racialisation, one user wrote, 'you ever just look at someone and know they hate Palestinians',[111] which was liked over 1,300 times. This comment was only posted because this user identified Emhoff as Jewish.

It is no longer the case that to leave Judaism and the Jewish community, one must convert to another religion. This is the modern manifestation of denial. Clearly, Emhoff is free to choose whatever identity she feels best fits her. However, her decision to deny her indisputable connection to Jewishness is an act of denial that seems to have been brought about through non-Jewish ideas of Jewish identity and Jewish reactions to Jew-hate. Emhoff's decision highlights the desperate necessity for Jews as a collective to define their own identities and to properly educate themselves about who they are, without utilising non-Jewish perceptions. If Ella Emhoff was able to understand that to be Jewish is to be a member of a people, a nation, a civilisation as well as a religion, then perhaps she might feel proud to stand next to her stepmother, the Vice-President of the United States, as a proud Jew.

MAIN MANIFESTATIONS: DEPLOYMENT OF JEWISHNESS AS A WEAPON

The third, and perhaps most overtly harmful, form of internalised Jew-hatred is the deployment of one's Jewish identity as a weapon in order to harm. Although this is not always the case, denial and the deployment of one's Jewish identity can go hand in hand. This was the case with Johannes Pfefferkorn, who denied his Jewishness but then deployed his former Jewishness as a weapon against other Jews in order to prove his worth as a Christian. However, not every ideology necessitates the denial of one's Jewishness in order to be accepted. As we have explored already, there are those that will tolerate – and even attempt to exploit – Jewishness as long as it conforms to their own aims and values. However, this pressure to conform can lead these good Jews to deploy their Jewishness as a weapon to demonise bad Jews.

Yevsektsiya

No discussion on internalised Jew-hatred, and specifically the deployment of one's Jewish identity as a weapon, would be complete without a brief review of Yevsektsiya, whose story I described in *Jewish Pride: Rebuilding a People*. In many ways, the Yevsektsiya's members are no different from any of the other Jews discussed in this book. Like all Jews suffering from internalised anti-Jewishness, they tried to prove their membership of their version of the community of the good. They were trying not to be specifically Jewish, and they were working hard to demonstrate that their Jewishness was not an impediment to belonging to the new Soviet Union.

Created in 1918 in order to bring Jews into the Russian Revolution, the Yevsektsiya has gone down in Jewish history as a movement of Jews who contributed to the destruction of Jewish life. Although the Jews in Russia benefited greatly from the February 1917 revolution (which immediately resulted in the emancipation of the Jews), they did not immediately flock to socialism come November 1917. In order to force them to abandon their other ideologies and to encourage them to join the Bolsheviks, the Yevsektsiya's own mission statement included the commitment to the 'destruction of traditional Jewish life, the Zionist movement, and Hebrew culture'.[112]

In *Der Emes* (The Truth), its Yiddish language Soviet newspaper (which often repeated the lie that Rabbis were sexual predators), the Yevsektsiya attempted to spread Bolshevism to the Jewish community and remake the Jewish community according to the Soviet 'ideal'.

The Yevsektsiya's attempt to prove their Bolshevik credentials resulted in the destruction of much Russian Jewish life. It shut down *kehillot* (a kind of Jewish municipal council) and then burnt their buildings. It then set its sights on destroying Zionism in Russia. It raided Zionist organisations and arrested its leaders. The study of Hebrew, the indigenous language of the Jews, was also threatened. The Yevsektsiya created schools that taught Sovietised Yiddish, and even respelled classic Yiddish words to erase their Hebrew origins and it shut Hebrew schools and destroyed Hebrew culture.

Although they caused huge damage, we must recognise that these Jews were suffering from intense trauma and were desperately seeking a solution to their Jewish handicap. The Russian Empire was the site of some of the worst Pogroms in Jewish history and an estimated 250,000 Jews were murdered during the 1918–22 Russian Civil War alone. It is unsurprising that some Jews would have hitched their wagons to the Bolsheviks when the ultra-monarchist White Russians were (and had been) so intent on murdering them. Although the Bolsheviks also massacred Jews during the Civil War (they are esti-mated to have murdered 8.5% of Jews killed during this period), their utopian vision of the future would still have represented hope for

Jews. Like all Jews suffering from internalised anti-Jewishness, there are a variety of explanations for their actions. Similarly, to Jews who converted to Christianity, we cannot understand their actions via the pull factors alone: their ideological support for Bolshevism. This is not enough to explain their fervour. Instead, while they may have supported Bolshevism, they were trying to prove that their Sovietised version of Jewishness was compatible with the Bolshevik revolution (just like the 19th-century German Jews tried to prove their universal and rational Jewishness was compatible with modern German society). This means, like so many that came before them, they had to remake Jewishness as an extension of the dominant ideology. Hence, the determination of the Yevsektsiya to destroy all Jewish life not seen as being compatible with the new Soviet State.

In an added tragic layer to this story, as is so often the case, these attempts to be 'good Jews' did not work. The Jewish leaders of the Yevsektsiya were purged by Stalin, despite their devotion to his cause. These Jews have gone down in history as archetypal Jewish betrayers of the Jewish people. And they are. Their actions caused enormous damage to their own people. We can and should judge them, but if there are lessons to be learned from their experience, we must understand why they did what they did. They were Jews traumatised and shamed by non-Jewish attitudes towards their Jewishness and who sought acceptance in a new world of possibility. Like all Jews who deploy their Jewishness to harm other Jews, they occupy dual roles as victims as well as perpetrators.

Éric Zemmour

Éric Zemmour, a far-right, Jewish candidate who stood for the French presidency in spring 2022, is significant because much contemporary discourse, including my own, focuses on Jew-hate on the Left. However, like all things connected to Jew-hatred, internalised anti-Jewishness is not just a product of the Left, and its manifestations on the Right must be recognised and explored to truly understand the scope of this phenomenon.

France has a complicated and painful history when it comes to its relationship with Jews. In 1306, like most other Western European countries at various points, France ethnically cleansed its Jews and then after briefly permitting them to return due to perceptions of Jewish wealth (the Economic Libel), they were expelled again in 1394. By the 17th century, the Jews had begun to illegally settle in France and her colonies again, which led to the 1615 Edict which barred Jews from French colonies. This was reiterated in The Code Noir in 1685, which stated, 'we enjoin all of our officers to chase from our islands all the Jews who have established residence there.'[113] Though Jews eventually returned to France and were emancipated in 1791, Jew-hatred continued to fester. Most famously, it manifested itself in the Dreyfus Affair. In 1894 Alfred Dreyfus, an assimilated Jewish officer in the French army, was falsely accused of conspiring against France by selling military secrets to the Germans. He was court-martialled and sent to Devil's Island, the French penal colony. Dreyfus was later released and pardoned.

Moreover, even though French Jews had acquiesced to the state's demand to shed Jewish nationhood and Jewish specificity, the Jews in France were not – and still aren't in certain quarters – seen as being fully French. One of France's most shameful moments in their century-old abusive relationship with the Jews was during the Shoah. Around 72,500 French Jews were murdered in the Holocaust. But this genocide was not just imposed on the French by the Germans. The French themselves are known to have played an active role in the deportation of their own Jews. The 1942 Vel' d'Hiv Roundup, which resulted in the arrest and deportation of 13,152 French Jews in Paris, was carried out by the French police. In the south, Marshal Philippe Pétain's Vichy regime passed laws in 1940 which mimicked the Nazis' racist 1936 Nuremberg Laws. These measures were passed into Vichy French law without any involvement by the Nazis. The General Commissariat for Jewish Affairs, created by Vichy France in March 1941, coordinated the seizure of Jewish belongings and organised anti-Jewish propaganda. The Vichy government itself created concentration camps and Jews in Vichy France were deported to be murdered by the Nazis. Pétain also deprived Algerian Jews (from whom Zemmour descends) their French citizenship and would almost certainly have deported them if it had not been for the Allied invasion in November 1942.

Following the war, France was an intellectual centre of Holocaust denial where Maurice Bardèche and Paul Rassinier flourished. And in recent years, French Jews such as Ilan Halimi, Mireille Knoll (a Holocaust survivor) and Sarah Halimi were murdered because they were Jewish, and on 16 February 2022, Jeremy Cohen was run over by a tram when he was reportedly fleeing an anti-Jewish attack. Today, due to ongoing Jew-hate, large numbers of Jews are leaving France, mostly returning to Israel.

Given this dark history, a Jew running for President in France should be a cause for celebration. However, his internalised anti-Jewishness means he poses a specific threat towards French Jews. Zemmour has, for instance, made the fantastical claim that Pétain protected French Jews by only deporting foreign Jews, as if that would exonerate him from his crimes against the Jewish people. This is also not true: from 1942 Vichy deported both French and foreign Jews. As Ariel Weil, the Jewish mayor of a Parisian district, stated, 'History is complicated but this is very simple: Pétain did not protect the French Jews.'[114]

Yet another example of Zemmour's dangerous perspectives on France and its Jews reveals the manner in which he prioritises France and Frenchness over Jewishness. He has referred to the Jewish French intellectual Bernard Henri-Levy as 'cosmopolitan'[115] and 'traitor par excellence'. 'Cosmopolitan', as described by Russell Valentino, Professor of Slavic and East European Languages and Cultures, and Associate

Dean for International Affairs at Indiana University, 'was a codeword in the Soviet Union for Jewish ... Anytime a Soviet apparatchik wanted to criticize a Jewish intellectual, he or she accused him or her of being a rootless cosmopolitan. They did not need to say Jewish. Everyone understood.'[116] Though initially an anti-Jewish dog whistle on the Left, it has now crossed over and is – clearly – used on the Right.

'Traitor par excellence' is an example of the accusation of dual loyalty, rooted in the Conspiracy Fantasy, which paints Jews as being incapable of loyalty to the countries of their birth because they are only loyal to Jews and Israel. The notion of Jews being considered traitors is especially painful in France given the Dreyfus Affair. Staggeringly, Zemmour cast aspersions on Dreyfus's innocence by stating 'We will never know'[117] whether he was guilty or not.

Zemmour's rhetoric reinforces the idea that Jews are disloyal towards France. This was also exemplified by his comments about four of the victims of the devastating 2012 terrorist attack on a Jewish school in Toulouse who were buried in Israel. On these Jewish victims of Jew-hate, Zemmour stated: 'Murderers or innocent people, persecutors or victims, foes or friends, for them, France was suitable to live in ... but they wouldn't leave their bones in France, they are foreigners first and foremost and they wanted to remain foreign even after death.'[118]

Jean-Marie Le Pen, the infamous far-right French politician, presidential candidate and former National Front leader, understands well the power of the token Jew and has suggested 'the only difference between Eric and me is that he is Jewish. It is difficult to call him a Nazi or a fascist. This gives him more freedom'.[119] In an article for *The Conversation*, Hannah Rose, a research fellow at the International Centre for the Study of Radicalisation wrote: 'In the course of my research, I came across multiple illustrative comments on right-wing forums on 4chan's politics boards, where Zemmour was described as "100% /ourjew/".'[120]

Just like token Jews on the Left, Jews like Zemmour on the far-right kosher and legitimise Jew-hatred while failing to understand that once their use has expired, just like the Yevsektsiya, they will most likely be cast aside. Zemmour's comments are reprehensible, but they reveal an interesting component of his psyche. As per Comte de Clermont-Tonnerre's diktat on the shedding of Jewish national identity in 1789, and the abandoning of the nationhood aspect of Jewish identity, Zemmour sees himself as French first. His primary identity in the Identity Salience Hierarchy is French. His Jewishness is not a priority. Indeed, the false notion that Pétain protected French Jews while only participating in the murder of foreign Jews is, according to Zemmour, a defence because he sees French Jews as more connected to non-Jewish French people than foreign Jews. This is why he sees Jews wanting to be buried in Israel as traitors. These murdered Jews are openly flouting Napoleon's demand that Jews 'should consider Paris to be your Jerusalem.'[121] The French are French first. French Jews are French first. But the problem is, as we have discussed at length, being Jewish is specific. And many Jews, on some level, are aware of this. We are aware that our specificity has burrowed deep into our Jewish souls and hearts. It's part of our (cultural, ethnic and genetic) make-up. Deep down we know this, and this is why we struggle so much.

Zemmour was also handicapped on another level by his Algerian Jewishness. Not only was he a Jew, but he was also an Algerian Jew. And though they had been French citizens since 1870, the Algerian Jews were accepted even less into French society than the French-born Jews. As David Haziza wrote in his 2022 *Tablet* article titled 'The Wicked Son', 'While Algerian Jews no longer belonged to Africa or the Arab world, and their Jewish knowledge was often scarce, they never really made it in French society. Marginalized in 1940 after decades of humiliation – including pogroms – the vast majority still chose France in 1962, only to have their accent, their complexion, and their strange manners thrown back in their face.'[122]

It is no wonder that in yet another desperate attempt to prove his Frenchness, Zemmour tweeted, 'Napoleon is my grandfather, and Joan of Arc my grandmother.'[123] This isn't quite true though, is it? Whether he likes it or not, Zemmour's grandfather was Abraham, and his grandmother, Sarah.

The emphasis on universal Frenchness was the milieu out of which Zemmour emerged and tried to navigate in a French society that really, deep down, didn't trust 'his kind'. So what did he do? Like every Jew coping with the same identity crisis, he attempted to remake himself as more French than the French. Zemmour's internal battle was illuminated, by a user quoted by Hannah Rose, who, in seeming shock, states, 'despite being Jewish, [he] seems to truly love France'.[124]

In their article on Zemmour in *Tablet*, Mitchell Abidor and Miguel Lago claim that 'Zemmour's inflammatory remarks are not the product of Jew-hatred.'[125] This is wrong. Zemmour's comments are absolutely an expression of Jew-hatred. Jew-hatred was absorbed by Zemmour from the society in which he grew up. It is a French form of Jew-hate that sees Jews as outsiders who have to bend and contort themselves to prove their loyalty. But this was never enough. As I detailed in *Jewish Pride: Rebuilding a People*, decades after Comte de Clermont-Tonnerre insisted that Jews shed their nationhood, in 1806 Napoleon questioned a collection of Jewish elders on whether they were more loyal to France or other Jews. Despite Jewish efforts to integrate, the suspicion never ends.

Zemmour is a Jewish tragedy. An incredibly dangerous anti-Jewish Jewish tragedy, but a tragedy, nonetheless. He is a Jew, whose parents were Berber Jews from Algeria who fled to France during the Algerian war. In attempting to integrate into French society and become what he perceives as being fully French, he internalised France's historic anti-Jewish sentiment. This then led him to deploy his Jewish identity against other French Jews in order to demonstrate, as French Jews have often been forced to do, that he above all else, is French.

THE LAST D: DEFENCE

Internalised anti-Jewishness manifests in three major ways: **Diminishment**, **Denial** and **Deployment of Jewishness as a Weapon**. These various manifestations are a factor in the difficulty of combatting it. It may be our natural instinct to focus our attention on defending ourselves against Jews like Zemmour or highlighting the dangers of groups like the Yevsektsiya, Jews who pose a clear and present danger to our peoplehood. They are the most overtly harmful and dangerous. But we are also battling a silent and more insidious enemy. The more subtle forms of internalised anti-Jewishness must not be allowed to pass under the radar. They infect us and slowly chip away at our Jewish self-esteem until we are shells of our former proud Jewish selves. And they can ultimately lead us to deny our Jewishness entirely. It is a tragedy that someone can belong to a community that has survived and thrived for thousands of years, despite facing almost unbelievable oppression and persecution, and can still feel ashamed of, or even deny they belong to, this group.

The road to combatting internalised anti-Jewishness is long and difficult. But we must do the work necessary to confront and defeat this scourge that has impacted our people for millennia. The task ahead of us is intimidating, but we must not let ourselves be scared into inaction. If Jewish Pride is the Jewish future, then we can only achieve this through the defeat of internalised anti-Jewishness. This, in all its various forms, is one of the most serious threats facing our peoplehood today. We must not allow it to win.

Chapter 3

FROM PRE-MODERN TO PRE-WAR

'There isn't a single Jew who doesn't carry within himself at least the beginning of Jewish self-hatred.'

Theodor Lessing, 1929

As with all aspects of Jewish history, it is the repeated patterns that inform our understanding of our experiences today. Though seemingly disparate, it is these sequences that help us understand concepts and ideas that emerged over time in relation to our peoplehood. Similarly with Jew-hate, though modern manifestations of internalised hatred may seem different on the surface, if we adopt a wider perspective, we see patterns emerge across Jewish history which are all rooted in the same core. These various responses are manifestations of our own definition of internalised anti-Jewishness: **'When Jews absorb non-Jewish perceptions of Jews, Jewishness and Judaism and allow the non-Jewish world to define our narrative.'**

Tragically, there are countless examples of Jewish individuals and communities that have absorbed non-Jewish perceptions of Jewish identity and have in turn experienced internalised anti-Jewishness. The examples chosen in this chapter are simply intended to highlight the endless pattern of internalised Jew-hatred that has blighted our collective and individual experience.

It is important to remember that we are not approaching these stories with the intention of judging or demonising those who feature in them. We are treating them with empathy, even though the individuals or organisations featured may have caused huge amounts of damage to our people. We must understand that they were Jews living in the violently oppressive anti-Jewish world, and though they are responsible for their own actions, we cannot divorce those actions from the wider context.

Though this phenomenon has been experienced by Jews for several millennia, it reached a crescendo in the period that followed Europe's staggered emancipation of the Jews who lived within its boundaries. As we will see, it is specifically within this era's milieu that the real and reflective conversations surrounding the issue of internalised Jew-hate began.

HELLENISED JEWS AND EPISPASM

The history of internalised Jew-hatred runs alongside the history of externalised Jew-hate. It stretches far back to the ancient world, long before the Jewish expulsion from Jerusalem when Jews still lived in our indigenous homeland.

In the late 330s BCE, the Greeks, under the famed Alexander the Great, defeated the mighty Persian Empire and took control of its possessions in the Levant, including the Jewish state of Judah (renaming it Judea). This was the backdrop to the events that led to the now legendary Jewish uprising of the Chanukah story. Jewish Zealots under Judah HaMaccabee defeated the Seleucid Empire, a Greek state in western Asia, under Antiochus IV and re-established a Jewish independent Kingdom in our homeland. Although they were Zealots, the Maccabees were responding to the legitimate and overt threat of cultural genocide that was being carried out by the Greeks which aimed to stamp out and destroy Judaism and Jewishness.

This Greek attempt at overt cultural genocide was not, however, always the policy that governed interactions between the Greeks and their new Jewish subjects. The Greeks initially allowed Jews to live as Jews, although, rather crucially, as they did with all their colonies, they imposed Greek culture onto them. This imposition, along with a natural desire to fit in and be accepted by those in positions of power, led to Jews identifying with the culture of their new overlords, eventually resulting in the creation of Hellenised Judaism, which itself can thus be read as an example of internalised anti-Jewishness.

One of the most extreme manifestations of internalised anti-Jewishness during this period was the practice of Jewish men attempting to reverse their circumcisions. According to the book of *Maccabees*, King Antiochus IV granted Jason (formerly known as Yehoshua), a High Priest in Jerusalem, the right to build a Greek gymnasium adjacent to the Second Jewish Temple. Ancient Greek gymnasiums were the social centre of male life. Sports took place there, business deals were conducted and there were spaces for education and socialising. Entry to such an important place was therefore vital if one was to advance through society. Importantly, Greek men participated in life at gymnasiums naked (the literal translation of gymnasium is a school for naked exercise). But due to being circumcised, Jewish men were automatically singled out as different and were not allowed to compete in public competitions. As scholar Holly Ann Jordan stated, 'reversing one's circumcision would have been necessary only in a society that practices public nudity and does not practice circumcision, such as the Greeks'.[126] They were excluded from a vital component of Greek social life. As Jonathan Goldstein, the biblical scholar, states, 'in a Greek Gymnasium all the physical exercises and sports were performed in complete nudity ... Many peoples of the Near East besides the Jews practiced circumcision, but Greeks tended to view it as an unseemly mutilation. Hence, some of the Hellenized Jewish youths who had to strip in the gymnasium were willing to submit to painful operations to disguise the fact that they had been circumcised.'[127]

Epispasm, the recreation of a foreskin, is an extreme attempt to fit in with the wider world. However, it is not entirely different from Jews engaging in rhinoplasty to be accepted and to 'look less Jewish' and to fit into Eurocentric beauty standards. Greek beauty standards, and the perception that circumcision was a form of mutilation, deepens our understanding of these ancient Jews' motives. It is not only the desire to be accepted into the Gymnasium and ancient Hellenised society that influenced this painful attempt to reclaim their lost foreskins. Jewish men were confronted with a dominant society that viewed their bodies as being mutilated. As Josh Law wrote in 'Reverse Circumcision in Hellenistic Judaism: The Case for a Gender Critical Readying', the 'Ancient Greeks are famous for their celebration of male beauty, and those who mutilated their male form were subject to mockery and isolation.'[128] To understand them from a modern context, these men wanted to 'pass'. They wanted to fit in and not be recognisably Jewish any longer.

These Greek perceptions of mutilated Jewish bodies may have also led these Jewish men (as other Jews have done throughout history) to perceive Jewish culture as less civilised and more barbaric than Hellenistic culture. Thus, we have a situation where Jews, although still in their indigenous homeland, were ruled by those who had specific disdain for Jewish culture, and as such ranked their own civilisation below that of their colonisers.

Whether these Jewish men absorbed negative Greek perceptions of circumcision or whether they engaged in epispasm simply to get ahead or avoid potential humiliation, the result was the same. Let us not forget that the instruction for circumcision was said to have come from God himself and is still a crucial element of the Jewishness of Jewish men all over the world. In Genesis, it is written, 'Any uncircumcised male who is not circumcised on the flesh of his foreskin shall be cut off from his people; he has broken my covenant.' So said God to Abraham, establishing the covenant of circumcision, a covenant 'between me and you and your descendants after you' (Genesis 17:10,14).[129] Thus, in abandoning circumcision, they effectively abandoned their relationship with God. Before the emergence of atheist Jews, this would have been seen as a staggering act of denial and an almost outright rejection of Judaism and Jewishness.

Through these procedures, these Jewish men were attempting to conform to the Greek masculine ideal and were rejecting their own Jewish ideas of masculine physicality which connected them to thousands of years of Jewish practice and heritage. It was also clearly seen as something which could be swept aside. It was possible for these men to disregard one of the most pivotal aspects of Jewish masculinity to be accepted, and to prosper, in Greek society.

More widely, as educator and author Jennifer Michael Hecht argues in her book, *Doubt: A History*, 'The secularist Jewish community began to see the empire and the Greek philosophical tradition as a significant part of their identity … the Jews who enjoyed Hellenistic culture may not have felt any less Jewish, seeing nothing ill in the Greek invitation to civic celebrations, universalist moral philosophy, exercise and education in the Gymnasium, a sense of progress, and a prosperous future for the kids.'[130] These Jews offer us a fascinating look into the psyche of those who suffer from this specific manifestation of anti-Jewish sentiment. By attempting to warp Jewishness through their own altered practice, they are then not compelled to emotionally process their own internalised Jew-hate. They can still profess to be Jews, even though we can see their internalised anti-Jewish sentiment play out in a very real, physical and painful way.

Ultimately, however, the act of epispasm and the emergence of Hellenised Judaism could not save these Jews from an intensification of anti-Jewish rhetoric. The Chanukah story, a defence against cultural genocide, took place after these events. Here, as in so many other stories, we see the same pattern where the Jews sacrifice so much to be accepted, but their sacrifices are not deemed sufficient by non-Jewish society.

The Hellenised Jews – and the men who engaged in epispasm – are one well-known ancient example of this phenomenon. But their experience offers us frightening insights into internalised Jew-hate. If Jewish men, living in the Jewish homeland, even though it was colonised, could fall prey to such extreme internalised anti-Jewish sentiment, how much more difficult is it for Jews torn from their indigenous land and living as a minority in the Diaspora?

CONVERTED JEWS

Like Pfefferkorn from the previous chapter, the following story features a Jew who denied his Jewishness and then deployed his former Jewishness as a weapon against other Jews. As we discussed, there are both 'push' and 'pull' factors regarding the conversion of Jews to other religious communities. The acceptance of, and preference given to, other religious doctrines is a pull factor, while the pressure of Jew-hatred and internalised anti-Jewishness is one of the push factors that can propel a Jew to convert out of Judaism.

As we saw with Pfefferkorn, non-Jewish societies can be so hostile that even when Jews formally abandon Judaism and Jewishness, they still feel compelled to demonise other Jews to prove their loyalty to their newfound co-religionists. This is a warped version of the 'good Jew'/'bad Jew' dynamic, and even though they were no longer Jews (aside from in an ancestral sense), they still had to prove their worth. Moreover, proving their worth did not focus their attention on being pious Christians who diligently followed the word of Christ, it led them instead to demonise Jews.

Similarly to Jews we encounter today who use their Jewishness to justify their anti-Jewish demonisation and delegitimisation of the Jewish state (and the vast majority of the Jewish people), the following former Jews also used their proximity to Jews to legitimise and promote anti-Jewish hate. In our time, Jews like these, namely antizionist Jews, are thankfully in the minority. But as we understand from the experience of the following individuals a small number of people can cause a great amount of harm.

One of the methods the Catholic Church in the Middle Ages engaged in to 'convince' Jews that Christianity was the true path to God was through disputations, which were public debates on religion between Jews and non-Jews before a sovereign. Given the power of the Church and its overt Jew-hate, Jews were never victorious in these debates that took place all over Europe. In these disputations, Jews were defending Judaism in an inherently and overtly hostile Christian society. The very best they could hope for was 'a draw' and the avoidance of pogroms that so often followed these public humiliations of Jews and Judaism. This was often a catch-22 situation for Jews. They could lose the debate and be attacked, or they could try and win the debate, but still be attacked. As author Michael J. Cook argues in *Jesus Through Jewish Eyes: Rabbis and Scholars Engage an Ancient Brother in a New Conversation*, 'since "winning" a debate could well jeopardise the security of the Jewish community at large, political considerations certainly entered into what Jewish disputants publicly said or refrained from saying.'[131]

Although this style of debate had been occurring since pre-Christian times, a particularly significant disputation took place in Paris in 1240. As with many disputations, the Christian side of the argument was defended by a former Jew who had converted to Christianity and who, because of his former Jewishness, supposedly had intimate knowledge of the evils of Judaism. The tragic traitor in the case of the Paris Disputation was Nicholas Donin.

Donin's journey towards the demonisation of the Jews began with his excommunication for doubting the value of Oral Traditions, i.e. the *Mishnah*, which makes up one half of the Talmud (the other half, the *Gemara*, is a record of the Rabbi's commentary on the *Mishnah*). Though by today's standards, doubting tradition does not warrant excommunication, Donin's doubt was during a time where such questioning was not tolerated. Though this action may seem harsh, his excommunica-tion does not justify Donin's total betrayal of his former community. Baruch Spinoza, the famed Sephardic Dutch Jewish philosopher, was controversially excommunicated in 1656 but did not turn on his people in the way Donin eventually did.

Though he initially clung to his Jewish identity, Donin lived a half-life of an excommunicated Jew, and he eventually succumbed to the pressures and propaganda of Christianity and converted. In a tragic about-face, Donin's work became focused on demonising and destroying Jews and Judaism. His first act of anti-Jewish hatred was to whip up and encourage the crusaders to massacre 3,000 Jews in Brittany, Poitou and Anjou. By 1238 he had travelled to Rome to denounce the Talmud before Pope Gregory IX. Like Pfefferkorn, who demonised the Talmud, Donin wrote 35 articles where he stated his own charges against the Talmud.

Following his conversion to Christianity, Donin became a Domin-ican Brother of La Rochelle, and described the Talmud as mocking Christianity. The demonisation of the Talmud as an especially evil and dangerous document was not created by Jews like Donin, but it certainly was promoted by them, and the legitimacy of his accusations rested on his former Jewishness. He was intimate with the Talmud; he had presumably read it during his studies, and he understood it. Therefore, he (and other converted Jews) could alone identify the danger it posed to Christianity.

Donin's testimony is not dissimilar to Theobald, the English monk (also a former Jew), whose support for the accusation of blood libel in England in 1144 was legitimised because he had been Jewish. In fact, Thomas of Monmouth, who interviewed Theobald when he was writ-ing *The Life and Miracles of St William of Norwich* stated, 'As a proof of the truth and credibility of the matter we now adduce something which we have heard from the lips of Theobald, who was once a Jew, and afterwards a monk.'[132]

Based on Donin's articles, the Pope ordered copies of the Talmud in Paris to be seized. Although Donin clearly made a compelling case against the Talmud, a Pope in the Middle Ages did not need much cajoling to order the persecution of Jews. It is in this way that Donin and other former-Jews like him appear as the good (former) Jew or the token (former) Jew to their respective non-Jewish societies. We see this pattern emerge repeatedly. This token figure is a component of many different examples of internalised hatred. Again though, we must view Jews like Donin with an element of empathy, and we must also acknowledge the realities of their backgrounds, the hatred and racism of the world around him that advocated for the destruction of the Jews (in whatever way appropriate to that specific period).

In March of 1240 the Jews of Paris were forced, under pain of death, to hand over their copies of the precious Talmud to the Dominicans and Franciscans. Following this, Louis IX forced four of the most eminent French rabbis, Yechiel of Paris (who was responsible for the excommunication of Donin), Moses of Coucy, Judah of Melun, and Samuel ben Solomon of Château-Thierry, to debate Donin in a disputation in the presence of the Queen. The rabbis argued against Donin's accusations that the Talmud contained anti-Christian messages in vain, but Jew-hate meant that the odds were never in their favour. They lost the argument against their former brother, Donin, and the Talmud was burned publicly in Paris and Rome in 1244. These burnings were not simply the destruction of Jewish literature, they were a direct attack on the intellectual nature of Judaism and on Jewish law. They destroyed the views, the arguments and the commentary of great rabbis. It was an act of deeply anti-Jewish cultural destructions, and as journalist David B. Green describes, '24 wagon loads included up to 10,000 volumes of Hebrew manuscripts [were burnt], a startling number when one considers that the printing press did not yet exist, so that all copies of a work had to be written out by hand.'[133]

The Paris Disputation was the result of Donin, a former Jew, enacting revenge on his former community while trying to cleanse himself of his Jewishness. And just as Theobald's testimony was used to justify accusations of blood libel that erupted all over Europe, Donin's actions precipitated a change in the perception of Jews in France. It presented Jews, who had previously been viewed as the keepers and followers of the Old Testament and Mosaic Law, as blasphemers, which ultimately resulted in the expulsion of Jews in France by King Philip IV on 22 July in 1306.

As the experiences of Pfefferkorn and Donin tell us, converting isn't always enough for Jews to be fully accepted. This also reveals a crucial component of our relationship with non-Jewish societies. As we discussed in Chapter 2, it speaks to Jewish ancestry and an aspect of Jew-hate, which tells us that abandoning Jewishness is not that simple. A Jew retains a residue of their former Jewishness (in the form of their Jewish ancestry) even after denying it or formally denouncing it. Suspicion and hatred often followed them wherever they went. Victor of Karben, a German Jew from the 16th century (a former rabbi no less), who had converted to Christianity expressed this constant suspicion when he wrote:

'And some come to me and ask craftily, "Were you a Jew?" When I answer in the affirmative, they mock me and say, "Go to St Andrew's Church in Cologne. A cat and a mouse. A dog and a rabbit." This means that as little as a cat and a mouse, or as little as a dog and a rabbit can be friends, so little could I become a good Christian. And they said with satisfaction, "Though you may act like a Christian, you are still a Jew at heart."'[134]

This was the experience of Jews who had abandoned their Jewishness and converted to Christianity. They are undoubtedly tragic figures. They, like so many before and after them, wanted desperately to be accepted by those around them. They were not able to find self-esteem in their own community and in their own Jewish anchor. Though Pfefferkorn and Donin (and many others) endangered their former community and are undoubtedly villains in our story, they have, like so many other villains, tragic origin or backstories.

Sadly, Jews continued to experience internalised Jew-hate as history unfolded. Indeed, it intensified during the period of the 18th and 19th centuries, which saw an explosion of this phenomenon and, crucially, saw conversations begin that aimed to identify and address it.

THE POST-ENLIGHTENMENT IDENTITY CRISIS

The Enlightenment changed much for the Jews living in the Western world. These changes are often deemed to be positive for Jews, and they were in some important ways. But Jewish hopes of acceptance were ultimately dashed, not least by the unintended consequences of emancipation and the persistence of Jew-hate.

At this stage of our historical exploration of internalised anti-Jewishness, our focus will be the impact of the Enlightenment on Jews in Europe, but it also had an impact upon the lives and identity of Jews across the Atlantic. In the new United States, American Jews, like their French brethren, responded to the guarantee of religious freedom by George Washington in 1790 by adopting a solely religious identity. This culminated in the 1885 Pittsburgh Platform when the American movement of Reform Judaism stated, 'We consider ourselves no longer a nation, but a religious community', officially shedding Jewish nationhood (and our connection to and yearning for our indigenous land) as part of Jewish identity.[135] As was the case with Ella Emhoff, this framing of Jewishness, as a solely religious identity, continues to have an impact upon both Jewish and non-Jewish perceptions of Jewishness to this day.

In the 130 years after the French Revolution, Jews living in Europe were emancipated. To truly understand the significance of this, we must first understand what their lives were like before. Throughout the Middle Ages, being a Jew in Europe, indeed being a Jew anywhere, was incredibly precarious. Jews lived lives of legal segregation and oppression and were routinely murdered in genocides, such as the Spanish and Portuguese Inquisition. We were often ethnically cleansed from the lands in which we built our homes, including much of Western Europe and other places, such as Morocco. Crucially, Jews living in Europe prior to emancipation were not European (just as Jews living in Arab lands were not Arab). They were Jews permitted to live in Europe. This is an important distinction. To Jews in Europe, emancipation would have been the most significant change in their circumstances in 2,000 years. As a 1791 letter to *La Chronique de Paris*, a monthly literary review, stated, emancipation meant the recognition 'that Jews were equal to other citizens and working toward the legal abolition of disabilities and inequities.'[136] Unlike their previous status, they were now citizens of non-Jewish European societies, supposedly the equals of non-Jewish Europeans.

However, the newfound freedoms enjoyed by Jews in Europe came at a cost and triggered a Jewish identity crisis. And despite appearances, emancipation was not really an act of altruism. It was not a case of non-Jewish European societies openly welcoming Jews into their midst just as they were. Although they had been emancipated legally, Jews were still expected to uphold their end of a bargain they did not agree to. They were expected to conform to non-Jewish definitions and expectations of what it meant to be a Jew in post-Enlightenment Europe. They discarded or weakened their Jewish anchors. They shed their nationhood and their specificity and diminished their own more traditional Jewish identities to be accepted.

This discarding of Jewish nationhood in order to be accepted demonstrates the harsh conditions put on Jews. In response to

Johann Gottlieb Fichte, the German philosopher who stated the Jews cannot have a separate national identity, German Jewish psychologist Moritz Lazarus argued, '… We are Germans and nothing but Germans, when we speak from the concept of nationality, we belong to only one nation, the German'.[137] We must not condemn or demonise Jews like Lazarus who also stated, 'The Jews no longer have their own nationality'. They only wanted the Jews to be treated as equals. But we must also recognise the inherent danger of shedding integral aspects of your Jewish identity to be accepted by the wider world. As we will see, it never works.

This is where the Broken Mirror of Jewish identity went into overdrive. Jews were expected to acquiesce to the demands of their respective non-Jewish societies. Their new-found freedom alone is not sufficient in explaining the identity crisis that ensued. If the Jews had been permitted to remain authentically Jewish without being coerced into being a 'good Jew', then this discussion may not be as relevant today as it is. However, the identity crisis was a result of the coercive nature of the emancipatory promise. Sadly, this period of emancipation and assimilation can be summed up by the German Jewish writer Conrad Alberti, who described the struggle of the assimilated Jew as 'the unceasing struggle with ourselves' as they sought acceptance from a world who would never embrace them.[138] Of course, there were some Jews who continued to live their lives as they had done before, but many did not. However, expecting Jews, who had lived lives of legalised oppression, to resist the allure of freedom and emancipation is perhaps unreasonable when considering the reality of their circumstances.

Moses Mendelssohn and the Haskalah
One of the Jews who embodied, and helped create, this Jewish post-emancipation identity crisis was Moses Mendelssohn, often considered the father of the *Haskalah*. Mendelssohn was born in

1729 in the city of Dessau, in the principality of Anhalt-Dessau (in modern-day Germany). He was short in stature and had a hunched back and his disadvantages were intensified by being Jewish. He was educated by David Frankel, who, when Moses was just 14 years old, was appointed the Chief Rabbi of Berlin. When Frankel moved to the then-Prussian capital to take up his post, Moses was allowed to follow to continue his learning. This was Berlin, prior to the Enlightenment and prior to emancipation. Only 2,000 Jews deemed to be economically useful were allowed to reside within the city walls, while the rest were confined to the ghetto and segregated from the Christian majority. Moses, though, was exceptional and was later referred to as the 'Jewish Socrates', which helped him to navigate this racist system.[139] To gain acceptance and recognition, while he did publish work in Hebrew, he was not loud about his Jewishness. However, his brilliance and the Jew-hatred of those around him who couldn't believe a Jew could produce such important works forced him to publicly address his Jewishness.

On 12 December 1769, Mendelssohn wrote a letter to Zurich Pastor Johannes Caspar Lavater refusing to engage in a public disputation about religion. This was an impressive act by an aware man. As we saw previously from the example of Donin, public debates between Judaism and Christianity were designed by the Christian majority to demonstrate their superiority. Mendelssohn strongly disliked such displays. 'I hate all religious disputes, especially those conducted in the eyes of the public. Experience teaches that they are useless. They produce hate rather than clarification,' he argued.[140] Reading between the lines, we can infer that he believed that not only were religious debates useless, but they were also, generally speaking, very dangerous for Jews.

Following the Lavater Affair and the French Revolution, Mendelssohn began publicly advocating for Jews. Although, like most Jews in Germany, he initially spoke only Yiddish and Hebrew, he learned to speak German. And, in one of his most important contributions to the German Jewish community, Mendelssohn translated the Torah into German, saying it was a 'first step towards culture'[141] for the Jews. This translation is significant because the only other translations of the Torah into German were undertaken by Christians. This was an attempt to Germanise the Jewish community but by a Jew. Similarly to the characters used in Yiddish, Moses' translation used Hebrew characters. Although it is almost moving to see Mendelssohn's hope in a future where Jews and Germans could coexist, this misguided faith ignored the deep history – and continued presence – of Jew-hatred in Europe. It is tragic, seeing the hope that existed in Mendelssohn despite the fact he continued to operate in an ever-hostile world.

Mendelssohn's translation was rooted in discussions about belonging. During the 18th century, conversations on identity were rooted in language. You could not be a German if you did not speak German. And, for Jews, as we saw in Chapter 1, despite their best efforts, learning or speaking German did not necessarily result in them being considered German. They were 'othered' because they were Jews. But just like the Hellenised Jews' translations of Hebrew into Greek, Mendelssohn's translation of the Torah was an attempt not just to Germanise Jewishness and Judaism, but to move Jews towards what was considered by non-Jewish society at the time as higher culture. And this is where the problematic nature of Mendelssohn's work emerges.

There is obviously nothing inherently wrong with translating the Torah into German. However, Mendelssohn's thinking placed the 4,000-year-old Jewish civilisation and culture below that of Germany. Thus, Mendelssohn argued that Yiddish was 'a language of stammers, corrupt and deformed, repulsive to those who are able to speak in a correct and elegant manner.'[142] Nor was he alone in this way of thinking. As Professor Dovid Katz argues in his *Words on Fire: The Unfinished Story of Yiddish* (2004), 'Many antisemitic books appeared accusing the Jews of having a secret language that they used to fool

Christians in commerce and commit blasphemy against Jesus Christ and Christendom. These books usually attacked the language of the Jews with an aesthetic judgment that Yiddish was an ugly, barbaric "jargon" emblematic of the Jews' lack of civilization.'[143]

Such perceptions were wrong; Yiddish is not barbaric. It was the language of our Ashkenazi family and it represented the diverse beauty of Ashkenazi culture. But, to Mendelssohn's mind, to be traditionally Jewish was to be a 'bad Jew', and to be integrated was to be a 'good Jew'. It is here, and in many other examples, we can see that Mendelssohn's actions were driven, at least in part, by the internalised anti-Jewishness.

In some ways, Jews like Mendelssohn are perhaps even more tragic than Pfefferkorn and Donin. They discarded their Jewishness because they could not exist as Jews in a Christian world. It is likely that they had no illusions of how Jews were treated and they saw no other choice but to convert to Christianity. But Mendelssohn tried desperately to keep hold of it. He wanted to be Jewish. He did not want to discard it and he lived his life as an observant Jew. As Gilman writes, '… Mendelssohn also felt he had to be accepted by the Jewish community. Unlike Spinoza who was excommunicated by the Dutch Jews, Mendelssohn wished to restructure the very definition of the Jew as to make his new splitting of the good Jew from the bad Jew the norm rather than the exception.'[144] And in hopes of saving it, he inadvertently went to great lengths to destroy aspects of Jewish culture and civilisation. Though Mendelssohn, in his own complicated way, was an advocate for Jews, he chose to recreate Jewish culture as simply an extension of modern German culture. He sought to be a 'good Jew'. His impact, as historian Paul Kriwaczek argues in *Yiddish Civilization: The Rise and Fall of a Forgotten Nation*, was thus a malign one:

'This towering genius … [who] could have helped establish the Yiddish civilization among the founders of the modern

European world, was so subject to the prejudices and antago-
nisms between the German and Slav-influenced halves of the
Yiddish realm, that he colluded in denigrating the major part of
his own nation. Indeed, one could say that he unwittingly began
the process by which the Yiddish civilization would eventually
be written out of history.'[145]

While Yiddish survived in Eastern Europe, mainly due to the legal
restrictions in place against Jews until well into the 20th century,
many enlightened Jews shared Mendelssohn's disdain for traditional
Jewish culture. Isaac Dov Levinson, a Russian follower of Mendelssohn, wrote in 1828 that Yiddish is 'completely corrupted … If we wish
to formulate concepts about higher things, Judeo-German will not
suffice.'[146] And as Rabbi Eli Kavon suggested in his article 'How Moses
Mendelssohn killed Yiddish in Germany', 'most German Jews agreed
with Mendelssohn that Yiddish presented a stumbling block to being
good, emancipated German citizens.'[147] Jews, like Mendelssohn and
Levinson, had absorbed non-Jewish ideas that argued Jewish culture
is inferior to non-Jewish culture. As a result, they supported the denigration of the Jewish language (and culture) by the Christian world.

As discussed in Chapter 1, despite our experiences, many Jews
continue to put our trust in the non-Jewish world. Mendelssohn was
no different. He lived at a time of great upheaval but, like other Jews,
he forgot the historic Jewish experience. He did not understand that,
regardless of space or time, Jews are rejected and demonised by the
world around them. He put his faith in the non-Jewish world. Like
many Jews who came before and after, it is clear that he felt that
diminishing parts of Judaism and Jewishness were a sufficient sacrifice in order to join non-Jewish society. He thought that with a little
tweaking, Jews would be accepted by the wider world. Ultimately,
Jews of the Haskalah were willing to almost de-Jewify Judaism in
order to remake it, and themselves, as compatible with the modern

world. They changed their dress, their religious practice, their jobs and even the language they spoke. But these efforts did not result in an acceptance of the Jews.

Although Mendelssohn advocated for emancipation, this process did not begin until 1808 with the emancipation of the Jews in the Grand Duchy of Hesse. Advocating for equality and the Jewish compatibility with Germanness, Mendelssohn published *Jerusalem* in 1783. In this work he stated: 'The supreme Being has revealed [religious doctrine and tenets] to all rational creatures through concepts and events inscribed in their souls with a script that is legible and intelligible at all times and in all places.'[148] Ultimately, he argued that Judaism was a rational religion and, as such, was not contradictory to the ideals of the Enlightenment. Therefore, Jews could be citizens of modern society.

Mendelssohn's efforts to prove that Judaism was a rational religion eventually became key to the work of *Wissenschaft des Judentums* and played a significant role in the creation of the new movement of Reform Judaism that emerged in Germany in the 19th century. Reform Rabbi Kaufmann Kohler wrote that Reform Judaism allowed Jews 'to be perfectly at home in our Western civilization and to be at one with their fellow citizens, not an alien and a stranger with a foreign tongue.'[149] The idea that Judaism was a modern rational movement was demonstrated through the remaking of it as a universal ideology. As we know, this tension between the universality of the modern world and the specificity of the Jews had created pressure for the Jews to shed what made them specific and to adopt universal perspectives. Not dissimilar to modern Jews who root their Jewish identities in Tikkun Olam (which we will explore in the next chapter), the Judaism that emanated from Mendelssohn's work was focused on the idea of a universal tolerance. This was promoted by Kohler, who argued that the commandment of love thy neighbour applies to all humans and not just Jews. He wrote:

'On the contrary, the Talmud expressly states that the basis of that law is the chapter of Genesis which declares that man was made in the image of God. And to avoid all misunderstanding the Law reiterates the command: "Love ye stranger, for strangers ye have been in Egypt."'[150]

Having love for humanity and using one's experiences to advocate for others does not necessarily mean you are suffering from internalised anti-Jewishness. Philosopher Emmanuel Levinas wrote, 'The traumatic experience of my slavery in Egypt constitutes my very humanity, a fact that immediately allies me to the workers, the wretched, and the persecuted people of the world.'[151] As Levinas describes, our specificity can contribute towards notions of universality as we can use our experiences to empathise with other parts of our community, which, in turn, supports the idea of a community made up of distinct elements. However, what is problematic about Mendelssohn and those who followed him was the manner in which Jewish practice and ideology evolved specifically in order to be accepted by the non-Jewish world, as well as his perspective of 'good Jews' and 'bad Jews'. It is the ranking of culture and the altering of Jewish identity to be accepted that is a symbol of his internalised anti-Jewishness.

Although he – and many of those he inspired – clearly had love for Jewishness and Judaism, the work that he contributed to German Jewish life did not succeed in allowing German Jews to escape Jew-hate. Despite its promise, emancipation failed in creating a world where Jews could live freely as Jews. The continuing nature and evolution of Jew-hate continued to harm Jews to such an extent that many Jews felt as if they could not even live lives as assimilated Jews. They had to convert to Christianity in order to truly overcome their supposed Jewish handicap. In fact, author Daniel B. Schwartz describes an 'epidemic of baptism'[152] among the Berlin Jewish elite and 100,000 Jews were thought to have converted to Christianity in Germany during the late 18th and 19th centuries. Mendelssohn's own daughter, Dorothea Schlegel, converted to Protestantism, and Schwartz notes that 'Of Mendelssohn's six children, four converted [to Christianity], all following their father's death in 1786. Of his grandchildren, only one went to his grave as a Jew.' In a letter to his daughter, Abraham Mendelssohn, Moses' son, wrote, 'We have educated you and your brothers and sister in the Christian faith, because it is the creed of most civilized people.'[153] Though they clearly differed on their identity, both Moses and Abraham ultimately agreed that Jewish culture was less civilised than others at that time, namely German and Christian. But, like Pfefferkorn 400 years earlier, even following conversion, Jews were not able to overcome their Jewishness. Although the famed poet Heinrich Heine argued 'the baptismal certificate is the ticket of admission to European culture', he later regretted his conversion.[154] Echoing the Hellenised Jews who engaged in epispasm to get ahead, Heine hoped that conversion would help him with an appointment to a much sought-after academic position, but he was unsuccessful. In a tragic letter to his friend Moses Moser, Heine wrote, 'I just converted to Christianity and already they are angry at me for being a Jew?'[155] Ultimately, Heine's sacrifice, and the sacrifice of so many Jews, just to be accepted by the non-Jewish world was, rather heartbreakingly, in vain.

The fact that Mendelssohn's own children converted to Christianity underlines the naivety in his work. He put faith in a world which he should never have trusted. It was not Mendelssohn's fault that he failed to create a world where Jews could be both proudly Jewish and proudly German. In his calls for Jews to 'adapt yourselves to the morals and the constitution of the land to which you have been removed; but hold fast to the religion of your fathers'[156] he failed to understand that this was not easy, not because being Jewish was somehow incompatible with being German, but because the non-Jewish world was anti-Jewish. He failed to address the pressure, both in terms of internalising Jew-hate and the basic facts of society that caused Jews to convert to Christianity, as Rabbi Eli Kavon describes, 'to be cured of the disease of a primitive and ossified Judaism.'[157] It is not hard to see why Abraham Mendelssohn converted to Christianity, when his own father, though proudly Jewish, felt that Jewish culture was inferior to that of Germany.

Indeed, while Mendelssohn and others fought for a place for Jews in German society, continuing and developing Jew-hatred meant that they were ultimately unsuccessful. Jew-hate continued to evolve with others arguing against emancipation. Prior to emancipation, Christian Europe thought of Jews as obstinate. They were perceived as having purposefully rejected Christ and were seen as wanting to remain separate and distinct. This is why Pfefferkorn spoke of forcibly converting Jews in the 16th century.

However, following emancipation and the development of modern science, race theory emerged as a pseudoscientific offshoot. This was a modern expression of the historic racialisation suffered by Jews. This was used to justify the idea that Jews were unable to join Christian society, even if they wanted to. An output of the scientific evolution of the 19th century, race theory, a product of social Darwinism, created the modern notion of races and racism. Thus Jews were framed as a biologically inferior race who were unable to shed what made them Jewish and were therefore an inherent danger. As German anti-Jewish pamphleteer Karl Wilhelm Friedrich Grattenauer argued, the 'mentality of the Jews was unalterable even through the act of baptism.'[158] This exclusion of Jews was rooted in the German notion of *Volk* (folk), created by the German philosopher Johann Gottfried Herder, which argued that Germans are one race that can trace their ancestry back to the ancient Teutons. They were racially pure, and Jews were foreign interlopers. As historian Richard Weikart stated, 'toward the end of the nineteenth century quite a few biological racists radicalized racial distinctions by stressing the supremacy of the

German or "Aryan" race and simultaneously denigrating the Jews.'[159] Indeed, this era saw the creation of 'antisemitism' as a word, which was rooted in racial theories focused on language as an indicator of biology and as a sign of belonging. With devastating consequences, this modern expression of anti-Jewish racism later became the basis for the Nazis' ideology.

It is tragic to consider that just over 150 years after Mendelssohn died, and after the immense effort made by German Jews to be accepted, his beloved Germany (assisted by its allies) began mass-murdering Jews in Europe based on race theory. Mendelssohn and his followers believed that if they fulfilled their end of the bargain, to remake Jewishness and Judaism, then the non-Jewish world would fulfil theirs.

The tragedy is it did not.

RECOGNITION: THEODOR LESSING AND *DER JÜDISCHER SELBSTHAß*

Against this backdrop of assimilation and unhealthy forms of integration, conversations began surrounding the issues of internalised Jew-hatred. While, as we have explored, many Jews promoted assimilation, there were also those who argued against it and who criticised the efforts that assimilationist Jews were going to in order to integrate into the non-Jewish world.

Initially, the conversations focusing on the issues of internalised anti-Jewishness were not as evolved as our own. As I outlined in the Introduction, the common phraseology to describe this phenomenon was 'self-hatred'. This, as historian Shulamit Volkov explained 'was typical of a certain particular phase in the history of German Jews, following the completion of their emancipation especially during the years immediately preceding World War 1'.[160]

However, these conversations are the intellectual roots of the one that we are having today, and although we may disagree on the correct language to use, we must acknowledge the history of our own discussions. The phrase 'Jewish self-hate' was utilised by many, including Anton Kuh, the anti-assimilationist Austrian Jewish writer, but it entered into our collective lexicon due to the work of Theodor Lessing with the publication of his seminal 1930 book, *Der Jüdischer Selbsthaß* (Jewish Self-hate)

Like Kuh, Lessing was born into a highly assimilated Jewish German family in 1872. His parents were so keen on 'passing' as German that he only found out he was Jewish when he was scolded for racially abusing a Jew. 'You're one too,'[161] he was told. In fact, as author Paul Reitter suggested, 'Sigmund and Adele more or less instructed Theodor to see his Jewish heritage as something repellent, as something to be kept "covered"'.[162] In his own words Lessing described that he 'went through a period of *Deutschtum* and total reaction against *Judentum*'.[163] This ultimately resulted in his 1895 conversion to Protestantism.

As Sander Gilman states, the struggle against Jewishness is rooted in 'the denial of the essential Jew within'.[164] This caused Lessing to grapple with his own Jewish identity, and he asked questions that are still relevant to us today. 'Can a plant disown the soil out of which it grew? Am I myself not the fruit of a people and circumstances I hate and want to wipe out? Am I not damaged, lowly ill-bred, ruined?'[165] Lessing's eventual embrace of his Jewishness and his abandonment of Protestantism was, unlike Kuh, who rejected Zionism as being a product of European nationalism, tied to increasing identification with Zionism, which he called, 'the great work of the Jewish people'.[166] More widely, from 1896, the Zionist movement reignited the spark of Jewishness that had been extinguished by emancipation. Lessing noted that as some of the assimilated Jews of Europe began to dream of a Jewish homeland, they founded the Jewish Agency in 1908.

Lessing's 1930 book, *Der Jüdischer Selbsthaß*, popularised the concept Kuh had outlined a decade earlier. In it, he breaks down reasons for this Jewish affliction while offering a path to redemption. This work is crucial in understanding both the origins of 'Jewish self-hate' and its historic prevalence in our community. Although published over 90 years ago, parts of Lessing's work seem as if they were written today.

When discussing the German Jewish community, there is a tendency to judge them for their assimilation. This is extraordinarily lacking in empathy. When it opened up to Jews, the lure of the new world could not be resisted. And, similarly, oppressive pressure that European non-Jewish culture imposed on Jews to conform was simply too great. Jews could not stay in the ghetto, when the world, the bright, shiny new world, was now open to us. As Lessing described, 'One would have to think of people as better than mere human beings if one wished to blame Jews for mass conversion to Catholicism or Protestantism during the Age of Enlightenment. They really believed in love, at the very least in "tolerance"'.[167] And, as he also argues, we cannot judge those like Mendelssohn too harshly. They were trying to overcome the perceived handicap of being Jewish, to become citizens of the global world. But despite the promise offered by emancipation and the fact that the French Revolution and the Enlightenment greatly reduced the power of the Church in Europe, Jew-hate did not disappear. The reason the modern Western world continues to be so embedded with Jew-hate is because Christianity was the seed from which Western culture grew. As Lessing states, 'the development of "modern culture" is inseparable from that of the history of Christianity.'[168]

As we know, a major difficulty that Mendelssohn and the like were attempting to overcome was the specificity of Jewishness, as opposed to the universality of the new Europe. It is why they worked so hard to warp and change their Jewishness. Not only did they want Jewishness and Judaism to fit in with the new world, but they also wanted to create a situation where, as Lessing argued, 'Judaism becomes the bearer of universal teaching'.[169] Referencing the work of

Moses Mendelssohn and the Reform movement, this was an attempt to make Judaism compatible and relevant to the new universalistic values promoted during and following the Enlightenment. However, as we have previously seen, this caused significant damage to Jewish specificity and Jewish self-perception.

Despite the prevalence of Jew-hate, in *Jewish Self-Hate*, Lessing envisions a Jewish response to the demands of the non-Jewish world. He imagines the Jews rejecting the offer of so-called friendship because they refuse to sacrifice, warp or diminish their Jewishness to be accepted. Sadly, for most, this was not the response. But we can allow ourselves a moment to imagine if it was. What might have been the outcome? Lessing envisages the following speech:

'For the past two-thousand years, we have lived for the coming of the Messiah, who has been promised to lead us back home. Now your benevolence and friendship offer us beautiful Europe and great America as fatherlands. But, as payment, we would have to break with our own historic traditions, in order to adapt and grow into the Great Christian West. We cannot do this! We have never demanded of you that you convert to our religion. We have never sent missionaries among the nations or been addicted to conquest. We want to bear our sidelocks and yellow patch undisturbed. We want to preserve our Hebrew language and names. We refuse to participate in your holidays and memorials, each of which can only remind us of past martyrs. You are welcome to your images and gods, but you should leave us to ours. We are, and must remain, different ... We do not follow the creed of the Holy Trinity. Our God has neither form nor name, beyond man and the abomination of world history. You are free to despise us, but we in turn refuse to accept your benefits: your offices and schools, your ways and means. We voluntarily carry forward the galut and ghetto, awaiting our Messiah to appear out of Bethlehem.'[170]

But, as Lessing asks, 'Would such a reply have been possible?' To some, it might have been, but to many others it would not have been. Not only was the gleam of the new world too bright but the pressure to join it was also oppressive. We cannot blame 19th-century European Jews for not giving this speech. But we can blame the non-Jewish world for forcing them to choose between their Jewishness and their membership in wider society. We should refuse to choose. We will not. Today, we do not need, as Lessing imagined, to consign ourselves to ghettos, we can integrate as proud Jews. This is not impossible, but we must recognise that it is not easy. We are attempting to integrate into a world that does not want us to be ourselves. They want us to be a version of ourselves that is, in reality, just a version of themselves. This is the 300-year-old conundrum posed by Jewish integration. It is difficult. But, once again, I must state, the fault does not lie with us. Yes, there are some Jews who do not wish to integrate, which is their choice, but many of us want to. Many of us already feel as if we have, to some extent, dual identities. But the explanation for this difficulty in Jewish integration lies in the behaviour of the non-Jewish world. It refuses to allow us to be proud Jews with an authentic Jewish identity based on Jewish experience, values and traditions. Lessing describes the tragedy of Jewish integration, 'But the price that Jews have paid to become European citizens is either ignored or spoken of in hushed tones: betrayal of their hopes, and sacrifice of their dreams.'[171]

Ultimately, as he asked, 'From what do Jewish self-haters suffer if not an unhappy love for an enemy?'[172] This unrequited love is what causes Jews to so aggressively hide, warp or even reject their Jewishness. They are desperately seeking approval, and perhaps they are also aware of how the world views Jews, which makes them try even harder to be accepted. This is the tragedy of these kinds of Jews suffering from internalised anti-Jewish hate. They are trying to achieve the unachievable. And as a result, as Lessing argues, 'all people of Jewish blood have a tendency to Jewish self-hate'.[173] Whether or not all Jews (and not just those who were born Jewish) have a tendency, they at the very least have the capacity to develop internalised anti-Jewishness.

Though Lessing spoke of Jewish blood, it is not only Jews with Jewish ancestry who can experience internalised Jew-hate. Even Jews by choice, people who have made the decision to join the Jewish people, can still experience internalised anti-Jewishness. This is simply because prior to their conversion, they lived as non-Jews in the non-Jewish world. For however long they lived this way, they were not dealing with the challenges of being a Jew in the Diaspora. They were part of the majority and a majority that is taught to view Jews in specific, negative ways. Therefore, without serious introspection it is possible that certain anti-Jewish perspectives could stay with someone, even after their conversion. This may seem contradictory, but, as we must always remember, these issues are immensely complex. Though specific anti-Jewish ideas may originate while these Jews were still living as non-Jews, we must consider this as a form of internalised anti-Jewish hate once they convert. Jews by choice and Jews with Jewish ancestry must both investigate, and overcome, any feelings of internalised anti-Jewishness they may have.

Anton Kuh and Theodor Lessing are the architects of our structural understanding of this issue in our community. Though the nuances and complexities of their arguments may be forgotten, the phrase they coined and popularised lives on. When I discuss internalised anti-Jewish sentiment, most people respond by referencing 'Jewish self-hate'. And although we reject this phrase, we must acknowledge their work and their contributions so we can create our own understanding of internalised anti-Jewish hate. We must also understand this work in its context. It emerged during a time of crisis where Jews were suffering the most intense period of internalised Jew-hatred in several millennia.

Due to the origins of the discourse, many commentators believe that internalised anti-Jewish sentiment or 'Jewish self-hate' is a result of the fin de siècle. However, we must acknowledge that while these conversations may have begun in earnest in the 19th century, the phenomenon has been a part of the Jewish experience for thousands of years. It is this acknowledgement that deepens our understanding of why this issue has plagued the Jewish community, in varying degrees, for almost 3,000 years.

Tragically, Jewish attempts to be part of German society continued even after Hitler became Chancellor. Jews continued to put trust in the wider non-Jewish German society and on 31 January 1933, the day after Hitler's appointment, the *Jüdische Rundschau* argued 'within the German nation still the forces are active that would turn against a barbarian anti-Jewish policy.'[174]

In yet another demonisation of the Jewish language, the official German student organisation displayed posters in April 1933 that said Jews who write in German were liars, Jews can only write in Hebrew. Max Hermann, a Jewish professor of the history of the theatre of Berlin who later was murdered in the Theresienstadt concentration camp, was offended by this assertion that Jews were not Germans. In a letter to the Ministry of Culture, he refused to enter the theatre as long as the posters were displayed. He wrote, 'My honour is offended … by the reference to that group with which I am associated by birth, and about which it is publicly stated that the Jews can only think Jewish; that if he writes German, then he lies … I write German, I think German, I feel German and I do not lie.'[175] Again we see the idea that Jews speaking German are simply passing as German to cause Germany harm, and again we see Jews forced to assert their other identity and distance themselves from Jewishness to be accepted. But they are still seen as usurpers and they do not belong. For the Jew to use the language of the place in which he lives has one only aim. As Hitler himself claimed, 'For the [Jews language] is not a means for expressing thoughts but a means of concealing them.'[176]

Even after 11,737,021 Germans voted for the Nazis in November 1932, and even after Nazi Jew-hate had started to impact their lives, many German Jews still tragically put their faith, and rooted their identity, in Germany. Considering the history of German Jewish assimilation, it is staggering that the Nazis and the Holocaust emanated from Germany, where the Jews had worked so incredibly hard to be accepted. The extermination of six million Jews and the systematic oppression of countless other Jewish people was one of the most significant moments in Jewish history. It led to the realisation by Jews all over the world that no matter how much they acculturate they would not be accepted. We might think this shocking and frightening realisation may have propelled Jews to proudly proclaim their Jewishness, but in some quarters, particularly in America, it had, as we will see, the opposite effect.

Chapter 4

FROM POST-WAR TO PRESENT

'Today's un-Jews remain as engaged with parts of their Jewish heritage, as appalled by other parts, and as anxious for acceptance, as their predecessors.'[177]

Natan Sharansky and Gil Troy, 2021

As it has always been, the issue of internalised Jew-hate following the Shoah was a response to Jew-hate and an attempt to cope with being Jewish in the non-Jewish world. But instead of a return to Jewish Pride as a way of rejecting hate and reclaiming our identity following the destruction of 40% of the world's Jewish population, the post-Holocaust terrain threw up even more challenges. These challenges, and the internalisation of modern, post-Holocaust Jew-hate, are the context in which we live our lives today.

While our own battles with internalised anti-Jewishness are rooted in a modern context, they are an extension of our ancestors' historic experience. In this chapter we will see echoes of previous examples of internalised anti-Jewishness framed in our own current circumstances.

THE JEWISH COLD WAR

During the 1940s and 1950s, American Jews, like the pre-Shoah Germanic Jewish communities, were also focused on discussing and debating internalised Jew-hatred. These conversations became so heated that there existed what historian Susan Glenn describes as a 'Jewish Cold War'.[178] A response to the horrifying trauma of the Shoah, this was nothing less than a fight for the future of the Jewish community. Would Jews integrate, free themselves of their Jewish 'handicap' and become fully American, or would positive Jewishness, a 1940s version of Jewish Pride, be cultivated as promoted at the time by German American psychologist Kurt Lewin? As Glenn puts it: 'One side worried about Jewish weakness and self-hatred and insisted that group cohesion and loyalty were the keys to the survival of a distinctive Jewish culture. The other side framed its responses to the pressures for Jewish cohesion in terms of fears of totalitarianism and the loss of individual autonomy and freedom.'[179]

Of course, whether Jews can integrate or not is not really a choice for Jews themselves. This was true in Germany during the 19th century, it was true in the United States after the war, and it continues to be true today. And this is something most conversations on Jewish integration ignore or fail to recognise. They put the onus on the Jew, as opposed to the non-Jewish world. But how can Jews integrate if they are not allowed to integrate? How can Jews fully integrate if the Jewish Question on the status and role of Jews in society remains a contemporary discussion point?

In her work, Glenn describes a specific battle that perfectly encapsulates this Jewish tug of war. In 1952 sociologist and writer David Riesman published an article that detailed 'a very savage fight'[180] taking place at a Jewish hospital being constructed on Long Island. At this point, it was common for most Jewish hospitals to have a kitchen that could prepare food for non-Jewish patients as well as a smaller kosher kitchen for Jewish patients. However, Riesman describes how, at this specific hospital, 'a group of rabbis and Orthodox Jewish businessmen were demanding that the new hospital serve kosher food exclusively'.

Riesman's outrage was not primarily focused on the type of food that would be served. Instead, he believed that this fight represented something deeper and more significant about the future of the

American Jewish community. He saw that Jews were being forced from within their own community to mark themselves as 'different', and, specifically, non-American. Reisman argued that the Jewish doctors were being forced to decide whether 'they are physicians and efficient hospital administrators or policemen for a kind of "Israeli" extraterritoriality.'[181] Although Reisman blames the Jews for this choice, this is a constant bind that, ultimately, was forced onto Jews by the non-Jewish world. Would the Jews be defined by their Jewishness, or would they be full members of wider society? Would the Jews be specific or would they be universal?

While the Jewish Cold War can be illustrated by the fight at the Long Island hospital, this was just one battle in a broader conflict. Jewish Writers like Philip Roth, Isaac Rosenfield and Ben Hecht among many others were targeted by others in the Jewish community for their writings and their controversial depictions of Jews. In 1959 Roth wrote *Defender of the Faith*, which centred on a Jewish soldier who uses his Jewishness to gain advantage from his Jewish sergeant. In response, Roth was labelled a 'self-hating Jew' who caused 'irreparable damage to the Jewish people' by members of the Jewish community.[182] However, in a 1948 *Commentary* article, writer David Bernstein protested against the idea that Jewish writers were parroting Nazi ideology. He argued that '"overly emotional" Jewish leaders in the United States tended to distort the "realities" of American Jewish life by making constant reference to the fate of Germany's assimilated Jews.'[183] This was a time of much Jewish anxiety centred on survival and it focused on the eternal (imposed) Jewish conflict between specificity and universality. This battle was similar to previous, and even later, battles fought in the Jewish community for our future. And instead of turning on those who hate us, we turned on ourselves.

Ironically, there is a perspective, espoused by some American Jews such as former Anti-Defamation League director Benjamin R. Epstein and author Jonathan Sarna, that the period after the Shoah was the beginning of some kind of American Jewish Golden Age and a time of healing.[184] However, in truth, this was only ever a Gilded Age where a thin layer of gilding hid a period of contention for American Jews that was rooted in a desperate need to survive set against the backdrop of the worst genocide in recorded history.[185] And, in truth, as Abraham H. Miller, emeritus professor of political science at the University of Cincinnati and a distinguished fellow with the Haym Salomon Centre, argues 'the golden age of American Jewry has never existed.'[186]

In the 'savage fight' in Long Island, both the positions of the doctors and the rabbis were, in part, responses to the trauma of the Shoah. Indeed, the entire Jewish Cold War seems to be an attempt to come to terms with the unimaginable devastation of the Shoah. The aftermath of this cataclysmic event had put the very question of Jewish survival back at the forefront of debate with renewed urgency. And, put simply, the doctors and the rabbis in the Long Island story were debating something far more important than what food the hospital should serve. Instead, they were engaged in a bitter disagreement as to how best Jews could survive.

We cannot underestimate the impact the Shoah had on the Jewish people and it is clear why, following this catastrophe, the historic Jewish focus of survival became even more central. Although, as always, the wider historical context is also key. We also cannot underestimate the trauma – beyond the Holocaust – that we as a people are also collectively, and individually, coping with. American Jews, during this period, had experienced the same trauma the wider Jewish community faced. But they were also coping with the real anti-Jewish racism Jews faced in America in the 18th, 19th and early 20th centuries and the rise in American Jew-hate in the 1930s and 1940s.

Indeed, although there is a notion that American history was free of Jew-hate, this is not the case. There are countless examples of anti-Jewish racism from throughout America's long history, including, but not limited to, the 1924 Immigration Exclusion Act, the preaching of the 'radio priest', Father Charles Coughlin, who defended the Nazi November Pogrom in 1938, and the Nazi rally at Madison Square Gardens in 1939. Prior to the 1960s, overt Jew-hatred was still present and accepted in American society and it was not until then that American university quotas that targeted Jews were officially repealed (even though they unofficially continued until the 1980s). In 1962 an Anti-Defamation League of B'nai B'rith survey found that out of 803 country clubs, only 224 were found not to discriminate against Jews, 89 had quotas on the number of Jewish members and 416 admitted no Jews at all.[187] In an anonymous letter to the *Atlantic* on this issue, a concerned Jewish parent wrote, 'I find it rather difficult to make it clear to my children why we are not eligible, for from one point of view it isn't quite clear to me.'[188]

The horrors of the Shoah, and the failures of German Jewish integration, led American Jews to focus on learning the lessons of the German Jewish community. This was particularly so because many Jews from Germany had fled to the United States during the 1930s. Nonetheless, some members of the Jewish community believed that the Jew-hate of the previous two decades had led Jewishness to be seen as a source of shame. In an attempt to challenge this, in 1947, constitutional attorney Nathan A. Pelcovitz wrote, *What about Jewish anti-Semitism?: A Prescription to Cure Self-Hatred*. 'Judging from the common testimony of rabbis and novelists, of sociological surveys and table talk,' he argued, internalised anti-Jewishness was 'the neurosis' of the wartime generation. 'That many Jews who reached intellectual maturity in the age of Hitler reject and despise the fact of their Jewishness is a family secret we can no longer keep either from the children or the neighbors.'[189]

As had been the case previously, the struggle of American Jewish survival following the Shoah came to revolve around the struggle for integration. As Sander Gilman argues, it was 'the most momentous force to shape modern Jewish identity. Its force was felt not only among those Jews who directly experienced it but among individuals who could even remotely perceive themselves as Jews.'[190] The pre-Shoah Jewish notion – however inaccurate in reality – that a Jew who had integrated and who had diminished their Jewishness, shed their Jewish anchor and lived as an active participant in non-Jewish life could escape Jew-hatred, was over. No matter how secular they were, or how much they diminished their Jewishness, they could still be targeted. This fact made many Jews reconsider what it meant to be Jewish. This led some Jews to reject the promises of integration, drop their Jewish anchors and reclaim their authentic Jewishness through Jewish Pride.

However, many Jews in America followed a different course. As had been the case in Germany in the 19th century, many Jews turned their frustration and anxiety of their place in the world against their Jewishness, as opposed to against the intolerance of the non-Jewish world. In an act of self-blame, they saw their Jewishness as the problem, rather than recognising the problem of Jew-hate belonging to the non-Jewish world in which they lived. As Nathan A. Pelcovitz suggested, 'The central problem of Jewish anti-Semitism [a synonym for Jewish self-hatred], particularly among the youth, continues to be what it has always been: flight from Jewish identity' and the 'frantic … search for formulae of escape from the consequences of having been born a Jew.'[191]

The post-Shoah trauma was compounded by other questions regarding the role and status of American Jews in America. The Jewish Cold War, suggests Glenn, also stemmed from fears within the community caused by the establishment of the State of Israel in 1948 and the dynamics of the emerging Cold War and the threat of Communism. For parts of a community that was so focused on integration as a means of survival, the rebirth of a Jewish State was potentially problematic. It intensified pre-existing questions about Jewish loyalty. Reisman's piece on the Long Island hospital had even gone so far as to deride what he termed 'Israeli extraterritoriality'. This was intolerable to a community trying to demonstrate just how American they were. Conspiracy Fantasy and the canard of dual loyalty, as referenced in Chapter 1, continued to haunt American Jews.

Moreover, the alleged connections made between Jews and Communism also threatened Jews' place in American society. Despite Judeo-Bolshevism being a dangerous myth propagated by the Nazis among others, the Red Scare of the late 1940s and 1950s period had a distinctly anti-Jewish tinge. While purported to be focused against 'communist infiltration', there was an anti-Jewish subtext to its activities.[192] Hollywood was chosen to be a primary battleground for the House Un-American Activities Committee (HUAC), and its chairman Martin Dies made no secret of his committee's real aims. 'There are too many Jews in Hollywood!' he exclaimed.[193] Unsurprisingly, public perceptions of Jews were affected. 'Our evaluation of the general mood was that the people felt if you scratch a Jew you can find a Communist,' said Arnold Foster of the strongly anti-communist American Jewish Committee.[194] This, understandably, impacted Jewish American perceptions of their position in society, with Jewish organisations, such as the ADL, who were trying to end discrimination of Jews in employment, housing and education, forced to fight the 'Jew-as-Communist'[195] stereotype by 'demonstrating the anti-Communist credentials of American Jewry.'

In many regards, the post-war internal Jewish Cold War in the US, replayed aspects of the Jewish Question debates which raged in Europe in the 19th and early 20th centuries. Reisman's battle for universalism over Jewish particularism echoed Moses Mendelssohn and, to a considerable degree, what had occurred among emancipation-era German Jews a century before. Reisman describes his family as having 'severed all or virtually all Jewish ties.'[196] The trauma and self-blame was so strong in this era that the notion of Jews having to have 'group loyalty'[197] and to conform to one type of behaviour was described by the American essayist, Clement Greenberg, as no different from how 'the Germans made their Germanness.'[198] In other words, fear elicited by the idea of an imposed Jewish identity felt akin to the manner in which Nazi Germany attempted to create a *Volksgemeinschaft* (people's community). Reisman baulked at what he saw as 'ethnic culture dictators' and rejected what he saw as a Jewish 'chauvinism'.[199]

In a 1951 *Commentary* article on 'The "Militant" Fight Against Antisemitism', Riesman returned to these themes. 'Every threat or presumed threat to Jews anywhere in the world can be converted into a lever for the "militant minority" of Jewish organizational life, much as Russian threats to American interests anywhere reinforce the power of our self-proclaimed militant anti-Communists to put a blanket of "unity" over American life as a whole,' he wrote.[200] The Shoah, he believed, was being used to manipulate Jews into identifying in specific ways. 'If Hitler had not attacked and exterminated Jews, the physicians in the Long Island hospital would find it easier to resist fanatic politicians,'[201] Riesman argued; they would have been able to define their own identities in any way they felt comfortable. These 'fantastic politicians' were, of course, the Orthodox community leaders pressuring the doctors to be specifically Jewish (or even Israeli), rather than universally American.

While Reisman and Greenberg fought against imposing a uniform strong Jewish identity, others fought back against the development of internalised anti-Jewishness. As we have touched upon, Kurt Lewin, the founder of the Commission on Community Interrelations (CCI) argued for Positive Jewishness. According to Lewin, this 1940s version of Jewish Pride was not rooted in Jewish religion and ritual practice, but rather 'but the development of group "loyalty" that must constitute the basis for a "positive" Jewish identity'.[202] In sharp contrast to Jews like Greenberg and Reisman, Lewin wanted to promote a sense of 'belongingness' which would mean an element of co-dependency between Jews. To the dismay of Reisman, Lewin advocated for Jews to 'accept active responsibility and sacrifice for the group.'[203] The lesson of the Shoah, Lewin understood, was that the fate of one Jew was tied to the fate of all Jews. But Lewin wanted to reframe this terrible lesson in a positive way. He wanted to create a world where Jews could stand together and say 'Yes to being a Jew.'[204]

Lewin was not the only Jewish intellectual to grapple with these issues and to offer a solution to what they deemed to be Jewish self-hate. Lewin's positive Jewishness was a bulwark against internalised anti-Jewishness that was adopted by key figures in the Jewish community, such as Milton Steinberg, the Rabbi of the Park Avenue Synagogue in New York City. Steinberg wrote that without 'self- acceptance' the continuation of a separate Jewish identity in the United States was not guaranteed.[205] Although, unlike Lewin, who wanted to exclude the religious element of Judaism from Positive Jewishness, Steinberg argued that the answer to this problem was 'not less Judaism but more'. And although Jews are not just a religious group, we must not erase the importance of Judaism, the religion alongside ideas of Jewish peoplehood and civilisation when discussing Jewish identity and pride.

Conversations during the Jewish Cold War, as they must always be, should have been rooted in an empathetic understanding of the trauma the non-Jewish world had inflicted upon Jews. The error in these conversations was that they blamed the Jewish community itself for its circumstances. There were American Jews who were trying to conform to an American ideal of a 'good Jew' – being American and not being specifically Jewish, not being loyal to Israel and definitely not being Communist. But these preconditions for integration into American society were not set by Jews. Once again, as in 19th-century France, Jews were expected to uphold the end of a bargain they had not agreed to. This pressure created the Jewish Cold War. We fought ourselves, as opposed to fighting Jew-hate and those who were forcing us to warp and change ourselves.

Of course, discussing this with hindsight, it is easy to offer prescriptions as to what those American Jews should, or should not, have done. But we should not judge them. We must acknowledge that these Jews just wanted to survive. And to do this, many thought that integration was the way to do it. As we saw with Mendelssohn, for a people so persecuted, a post-emancipation promise of freedom would have been too great an offer to reject.

As Glenn writes, the evolution of the Jewish Cold War demonstrates the differing and developing perspectives on the issue of internalised anti-Jewishness. 'In the 1940s, émigreé social scientists like Lewin had given it broad intellectual authority and helped move the terminology to the center of American social thought where, by the early 1950s, its descriptive usefulness was defended and debated by the combatants of the Jewish Cold War.'[206]

Following the victory of the State of Israel during the 1967 Six-Day War, which we will explore later in this chapter, discussions around internalised anti-Jewishness in the United States focused on whether a Jew supported Israel or not. However, the backdrop to these debates was somewhat different from the immediate post-war years, with the roles American Jews were assigned in society changing during the 1960s. Moreover, despite the undoubted benefits which arose from this period of cultural emancipation, it also brought new challenges to the American Jewish identity.

A CULTURAL EMANCIPATION

The cultural emancipation of Jewish Americans began towards the end of the 1960s and, although specific to the wider context of the United States, has definite echoes of the other emancipations that swept through Europe in the 19th century and early 20th centuries. The official social and legal restrictions against Jews were mostly (but not fully) swept away, allowing Jews as a collective to feel as if they had truly and successfully integrated themselves into American society. This, in turn, led many Jews to think that Jew-hate in the United States was consigned to the pages of history or the fringes of society. For the first time, they were able to leave their ethnic enclaves in the American versions of the shtetls, move to the suburbs and, to an extent, join polite society (and the country club).

While Jew-hate in America persisted, unlike in Germany a century before, it did become, in some places, less overt. For various reasons, such as new legislation (at both a federal and state level), media, such as the 1947 film *Gentlemen's Agreement*, and the tabooing of overt Jew-hatred due to its association with Nazism, overt Jew-hatred declined throughout the 1950s and 1960s. As historian Leonard Dinnerstein recorded, the number of Americans who heard 'criticism or talk against Jews' declined from 64% in 1946 to 12% in 1959.[207] And in 1950 the *American Jewish Yearbook* wrote: 'Organized anti-Semitic activity, which began to decline after the war, continued at a low ebb during the year under review.'[208]

But as was the case in Europe, this new-found freedom came at a price. It led to the continued alteration of Jewish identity and Jewish understanding of their own experience. It was a barrier preventing them, once again, from processing their own trauma and experience. How could they come to terms with all the trauma these Jews had experienced when America was finally opening its doors, literal and figurative, to its Jewish citizens?

The process of Jewish integration also bears certain similarities to the experiences of other diasporic communities in the United States, such as the Italian. During the same period, the Italians, among others, are also considered to have 'become white'. In fact, my Italian American friend's father used to tell her that 'he became white in his lifetime'. However, the ramifications, and the context, of this cultural emancipation were different in non-Jewish communities.

In the 19th century many different communities, like the Italians, Irish and Chinese amongst others, moved to America to build new

lives. Despite their clear similarities, though, there is a nuanced difference between the Jewish experience and that of other ethnic groups.
The Jews were refugees, already living outside of their indigenous homeland, who had often fled genocidal racism. They were not
economic migrants simply seeking the land of opportunity. Nor were
they fleeing a famine in their own homeland, as was the case with the
Irish. They had already been in exile for thousands of years by that
point and were escaping the latest in a long line of attempts to destroy
them. The Jews had no other choices. Where were they to return to if
their American dream failed? For 2,000 years they had been forced to
wander the world seeking the elusive dream of peace and acceptance.
And despite 2,000 years of hope, this dream was never realised. America was their last chance saloon.

Additionally, the identities that Jews had cultivated and protected
for thousands of years are precisely what had allowed us to survive
in exile. Because we were driven from our indigenous land 2,000
years ago, our Jewish anchors were especially significant. But with
the promise of a new life in America, many Jews were willing to
shed their anchors to be accepted. The context of Jewish integration
(whether in Europe or in America) thus led to the destruction or
weakening of the Jewish anchor, Jewish self-esteem and, ultimately,
led to an identity crisis.

In the United States, where so much discourse is clouded by the
binary of race, the apparent ability of American Jews, as a collective,
to integrate from the 1960s (whatever the limitations of that ability in
reality) also resulted in them being perceived as having joined the white
majority. Although there are many Jews (including Ashkenazim who
are so often incorrectly – and offensively – framed as 'the white people'
of the Jews) who do not pass as white, Jews, as a group, became thought
of as white. As it always has been, this notion was about perceptions of
Jewishness, rather than Jewish reality. It was a modern iteration of the
Jewish Question, once again rooted in questions regarding the status

of Jews in society. And while successful integration was what many American Jews had hoped for (and it certainly had its advantages), it was not without its costs and, as always, it did not result in an accurate reflection of their identity (or their experience).

Instead, it created a scenario where Jews, who have experienced all the traumas the world can throw at a people, are now, in many circumstances, perceived to be part of the privileged majority. The idea that Jews had joined the white majority also helped to cast them as a part of – even a leading player in – the oppressive majority.

America is a society founded on the persecution of many different minorities, but no groups have experienced as much systematic persecution as the Black community or the Native American community. The American system was created to advantage white people and, as a result, having light skin has always afforded some kind of advantage, even if it was just not to be persecuted based on the colour of one's skin.

But the emancipation of Jews led to a situation where, while some Jews could benefit from the advantage of being perceived as white, their entire historical and current experiences were erased. This idea of Jews as part of the oppressor class led Matt Fieldman, a Fellow of the inaugural class of the Civil Society Fellowship, to recently argue that Jews 'were the very definition of white privilege', and that, 'the American dream for Jews, to paraphrase Malcolm X, has been a nightmare for Black people.'[209] This is, in short, what these non-Jewish narratives argue about the most persecuted minority in the history of mankind. In a world defined by proximity to whiteness or Blackness, what space was there in the American discourse for light-skinned Jews to understand who they were or discuss the realities of their experience or process their trauma?

Moreover, the idea that Jews were able to fully integrate and become 'white' is not the whole truth. From the 1960s, while they could benefit from the advantage of being perceived as white in *some* circumstances, American Jews were still vulnerable to Jew-hate. There is a notion, as mentioned previously and as promoted by academic Jonathan D. Sarna, that in America, 'no anti-Semitism mars the Eden-like national landscape'.[210] 'The American Jewish experience,' Sarna thus argues, 'is unique.'

But this is incorrect. The American Jewish experience is not unique, nor was the US some kind of Eden for American Jews. The far-right in America and those who promote white supremacy, such as the KKK, have long viewed Jews as one of their primary targets. Their hate continued long into the cultural emancipation, which clearly demonstrates that there were always elements of American society that rejected the idea Jews were white and the notion they could integrate into American society.

This hate was not just ideological or rhetorical. In 1960 the Congregation Beth Israel synagogue (in Gadsden, Alabama) was fire-bombed with 160 congregants inside and another Beth Israel (this time in Jackson, Mississippi) was bombed by the KKK in September 1967. In his 1981 article, 'Anti-Semitism and American History', Sarna describes these violent attacks as 'occasional incidents' that 'tarnish this glowing picture' of American Jewish life. This is an extraordinarily naive view, although it is one most likely rooted in the American dream and what it represented for Jews, rather than the American reality. In his essay, *Anti-Semitism in the 1980s*, Earl Raab wrote in reference to American Jews, that recent events, namely the Lebanon war and the Palestinian terrorist attack on a synagogue in Rome, suggest that 'in the matter of anti-Semitism Jews have something to worry about.' And 'given their close study of the Holocaust, it is astonishing how naive so many Jews are about the nature of anti-Semitism. Yet naivete is an even worse defense in history than it is in the law, and naivete is at the root of dazzling confusions about the state of anti-Semitism in this country today.'[211]

As was the case for their European cousins a century beforehand, the American emancipation also led to an evolution of Jew-hate. The notion that Jews collectively became white continued the century-old trend whereby Jews were racialised based on non-Jewish perspectives of their physical appearance and what this meant for their role in society. The idea that Jews became white was never simply about the colour of some Jews' skin. It was about what the colour of our skin supposedly indicated about our position in society. And like most other forms of Jew-hate, it attributed power and privilege to Jews. The Economic Libel and the Conspiracy Fantasy specifically frame Jews as powerful and privileged. Therefore, notions of Jewish whiteness are simply modern iterations of millennia-old Jew-hate.

Today, the modern manifestations of these historic racist tropes create a very toxic formula for internalised anti-Jewishness and trauma. Despite the absurdity of this position, Jews have become, in some circles, the primary predator in American society. In 2017, for instance, a flyer was displayed at the University of Illinois at Chicago that stated, 'ENDING WHITE PRIVILEGE STARTS WITH ENDING JEWISH PRIV-ILEGE.'[212] This privileged Jew exists only in the minds of non-Jewish society. They do not reflect the Jewish reality. However, as has so often been the case, non-Jewish perceptions of Jewishness impact Jewish perceptions of ourselves. And, in the United States, many Jews have looked at their context and seen perceived affluence in their community while experiencing the dominant narrative that Jews are privileged and powerful. This has resulted in a kind of collective American amnesia about what it means to be a Jew, both historically and in the present, so much so that in 2021, a Pew Research Centre poll revealed that 92% of American Jews described themselves as white.[213]

Ultimately, although the cultural emancipation led to an improve-ment in circumstances for most Jews, they also seem to have absorbed narratives about their specific American experience cast against the wider backdrop of American race relations while ignoring (or forget-ting) the wider context of what it means to be a Jew. We can critique this experience, but we also have to have empathy and try to understand it. As German Jews in the 19th and early 20th centuries had been, American Jews were desperate to survive and be accepted. They lived on the hope that they would be the first generation to escape the continuous cycles of horrifying Jew-hatred. However, despite American Jews having felt that they were immune to Jew-hate (except on the fringes of the far right), they are today experiencing its familiar swelling. And they have now been awoken to the fact that, because their own cultural emancipation did not in fact allow them to escape Jew-hatred, America never really was what is sometimes referred to as 'the new Jerusalem'.

REPRESENTING JEWS: A CRITICAL PERSPECTIVE

As in Germany, the cultural emancipation of American Jews resulted in a shedding or weakening of their Jewish anchors. But how else has it impacted Jewish American self-image and self-esteem and how did Jews diminish themselves to fit with non-Jewish reflections of Jewish identity?

From the 1960s a version of Jewish culture became synonymous with American culture and in particular New York City. In fact, major aspects of American culture were created by Jews. The Great American Songbook was written primarily by Jews and the list of Jewish composers of famous Broadway musicals is endless. Jewish lyricists, writers or composers, like the late Stephen Sondheim, wrote:

Annie, Cabaret, Chicago, Dear Evan Hansen, Dream Girls, Gypsy, Les Miserables, My Fair Lady, Oliver, Porgy and Bess, Rent, Sunset Boulevard, West Side Story and the *Wizard of Oz* (among literally countless others).

In 1964 *Fiddler on the Roof* premiered on Broadway, later going on to win nine Tony Awards, becoming the 17th longest-running Broadway

musical in history. At the time of its release, its film version was one
of the most successful movie-musicals in history. But why did a Jewish
story about a shtetl in the Pale of Settlement become a much beloved
part of American culture?

In a similar fashion to perceptions of palatable Jewishness in
Germany, the American embrace of this very Jewish story shows
a defining facet of how American Jewish culture is perceived by
non-Jewish American society; Jewishness is accepted as long as it can
speak to an American understanding of universality rooted in ideas
of the American dream. It is this dynamic which facilitates the acceptance of American Jewish culture by non-Jewish America. In his book,
Acting Jewish: Negotiating Ethnicity on the American Stage and Screen,
author Henry Bial suggests that despite the clear Jewishness of Tevye,
he functions 'as a universal character for an American audience.'[214]
Bial also argues that Tevye is Jewish enough for Jewish audiences,
but not Jewish enough for non-Jewish audiences, thus ensuring his
palatability. This ambiguity allows non-Jewish (and Jewish) audiences
to impose their own meaning and perspectives on Tevye's story. In
'The Americanization of Tevye or Boarding the Jewish "Mayflower"',
author Seth Wolitz argues that 'Tevye encapsulated the world of
tradition coming to terms with modernisation, and in particular,
Americanisation.'[215] Tevye's Jewishness is not threatening because, in
the 1960s, the notion that America was a 'salad bowl' became more
prevalent. Unlike previous ideas of the 'melting pot', which 'produces
a society that primarily reflects the dominant culture'[216] the salad bowl
theory asserts that, 'rather than assimilating, different ethnic groups
now would coexist in their separate identities like the ingredients in a
salad, bound together only by the "dressing" of law and the market.'[217]
This means that this very Jewish story can represent something all
Americans can relate to without feeling threatened by its specificity.

Moreover, a natural result of migration is an evolution of culture.
In this case, this resulted in the creation of Americanised cultures

like Jewish American or Italian American, which are the American-ised versions of foreign cultures. This also helps us understand how non-Jewish Americans could embrace *Fiddler on the Roof*. It was an expression of Americanised Jewish culture, rather than of Yiddish culture from the Pale of Settlement. This Americanisation makes the foreign seem familiar, even if it is still rooted in a foreign culture.

Fiddler on the Roof celebrates a kind of Jewishness that comforts, rather than threatens, non-Jewish American audiences, who are now able to celebrate these stories as representing the universal American Dream. In fact, all Americans can use this story to feel pride in Amer-ica and Americanness. But the acceptance of American Jewish stories into the heart of America creates a trend whereby only specific Jewish stories (those that reinforce American ideas of Jewishness as well as American ideas of Americanness) are told and embraced. This results in the embedding of non-threatening Jewish stereotypes in American culture and sometimes, despite its ancient roots, the watering down of Jewish culture.

While Jews have long been represented in Hollywood, it has not been a wholly positive experience. As *Variety* magazine's features editor, Malina Saval, has suggested: 'you can be Jewish in Hollywood, but not too Jewish.'[218] You can be the Americanised caricature of a Jew that is palatable to the non-Jewish world, but you cannot be 'more Jewish' than that. This puts enormous pressure on Jews who create representations of other Jews to reflect the Broken Mirror of Jewish identity. Despite its clear Jewishness, Sheldon Harnick, the Jewish lyri-cist who wrote *Fiddler on the Roof*, reflected that he was worried it was 'too Jewish'[219] when he was writing it. Marshall Herskovitz, the Acad-emy Award-nominated director describes this Jewish attitude towards self-representation as 'self-censorship'.[220] Interviewed in 2003, Hersko-vitz argued that this censorship began in the studio system at the begin-ning of Hollywood. Jews like Louis B. Meyer worked hard to 'scrub out any ethnicism' in order to be accepted by the white majority.[221]

It is in this scenario where we must apply the nuance of positive representation. Yes, Jews, have been represented in media, but are they represented as whole complex human beings or are these characters rooted in non-Jewish stereotypes, perceptions and notions of good or bad Jews? Even the most Jewish of Jewish TV shows, like the *Marvelous Mrs Maisel*, which has Jewish life as its central focus, has been described by journalist Paul Brownfield as being rooted in 'shtick, stereotypes, and self-parody'[222] and by Molly Pascal as producing 'laughs, sometimes in self-recognition, [but] the traits perpetuate an ugly story about the nature of the Jewish people.'[223]

Richard Rosenstock, producer of *Arrested Development* and the *Big Bang Theory*, argued in 1992 that 'The key to comedy used to be "Write Jewish and cast Gentile"'.[224] At the same time, however, Larry Charles, supervising producer of *Seinfeld*, suggested in 1992 that 'we're allowing ourselves to be who we are, and not to be ashamed of exposing it.'[225] That is not necessarily the whole truth though. Despite the American 'salad bowl', depictions of Jews (frequently by Jews) often reinforce specific anti-Jewish stereotypes and only celebrate palatable Jews who are non-threatening to perceptions of Americanness. In *Annie Hall*, for instance, Woody Allen (as he does on other occasions) plays a caricature of a neurotic Jewish man. Irrespective of the various accusations about Allen himself, his various on-screen characters are the epitome of the nebbish, nerdy neurotic Jewish male who requires rescuing by non-Jewish women. His characterisation thus simultaneously rejects earlier threatening stereotypes about Jewish male sexuality which paint Jewish men as dangerous defilers of non-Jewish women. He exists in a castrated Jewish reality so as to be acceptable to non-Jewish audiences. This Jew in American culture is thus often a kind of non-threatening court jester. As author Henry Hoffman writes: 'Jewish critics were onto something when they noted that a funny yet negative trope about Jews might persist once it had entered the mainstream.'[226]

Jewish women are also demonised through the stereotypes of the 'Jewish American Princess'. In a 1970 episode of *The David Susskind Show*, Mel Brooks 'joked': 'If you meet a Jewish girl and you shake her hand, that's dinner. You owe her a dinner. If you should take her home after dinner and rub around and kiss in the doorway, right. That's already a small ring, a ruby or something.'[227] But, as Dr Gary Spencer, professor of sociology at Syracuse University, argued in 1988 because Jews, like Mel Brooks, utilised Jewish American Princess jokes, 'they gave permission to the wider society to tell such jokes and to elaborate on them. If Jews tell JAP jokes, then it must be okay for non-Jews to do so.'[228] Spencer went on to warn that these racist representations of Jewish women 'began to suggest actual discriminatory behavior, and even threats of physical and sexual violence.'[229] Spencer argues that Jews have incorporated anti-Jewish tropes into their self-image in an act of 'distancing oneself through self-denigration'[230] (or the act of self-blame). Just as assimilated Jews in 19th century Germany demonised the Eastern European Jews to demonstrate their own integration, American Jewish men did the same with Jewish women a century later. To become American, Jewish men had to demonise and discard Jewish women. As the writer Anne Roiphe has argued, 'Some Jewish men need only look at a Jewish girl and they hear the ghetto gates slamming shut.'[231] Jewish women themselves have also contributed to the spread of anti-Jewish tropes about Jewish women. Even the beloved Joan Rivers joked that 'If God had wanted us to bend over, He would have put diamonds on the floor.'[232] Tragically, the absorption of anti-Jewish ideas and the pressures to integrate and to be 'palatable' creates toxic relationships between Jews themselves.

Although the creators of *Friends* are Jewish, the TV show had a very problematic relationship with Jews. Ross is the classic effeminate Jewish nerd who is so cheap he steals the Christian Bible from the hotel he is staying in. Rachel is described as the 'quintessential' Jewish American Princess[233] who famously got a nose job, while Monica and Janice (and particularly Janice) are the loud abrasive Jewish woman with unruly hair. Each of these stereotypes (and more) are only utilised for comedic effect. These stereotypes are not threatening, are funny and as such are palatable to non-Jewish audiences. Another problematic representation of Jews in *Friends* (as well as other TV shows) focuses on the depictions of assimilated Jews. Although Monica and Ross's Jewishness is stated, Rachel, on the other hand, could be classed as 'Jewish-coded'. This is where a character's Jewishness is ambiguous and is only implied through Jewish stereotypes, again utilised only for comedic effect. This coding as Jewish reinforces the universality of Jewishness whereby Jews are no longer a distinct people, but rather a subset of the majority with 'quirky differences'. Of the Jewishness of Monica, Rachel and Ross, David Crane, one of the three *Friends* creators, stated, 'When we were creating the show, we were not thinking about Jewish characters. In the initial character breakdowns, we never mentioned religion.'[234] Yet, despite Crane's claims, the Jewishness of these characters is often referenced but *only* as a joke or a punchline. The infamous Holiday Armadillo episode, where Ross, unable to locate a Santa costume for his son during Christmas, dons an armadillo costume and proceeds to tell his son the Chanukah story, is a prime example of this.

Even Jewish characters who are perceived to be positive representations of Jews still reflect non-Jewish ideas of palatable Jewishness. In *Curb Your Enthusiasm*, Larry David is told, 'I like the wig. It hides the Jew'[235] when he wears a wig and a moustache, while the character of Susie is the classic overbearing Jewish mother-in-law. In this context, even if overtly Jewish, the good Jew is the non-threatening Jew. This does not mean that every example of Jews represented in Hollywood is negative, and we are of course allowed to laugh at ourselves and make jokes about ourselves. However, we must also recognise the more damaging aspects of this kind of representation and that even the more beloved characters, like Larry David, still reflect the prism of 'acceptable' Jewishness.

Beyond representing Jews as a punchline, Hollywood, and the media in general, also have an obsession with another kind of non-threatening Jew: the dead Jew. As Dara Horn described in *People Love Dead Jews: Reports From a Haunted Present*, 'as thousands of Holocaust books and movies and TV shows and lectures and courses and mandatory school curricula made abundantly clear, dead Jews were the most popular of all'.[236] These acts of Holocaust memory are important, but, in my own work over the last 16 years, I have noticed that much Holocaust education focuses on murdered Jews (which may be more of an accurate description than dead Jews). It often ignores Jewish life pre-war. It ignores the beauty and richness of Jewish culture and it frames Jews as passive actors in our own story. This martyrs these Jews. It recreates them, not as Jewish people who once lived and loved their Jewishness, but as a symbol of universal suffering that the non-Jewish world can use to learn something from. But those lessons don't ever actually include combatting Jew-hate. 'Murdered Jews' and 'Funny Jews', along with representations of Orthodox Jews, as 'Bad Jews' as discussed, make up what I call the Trichotomy of Jewish representation, and, sadly, there is almost nothing beyond this.

THE EVOLUTION OF JEWISH CULTURE

There is much beauty in the American Jewish community. There are many American Jews who are proud bearers of their Jewishness and who fight hard, in a myriad of ways, to ensure the continuation of the Jewish people. However, the similarities of the general American Jewish community to its Germanic predecessors require us to be critical about the place of Jewishness in America and how this has impacted the identity of American Jews.

Today, aspects of American culture (and specifically New York City) have been so fused with Jewish culture that many people are not even aware of their Jewish origins. When Leonard Nimoy died, the White House described Mr Spock's Vulcan salute as 'the universal sign for "Live long and prosper"'.[237] It is actually inspired by Nimoy's Jewish upbringing and seeing the Cohanim use this symbol in their priestly blessings in synagogue. Additionally, consider the bagel, now so synonymous with New York City, actually originated from Ashkenazi Jewish communities in Poland. Their popularity also coincided with this cultural emancipation of the 1960s when the *New York Times* stated that New York was 'the bagel center of the free world, and will doubtless be kept that way by the hundreds of thousands of residents who find that a bagel makes breakfast almost worth getting up for.'[238]

The absorption of aspects of Jewish culture into the centre of American life may appear to be a cause for celebration, and, in some ways, it is. However, it has also created a shallow version of acceptable Jewish culture that has stripped away our history, traditions and values that were developed over thousands of years. The Broken Mirror of Jewish identity has then reflected this 'altered' version of Jewishness back to the Jews. Because of this, Ashkenazi Jews became the default Jews. This is also an important perspective in diasporic conversations on 'Ashkenormativity', which describes how Ashkenazi culture dominates Jewish conversations at the expense of other Jewish experiences. In America, Ashkenazi Jewish culture dominates because the non-Jewish world has absorbed it, not necessarily because diasporic Ashkenazi Jews were purposely excluding other Jewish stories in a malevolent act of cultural dominance.

Like in all places, in America, Jewish identity has thus been shaped and defined by the non-Jewish world. So, like their German brethren two hundred years earlier, this unanchored Jewishness defined via the Broken Mirror of Jewish identity became the perfect breeding ground for internalised anti-Jewishness. Shockingly, there are American Jews who acknowledge the costs of the cultural emancipation but who see them as a worthwhile sacrifice in order to be accepted. In a truly tragic statement that demonstrates the diminishment of Jewish self-worth, author Howard Sachar was quoted in a *Los Angeles Times* article as saying, 'It's true, there's been an erosion around the edges of Jewish life ... but that's a cheap price to pay for the freedom we have enjoyed in this country.'[239] Sachar seems to celebrate basic human rights as if they were a 'gift' bestowed upon us that we should be grateful for. In *Jews and Other Differences: The New Jewish Cultural Studies*, Daniel and Jonathan Boyarin recognise this cost, writing that 'Jews who as a group have clearly achieved enormous economic success in the United States as well as accumulating cultural capital, whether in Hollywood or in Harvard Square, have done so by and large at the cost of deculturation. That deculturation is itself a source of pain and loss, vague and anecdotal at times, overwhelming at others.'[240]

Although American Jews are overwhelmingly Zionist and there is much beauty and Jewish Pride in their Jewish community, there are also Jews in the United States who have weakened or even shed their Jewish anchors. And sadly, for some American Jews, in their American journey, they went from a nation to a religion, and then to a culture. As we know from the 1885 Pittsburgh Platform referenced in Chapter 3, American Jews shed their nationhood. They were not, however, expected, as writer Will Herberg posits in *Protestant–Catholic–Jew: An Essay in American Religious Sociology*, to give up their religious identity (as religious freedoms were enshrined in the Bill of Rights in 1789).[241] This religifying of American Jews was set against the backdrop of normalised post-war religious observance in the United States more generally. In 1954 the words 'under God'[242] were added to the US Constitution and from 1956 'In God We Trust' became, what historian Jonathan Sarna describes as, the 'official national motto' of the United States.[243]

The post-war American religious boom resulted in the positioning of Judaism as one of *the* three faiths, alongside Protestantism and Catholicism, and, as Herberg stated, Judaism was part of the 'tripartite scheme' of religion in America and to be anything else was 'somehow not to be an American.' Thus, religious Jewish observance was promoted by the

United States through positioning Judaism as not just a religion, but one of *the* religions and Jews were thus 'enfranchised as the guardians of one-third of the American religious heritage.' This trend may have contributed to the revival of Jewish religious observance seen post-war. In 1950 writer Will Herberg noted that 'there is a religious revival under way among American Jews today.'[244] With reference to the alteration of Jewish identity from a nation to a religion, Herberg also noted that 'under American conditions, it is very difficult for the Jew to know himself as a Jew except in some sort of religious terms.'

However, in the modern age of secularism, 'Jews of no religion' are surging in America, as detailed by a 2013 Pew Research Center survey. And as a *Los Angeles Times* article stated, 'Among parents and guardians, two out of three "Jews of no religion" are not raising their children Jewish in any way.'[245] But what are the consequences of this diminishment of Jewish identity? In traditional circumstances, Jewish culture is an expression of our nationhood and our religion, but what does it mean if those elements of Jewish identity have been shed and erased via pressures to integrate and the Broken Mirror of Jewish identity? To be a cultural Jew, in this context, is perhaps to have an intangible Jewish identity. Although there are those who argue that cultural Jews are analogous to secular or atheist Jews, in this context that is not the case. Such Jews still engage actively in Jewish religious practice even if they do not base this engagement on a relationship with Hashem. When I say *Kaddish* (the Jewish mourners' prayer) for my late father on his *yahrzeit* (the Hebrew anniversary of his passing), I do so to honour his memory in the way Jews have always honoured those they have lost, not because I am exalting God's name. Cultural Jews are Jews who are Jewish predominantly via a celebration of Jewish culture, which is itself rooted in Judaism and Jewishness. But, for some unanchored American Jews what culture are we specifically referring to? Is it Jewish culture or is it the post-cultural emancipation of superficial Jewish culture defined via the non-Jewish world?

Being a cultural Jew in this context leaves one without a strong Jewish anchor and without literacy in what it means to be a Jew. As journalist Leon A. Morris writes, 'When American Jews say "I'm a cultural Jew" they tend to mean they like to pepper their speech with Yiddish words and expressions (often used incorrectly) and they have a fondness for lox and bagels. The attitudes and behaviors … are not the building blocks of a thick culture.'[246] Cultural Jews, in this context, are often rooted in a non-Jewish (non-threatening and universalised) version of Jewish culture. Tragically, American reflections of Jewish identity have reduced 4,000 years of Jewish civilisation to a smoked salmon bagel and a punchline. Whether it is Shabbat, our history, our texts, Israel, our values, our traditions, Jewish identity must be rooted in something tangible. After all, we are a people of action and of memory. If we refer ourselves to Yehuda Amichai's 'Poem Without an End'. It reads:

> Inside the brand-new museum
> there's an old synagogue.
> Inside the synagogue
> is me.
> Inside me
> my heart.
> Inside my heart
> a museum.
> Inside the museum
> a synagogue,
> inside it
> me,
> inside me
> my heart,
> inside my heart
> a museum.[247]

This is what it means to be a Jew. We move forward. We move on. But we remember. We remember our history, our land, our traditions, our culture, our texts and our faith and so much more. These memories are alive inside us. They are an inherent part of us and through education, we pass them on to the next generations. It is this inherent connection that the cultural emancipation in the United States in the second half of the 20th century helped to sever. Just like their ancestors who benefited from the 19th-century German emancipation, Jewish Americans certainly benefited from this emancipation, but the question we must ask is, at what cost?

THE LEFT AND JEW-HATE

Although there are still those who deny it, the progressive world is one of the greatest conduits for contemporary anti-Jewish racism. This has had a devastating impact on Jewish Pride for Jews all over the world. Though we know that sections of the Left (like the Right) have long been infected with the poison of Jew-hatred, rooted in the accusation of the Jewish obsession with money (Economical Libel), we have to understand some of the recent factors that have led to the deluge of Jew-hatred we see from parts of the mainstream modern Left. These events, though not all specifically related to Jews, have ushered in the renormalisation of Jew-hate. This, in turn, forced progressive Jews back into the never-ending Jewish bind; they can either belong to the progressive world or they can be proud Jews. In this context, it seems, they cannot be both. Importantly, this does not mean that these Jews have to drop their 'progressive' values, rather that they are made unwelcome in many Left or Progressive spaces.

Despite more recent developments in Jew-hate on the Left (and although Marxist ideology was partially founded on Jew-hate), there were times that different parts of the Left were more welcoming to, and supportive of, Jews than they are today. Historically, the British Labour

Party was solidly Zionist, even before the Balfour Declaration in 1917, and it also opposed the infamous White Paper in 1939 that put a quota on Jews fleeing Nazism to the British Mandate of Palestine, just before and during the Holocaust. For much of the post-war period, many Jews found Labour to be their natural home, and leading figures in the party – including former Prime Ministers Harold Wilson, Tony Blair and Gordon Brown – were both close to the community and strong supporters of Israel. Even on the Labour left, figures like Barbara Castle and Richard Crossman, were strongly pro-Zionist.

At the same time, the Conservative party – which became much more friendly to the community and Israel under Margaret Thatcher – had traditionally been seen as less welcoming to Jews and supportive of Israel. It, for instance, passed the infamous Aliens Act at the turn of the 20th century, while Ted Heath's government imposed an arms embargo on both Israel and the Arab states which were attempting to annihilate it in 1973.

While there has always been Jew-hate among elements of the Left, its promise of societal change has ensured that Jews have always been disproportionately represented in all kinds of Leftist spaces. Around 70% of American Jews vote Democrat, and in his book, *The Left's Jewish Problem*, Dave Rich states that in the 1940s and 1950s, Jewish workers in the East End of London were not only staunch Labour supporters, but also made up 10% of activists in the Communist Party of Great Britain, while being just 1% of the British population.[248]

The upswing of Leftist Jew-hate which began in the 1960s was driven by the Soviet and Arab effort to reframe Zionism as a form of imperialism; this, in turn, shaped the emerging New Left's perceptions of Jewish self-determination. As Rich notes, the New Left's primary focus was on the struggle against 'Western imperialism', colonialism and identity politics (the Old Left, by contrast, was more fixated on the 'class struggle').[249] The process of decolonisation that swept through Africa and parts of Asia drew enormous support from the New Left. But, in a modern iteration of traditional Jew-hatred focused on perceived Jewish power, Israel was not seen as an example of decolonisation (which, of course, it was), but rather it was framed as *the* symbol of Western (and white) imperialism. The notion that Israel was an imperialist force akin to the Nazis was spread by Arab and Soviet governments during this period. The Egyptian leader, Gamal Abdel Nasser, was fixated on the notion that Israel was a manifestation of Western Imperialism.

It is in this development of Leftist ideology that we see the birth of ideas still present today. For instance, Frantz Fanon, an Algerian psychotherapist and latterly, Ambassador for the Algerian Revolutionary Provincial Government, justified the violence of anti-imperialists when fighting their oppressors. And as part of the reframing of Israel as a colonialist power, Palestinian terrorists were thus added to a list of anti-imperialist 'freedom fighters', such as the Viet Cong, which were lionised by the New Left. But while the New Left began to see overthrowing the yoke of imperialism as its raison d'être, it was not, rather hypocritically, as interested in whether those who it supported actually shared its other values. We continue to see this hypocrisy today. Some LGBTQ+ activists call for the boycott of Israel (despite it being an oasis of gay rights in a region noted for its hostility to the LGBTQ+ community) and offer unquestioning support for the Palestinians, despite the fact that Palestinian society is oppressively LGTBQ+phobic. They proclaim Palestine to be an LGBTQ+ issue, which it is, but not in the way they understand it.

In terms of its domestic policies, as we saw with regards to the Yevsektsiya, the Soviet Union and its satellite states actively targeted Jews from the outset. During the 1940s and 1950s, Stalin promoted the Doctor's Plot, where he accused Soviet citizens with Jewish surnames of conspiring against Soviet leaders and implemented show trials, such as the Slánský trial in 1952, where Jewish (and non-Jewish) communists were accused of 'Zionism'. And in an example of official Soviet thinking, in 1963, the Ukrainian Academy of Sciences published *Judaism without Embellishments* which argued there was a global Jewish conspiracy working to destroy the Soviet Union. The book also pushed the Soviet line that the Nazis and Zionists had secretly collaborated, even claiming that Operation Barbarossa was a Jewish Nazi conspiracy. These two tropes of Israel pulling the strings globally and Zionists collaborating with Nazis, both of which are examples of Conspiracy Fantasy, are still peddled in various forms by high-profile figures on the hard left.

However, although these ideas had been circulating for a period, the major turning point for the global Left and Jews came in 1967, following Israel's victory over Egypt, Syria, Jordan, Iraq and Lebanon. Although Israel launched a defensive pre-emptive strike against the massing armies of its Arab neighbours, the war was deemed to be an act of Israeli aggression. In 1967 the PLO argued that Israel was created by the UN to create a 'colonial Zionist state in the Afro-Asian bridges, the Arab land of Palestine'.[250] This rhetoric, along with intense Soviet antizionist propaganda, embedded a specific form of Jew-hatred in major parts of the Left. The antizionist Left argued that their opposition was only to Israel and Zionism, not Jews, but this was not the case. In its propaganda, the Soviet Union persecuted Soviet Jews and long utilised classic anti-Jewish tropes such as accusations of Jewish power and greed and even included racialised depictions of Jewish noses and bodies.

It was during this period that we saw Israel being demonised as an apartheid state for the first time, an accusation still repeated regularly by figures on the Left. Both 2021 and 2022 saw major reports released by the Human Rights Watch and Amnesty International respectively that formally accused Israel of apartheid. Importantly, several countries such as Austria denounced Amnesty's report, stating 'We do not consider the use of the term "apartheid" in the context of the Middle East conflict to be appropriate. The serious crime of apartheid refers to a specific context. We reject the application of this term to the State of Israel.'[251]

However, this anti-Jewish demonisation of Israel has been utilised for decades. A 1968 article in *Race & Class* magazine, for instance, argued that 'Africa today lies encircled between two confident and aggressive white powers – South Africa and its satellites to the South and Israel to the North.'[252] The description of Israel as a 'white' state aims to purposefully and completely erase the connection between the Jews and their indigenous homeland. In this binary world of the New Left, for Israel to be, as it is described, an imperialist settler-colonial state, the Jews have to be white. This, of course, strengthened the United Nations General Assembly Resolution that declared Zionism to be a form of racism.

Of course, not every part of the Leftist spectrum is soaked with Jew-hate; however the ideological origins of some parts of the Left, as well as the developments in Leftist worldview in the middle of the 20th century, embedded these anti-Jewish ideas about Jews and Israel in important elements of the modern Left. This, as we will see, has had a devastating effect on the identities of Jews who also occupy these ideological spaces.

THE ROAD TO ZIONISM

Following the Six-Day War (and because of the persecution of Soviet Jews, who were held hostage in the USSR until Gorbachev came to power in the 1980s) American Jews reaffirmed their commitment to the international Jewish family and affirmed their commitment to Zionism. This took place concurrently with, and as a response to, the New Left, Soviet Union and the Arab world obsessively demonising Israel, and in the case of the Soviet Union, Soviet Jews. Initially, the hatred of the Left was only present on the far-left, it was not in the 'soft-left' or the progressive world, as we see today. This meant that most Jews in the West could continue to identify with the Left without necessarily being challenged in the way we are today.

Simply put, Israel's 1967 victory was a miracle. Prior to the war, the country was woefully underprepared to fight the five Arab armies that were actively planning an invasion. The fear, in Israel and beyond, was that the Jewish state would be defeated and there would be another Holocaust. This fear was not unfounded. It was not unreasonable to assume that the Jewish citizens of Israel would be massacred, or at the very least ethnically cleansed, following an Arab victory. This would have been a continuation of how Sephardic and Mizrahi Jews were treated by the Arabs for centuries, if not millennia. The fear of annihilation and the jubilation of victory brought Israel to the forefront of the minds of American Jews. This resulted in Zionism and Israel becoming a fundamental part of American Jewish identity (and indeed that of Jews in many other countries).

This evolution of Jewish identity is exemplified by the American Jewish Committee (AJC). Founded in 1906, the AJC was originally non-Zionist. As we explored earlier in the chapter, integration was a priority for the Jews of America, with attention focused on how best to become 'American', rather than maintaining connections to the global Jewish community. Although some members of the AJC were Zionist, the majority were not, and, during the Jewish Cold War, these Jews advocated integration as the primary method of securing Jewish survival.

The AJC's fears about supporting Zionism largely stemmed from concerns that Jews would be accused of not being loyal to the United States and could face additional Jew-hate at home (a fear which, as contemporary Trumpist accusations of dual loyalty demonstrate, was not unfounded). This is a tragic example of an abused people who fear that their actions bring hatred on themselves. Though the AJC eventually joined forces with the Jewish Agency, its attitudes to Zionism were far from enthusiastic. It feared Zionism being hoisted upon

American Jewry and rejected the idea of creating a democratic Jewish congress that would advocate for Jews as a collective in case it became a conduit for Zionism.

The AJC felt so threatened by Zionism that it couldn't even bring itself to be part of the desperately needed discussions about a post-war solution for Jewish safety, walking out of a 1943 conference that was to examine the demand for the creation of a Jewish state. The AJC eventually softened its position, leaving antizionist members to quit and join the ACJ (American Council for Judaism), which argued that Judaism was incompatible with 'Jewish nationalism'.[253] But the AJC's post-1948 shift did not necessarily mean it had embraced Zionism, it simply meant that it had accepted the reality of the modern Jewish state and opted to provide it with practical support. In the early 1950s, for instance, AJC President Jacob Blaustein helped secure $773 million in reparations from West Germany to the fledgling Jewish state. However, as former president of PBS and NBC News, Lawrence K. Grossman stated, despite this 'practical support',[254] the overarching message was that 'American Jews sole political allegiance was to the US'.

The non-ideological Zionism of the AJC even went so far as to lead to debates as to whether the organisation should remove the word 'Jewish' from its name and instead be called the 'Institute for Human Relations'.[255] As a result of the wider American context, by 1966 the AJC believed its principal raison d'être was civil rights – in the struggle for which Jews played a large and honourable role – and this thinking in many regards foreshadowed some contemporary debates. The assumption, in short, was that, as Grossman suggested, 'Jewish rights were safest when the rights of all were protected.'[256] However, the cultural emancipation of American Jews led to an inter-generational misunderstanding of Jewish identity and experience. The notion that Jews were still threatened – and that this had to be a primary concern for the Jewish community – went by the wayside. But as Albert Memmi, the great Jewish Tunisian writer, argued: 'No historic duty toward other men should prevent our paying particular attention to our special difficulties.'[257]

However, 1967 changed both American Jewry and the AJC. During the Six-Day War, American Jews (initially against the advice of the AJC) took to the streets to organise mass rallies in support of Israel. This was clearly a moment of reflection. The lingering traumas of the Holocaust reawakened the desperate need for Jewish survival which now became focused on the survival of the Jewish state. The day war broke out, lawyer Morris Abrams suggests, marked 'the beginning of the revival of a fearful collective unconscious in world Jewry'.[258] Rather poignantly he added, 'there appeared in the halls of the American Jewish Committee Americans of Jewish ancestry so totally assimilated as to have changed the actual pronunciation of their names, haunted by the specter of history and the common fate of Jews'.[259]

After Israel's victory, the AJC and the American Jewish community became actively Zionist. This was expressed not just through a continuation of their former financial support, but in terms of their values, ideology and identity as well. Actively supporting Israel became key to American Jewish identity, as Edward Shapiro noted, 'I am because I give'[260] became the fundamental definition of American Jewishness. To this day, the vast majority of American Jews, around 95% according to a 2019 Gallup Poll[261], see Israel as deeply connected to their Jewish identities (this is not just an American specific statistic, around 93% of British Jews feel that Israel plays a part in their Jewish identity[262]). In fact, following the war, the AJC organised for a committee of advertising agents to discuss how to market Israel to the rest of the world in a positive light, and AJC itself became – and remains – one of the leading Jewish Zionist organisations in the world. But, as we know, while the Jewish community was becoming more and more Zionist, the hard Left was becoming more and more antizionist. These diverging paths then began to converge in the first years of the new millennium.

THE ROAD FROM ZIONISM

Jews born after 1967 grew up against a backdrop of strong support for Zionism in their various diasporic communities. Israel had survived against the odds and Jews all over the world ideologically and practically supported the Jewish state. It became an integral part of the global Jewish identity, even among Jews who continued to live in the Diaspora. Of course, Jewish antizionism existed, but the question of Jewish support for Israel was neither a communal nor a mainstream topic. This is not necessarily the case today. A poll of US Jewish voters carried out in the summer of 2021, stated that 20% of responders under the age of forty said Israel does not have a right to exist and 'A third of younger voters agreed that Israel is committing genocide, a position that even human rights lawyers who are critical of Israel say is extreme'.[263] But what happened to precipitate this change in Jewish Leftists and why is the result a manifestation of internalised anti-Jewishness?

After the dashed hope of the failed 1990s Oslo peace processes, the beginning of the new millennium reintroduced New Left ideas about Israel to millennials and latterly, Gen-Z. Simply put, the early 2000s saw the previous divergence of Jewish Zionism and Leftist antizionism begin to converge. In September 2001 activists and NGOs gathered in Durban, South Africa, to discuss and promote the fight against racism. The conference degenerated instead into an orgy of anti-Jewish racism; Israel was (once again) branded as a white, racist, imperialist apartheid state in an effort to demonise and delegitimise it. In an interview with *Detroit Jewish News*, Michael Belling, a Jewish journalist from South Africa who reported on the Durban conference, stated, 'all the activities at the Durban I conference gave the Soviet KGB a posthumous victory.'[264] Belling also reports that copies of the infamous Protocols of the Learned Elders of Zion (a forgery purporting to show a Jewish plan to control the world) were 'freely available' and flyers 'lauding Hitler and

indicating that the outcomes would have been favorable had he won'
were also visible at this 'anti-racism' conference. Durban is infamous,
not just because of its overt anti-Jewish racism but because it helped
reopen the door of overt Jew-hatred into society, and in particular,
parts of the modern Left. Amnesty International – which has since
become a major conduit of Jew-hate, formally accusing Israel of apartheid, as we have seen – was, for instance, heavily involved in Durban.
The historic positions that we saw emerge with the Arab world and the
Soviet Union in the mid-1950s and 1960s and later the New Left were
once again being promoted by the modern Left.

The First Durban conference coincided with the September 11
attacks. The ensuing War on Terror and the wars launched by George
Bush and Tony Blair also shaped the attitudes of today's Left. In a
continuation of the anti-imperialist ideology of the New Left, the
Muslim and Arab worlds were supported as victims of Western imperialism. The Palestinians were, already by that stage, attacking Israel
in the Second Intifada. The false equivalence between Muslim and
Arab citizens experiencing the West's War on Terror and Palestinian
terrorists was made by Stop the War, a British anti-war organisation.
Incredibly, it saw Hamas and Hezbollah – both deeply anti-Jewish
and reactionary in the outlook – as part of the 'axis of resistance'
against Western Imperialism (which, of course, included Israel). The
idea that Israel was a white, imperialist entity was reintroduced and
reinforced. Along with the failures of the 21st century to yield any
progress on the peace process (and the blaming solely of Israel for all
its failures), these ideas have contributed to the disease of aggressive
and violent antizionism entering mainstream Leftist spaces, which has
had a devastating impact on Jewish identity.

Set against the backdrop of perceived Jewish whiteness, and
connected to Moses Mendelssohn's work to universalise Judaism,
many progressive Jews have utilised the notion of Tikkun Olam as
the basis for their entire Jewish identities. This idea, meaning 'repair

the world', is rooted in Jewish action such as carrying out mitzvot (this literally translates as good deeds but is connected to following Jewish law). Jonathan Krasner suggests that Tikkun Olam became a central Jewish concept in the mid-1980s. Krasner argues that 'the rise of Tikkun Olam was its power to give meaning to Jewish identity by articulating a post-Holocaust Jewish mission in the world and reinforcing liberal political and social values that were already deeply ingrained in the vast majority of American Jews.'[265] While Jews campaigning for social justice is, of course, not in itself a negative thing, the misunderstanding of this Jewish concept is much more troubling. Indeed, there are progressive US Jews who do not see their own community as the focus for any of their social justice work. Rooted in a rejection of Jewish specificity, they have bought into the notion that, as a privileged and powerful class, Jews are no longer deserving of advocacy. Instead, it is other oppressed communities that benefit from their campaigning while Jews are forgotten and the challenges we face are ignored and diminished.

Today, as with all forms of Jew-hate, various forms of Leftist Jew-hate are spread far and wide by the internet. Always evolving to fit the zeitgeist, it parrots the same ideas as its predecessors but tweaked slightly to frame it through the language and worldview of contemporary social justice movements. White privilege, Black Lives Matter (BLM) and hierarchies of oppression are the issues of our day. They, like their predecessors, paint Israel, and now more overtly Jews, as white, privileged, colonialist oppressors. Israel, and Jews, are seen, through the continuation and evolution of Economic Libel, Conspiracy Fantasy, Blood Libel and the Racial Libel, as the primary white predator who are controlling the world to oppress Black and Brown Bodies. As scholar Pamela Paresky wrote in *Sapir Journal*, 'In the critical social justice paradigm, Jews, who have never been seen as white by those for whom being white is a moral good, are now seen as white by those for whom whiteness is an unmitigated evil.'[266]

Social media has not only enabled the spread of misinformation, it has also allowed views, such as a race relations debate specific to American history and society, to develop a global reach. In a May 2021 *New York Times* article, for instance, Alyssa Rubin, an If Not Now volunteer, argued that during the 2020 Black Lives Matter protests (BLM), 'a whole new wave of people were really primed to see the connection and understand racism more explicitly,' she said, 'understanding the ways racism plays out here, and then looking at Israel/Palestine and realizing it is the exact same system'.[267] This is patently false. It is an absorption of non-Jewish narratives, rooted in the mis-alliance between parts of the Black Civil Rights movement and the Palestinians brought about by the Soviet Union in the 1970s.

The perception that the Black American experience is analogous to the Palestinian experience is still propagated by BLM today, which openly supports the racist BDS movement and demonises Israel as a settler colonial state. It is also yet another example of the racialisation of Jews. By painting Israel (and, by extension, Jews) as white, non-Jewish perceptions of Jewish ancestry are being imposed on to us in order to strip us of our indigeneity and our right to the Land of Israel. While Jew-haters may label the Jews as white and the Palestinians as Black, on a genetic level, as Cary Nelson, Jubilee Professor of Liberal Arts & Sciences emeritus at the University of Illinois states 'the Jews and Arabs of the Middle East offer no basis for racial differentiation.'[268]

Ironically, while Jewish survival was focused on the survival of Israel after 1967, for the wider non-Jewish world (and today even parts of the Jewish world) Israel was framed as all-powerful. It is no longer perceived to be the underdog – surrounded, as it was for so long, by hostile neighbours intent on its destruction – and Jews who were raised with Zionist and pro-Israel perspectives have since absorbed non-Jewish perspectives on Israel. They, in turn, have reported feeling cheated, with the comedian Seth Rogen stating that he 'was fed a huge amount of lies about Israel'.[269] The domination of antizionist and anti-Israel sentiment in mainstream media has led to Jews, like Rogen, to reject, or at the very least doubt, Zionism. These disillusioned, generally progressive, Jews then accept the narrative being disseminated on Israel (primarily by aspects of the Left, but also by some on the Right) and can go on to argue that Israel is an apartheid state and a perpetrator of genocide which does not have a right to exist. If we refer back to our definition of internalised anti-Jewishness, Jews, like Seth Rogen, have sadly allowed the non-Jewish world to define their Jewish identity. The prevalent non-Jewish narrative on Israel has led them to turn their backs on their ancestral connection to their indigenous land. As Dan Klein, a 33-year-old Jewish man, told the *New York Times*, 'It is an identity crisis ... Very small in comparison to what is happening in Gaza and the West Bank, but it is still something very strange and weird ... The Israel of their lifetime has been powerful, no longer appearing to some to be under constant existential threat.'[270] The article goes on to suggest that, 'The violence comes after a year when mass protests across the United States have changed how many Americans see issues of racial and social justice.'

However, just like German Jews 150 years ago and American Jews in the 1940s and 1950s, contemporary US Jews are faced with choices. They can be proud Jews who understand the Jewish connection to our indigenous homeland or they can be a member of the 21st-century 'community of the good'. Sadly, these ideas are mutually exclusive in parts of the modern Left. The pressures young Jews face with regards to Israel also extend to being held responsible for any Israeli action perceived as unjust by the non-Jewish world. Not only does this trend further the demonisation of Israel, but it can also force Jews to disavow Israel to demonstrate they are not party to these perceived crimes. This is not a uniquely American experience either. As a 2019 report suggested: 'Young Jewish Europeans surveyed indicate at higher rates than older Jewish respondents that people in their countries accuse or blame them for anything done by the Israeli government. Over half (52%) say this happens to them "all the time" or "frequently"'.[271] The report warned: 'Jews are being singled out for blame solely because they are Jewish.'

Like historic attacks on Jewish identity, the connection between Jews and Zionism continues to come under constant fire from the non-Jewish world. They both magnify the perceived Jewish debate about Zionism and present antizionist Jewish voices, which are a distinct minority, as somehow mainstream. Traditional media outlets have regularly written about the perceived split between Zionist and antizionist Jews as a means of promoting Jewish antizionism. Headlines such as 'Rabbi Attacks Zionism'[272], 'Discord among US Jews over Israel seems to grow'[273], 'Anti-zionist Jews Report US gains'[274], 'Feeling abandoned by Israel, many American Jews grow angry'[275] and 'Surge of violence in Mideast forces some young Jews to rethink a rite of passage'[276] have all been published by the *New York Times* since the rebirth of the Jewish state in 1948.

This alleged conflict between Jews about Zionism – which, as we have seen, the vast majority of Jews support – is sinister. We often see these trends as just being the consequence of how history has played out. But this is not the case. As in the 18th century, Jewish identity today is being actively manipulated and denigrated by non-Jewish societies. Fringe Jewish voices, such as representatives of the hard-left, antizionist Jewish Voice for Labour, have repeatedly been invited on major platforms such as the BBC. Naomi Wimborne-Idrissi, a leading figure in JVL, told one BBC radio programme that establishing an independent company process for dealing with accusations of Jew-hate in the Labour Party, 'means bring[ing] in the pro-Israel lobby to make sure that nobody says anything about Israel'.[277] This is a clear example of Conspiracy Fantasy and because she is Jewish, Wimborne-Idrissi was given an opportunity to spread it on a national platform.

But such discussions also give non-Jewish listeners the false impression that antizionism is a mainstream Jewish perspective and that debating Zionism is acceptable. Token Jews on the Left, like Éric Zemmour on the Right, can be used to kosher Jew-hate. In July 2020 Ken Roth, for instance, the former executive director of the Human Rights Watch, appeared to justify Jew-hate by tweeting, 'Anti-semitism is always wrong, and it long preceded the creation of Israel, but the surge in UK antisemitic incidents during the recent Gaza conflict gives the lie to those who pretend that the Israeli government's conduct doesn't affect antisemitism.'[278] This tweet gives credence to the idea that Jew-hate is a response to Israel's perceived crimes. It puts the responsibility on Israel, rather than the non-Jewish world for its continued crimes against the Jews.

But to be a quiet antizionist Jew does not seem to sate the appetite of many of those who hold these views. As Jarrod Tanny, Associate Professor and Block Distinguished Scholar in Jewish History in the Department of History, University of North Carolina, has suggested, they are, 'people with a profound interest in Israel, which they express in public with tenacity and malice.'[279] They are not happy for you or me to be Zionist and to celebrate our connection to the Land of Israel. Instead, they seem to be working to warp Jewishness and Judaism beyond recognition. And removing our connection to our indigenous homeland does just that. Like Jews who converted to Christianity in the Middle Ages or the Yevsektsiya in the Soviet Union, many of these Jews are fixated on maintaining their membership to the modern 'Community of the Good', so they often deploy their Jewishness to minimise and provide kosher cover to overt Jew-hatred. They are forced to denounce Zionism to be accepted.

The rhetoric of the Palestinian Campaign for the Academic and Cultural Boycott helps explain why many Jews on the Left feel compelled to totally denounce Israel and Zionism as opposed to call-ing for peace via a two-state solution. In 2011 it stated, 'We oppose co-operating with the leftist Zionists who take part in demonstrations or call themselves peace activists ... Those left Zionists do not care about the Palestinian rights.'[280] They have closed their movement to any kind of Zionism, even left-wing Zionism. So, to prove they belong, Jews in these spaces must be the harshest of critics and the most damning of commentators. They must prove their worth by wholly and unequivocally rejecting Israel, in any and all capacity. In 2021 Peter Beinart, the well-known antizionist Jewish columnist, tweeted a question to his 116,000 followers. It began, 'Do Zionists deserve a home on the American left?'[281] This question, by a Jew, legitimises the anti-Jewish notion that Zionists are not welcome in Leftist spaces.

The notion that Jews who reject Zionism are suffering from internalised anti-Jewishness is not to suggest that all Jews should have a monolithic perspective on Israel. Jews can and should criticise Israel, where criticism is justified, as they should do with any other country. It is unethical, and contrary to Jewish tradition, to force individuals into a monolithic way of thinking. We have always argued and debated our Jewishness, which is one of the most remarkable things about our peoplehood, and long should that continue.

However, we also have to recognise that we are working within parameters and boundaries. Jewishness and Judaism are driven by clear rules and though these have evolved over time, there is a limit to how far something can shift away from its core before it becomes something else entirely. This is why there are those, like historian Gil Troy and famed author and Jewish leader Natan Sharansky, who call such Jews Un-Jews.[282] This argument is rooted in the idea that these Jews have strayed so far from authentic Jewishness and Judaism that they are no longer Jews. Whether you agree with this assessment or not, ultimately, our individual choices cannot compromise the inherent truths about Jewish experience or identity.

Jews on the Left today are thus faced with what Lessing calls the 'eternal either or'[283] – the constant choice that Jews are forced to make between their Jewishness and their belonging to another society. The world will not let us be both Jewish and European/American/South African or Left. We are always forced to choose. Jews on the Left who have disavowed Zionism pose a danger to our peoplehood, but they are victims. Though they would not see it this way, many of these Leftist Jews are trapped in a toxic relationship with the world around them. They are gaslit and coerced into being a 'good Jew' and they internalise false and hateful narratives on Jews, Judaism and Jewishness from the non-Jewish societies in which they live. Narratives which, in turn, chip away at Jewish self-esteem and fuel internalised anti-Jewishness. Ultimately, antizionist Jews are victims of Jew-hate, and they clearly suffer from internalised anti-Jewishness, but our empathy for them and their experience must not lead us to underestimate the harm they can do to our peoplehood.

LOOKING FORWARD

The first half of this book has detailed the theory and history behind the Jewish experience with internalised hate, but this is ultimately a book of healing. Processing and overcoming internalised anti-Jewishness is a journey that involves real and consistent work. Ultimately, we cannot change the way non-Jewish society views us and treats us, but we can carefully consider how this treatment impacts us.

The following five interviews are with proud Jews from Australia, the United Kingdom and the United States. They are stories of Jews who have begun their healing journeys to overcome internalised anti-Jewishness. They are stories of healing, hope and harmony. Now that we understand the depths and manifestation of internalised Jew-hatred in our community, let us turn our attention towards overcoming it.

Chapter 5

RÓISÍN JACOBSON

RÓISÍN JACOBSON is a 22-year-old British Jewish woman who, in the last three years, has embarked on an extraordinary Jewish journey of healing.

Born in Cardiff, Wales, to an Irish Catholic mother and an English Jewish father, Róisín now identifies as a proud Zionist Jew. But this was not always the case and her relationship with Jewishness was initially fraught with pain and trauma.

Due to her father's traumatic relationship with his own Jewishness – he is the child of a Holocaust survivor – she recalls her Jewish upbringing as very complicated. Róisín's story is an example of how trauma, inflicted upon Jews by the non-Jewish world, can create a situation whereby our relationship with our Jewishness is reframed and we are unable to see its joy and beauty. Instead, we see only pain.

Although, by her own admission, Róisín's upbringing was 'very assimilated', she recalls moments where, as a family, they interacted with, and honoured, aspects of their Jewish identity. Even these, however, were complicated. She remembers every year, on the anniversary of the passing of her father's parents, he would put on a kippah and recite *Kaddish*, the Jewish mourners' prayer. During our conversation, Róisín reflects on the fact that even though her father, in many ways rejected his relationship with Jewishness and Judaism, there was still something inside him that compelled him to honour his own family in this distinctly Jewish way. For Róisín, it was also an important symbol of the specificity of Jewishness. She knew that, as a non-Jew, her mother did not honour her own family members in this way. These observations allowed Róisín in some way to recognise that being Jewish meant being separate from the majority who surrounded her, including members of her own immediate family. But this was a feeling that would only be truly realised many years later.

One of the few times she attended synagogue was during Pesach (Passover). While it was not immediately familiar to her, she felt an instant connection. She says that she 'found it exciting and I felt a connection to Jewish ritual and tradition as an expression of Jewish joy'. One thing that she still remembers being struck by, though, was how much she disliked the food. Her father used to tell her that Jewish food was not tasty or delicious, something she has since found to be untrue. Unsurprisingly, demonstrating the intergenerational aspect of these experiences, because her father told her that Jewish food was disgusting, she found it to be disgusting.

Róisín's family's trauma stems from the fact that over 90 members of her family were murdered in the Shoah. This incredible trauma almost completely reframed her family's relationship with Jewish-ness. Her grandfather, Marcus, was 17 years old when he was arrested during the November Pogrom (commonly known as *Kristallnacht*) in 1938. Along with 30,000 other Jewish men and boys over the age of 16, Marcus was deported to a concentration camp. In an act of incredible bravery, he managed to escape by beating a Nazi over the head with a shovel and then stealing his uniform. He then managed to travel to the UK, where he was later once again interned, but this time as a wartime 'enemy alien'.

In telling her grandfather's story, Róisín recalls how, even before his arrest, Marcus was beaten mercilessly by non-Jewish Germans, people who he had once considered to be his friends. This betrayal had a lasting impact – and one that crossed generations. Róisín says she always finds it hard to trust non-Jewish friends completely, always questioning whether they would ignore her suffering, beat her up, or hide her if 'things went dark again'. Particularly to our non-Jewish readers, this may seem like an extreme, or even unkind, mistrust of her friends, but the trauma and betrayals of the Holocaust, particularly in the descendants of those who survived, are so all-encompassing that they still impact friendships decades later. And as Bessel Van Der Kolk, author of *The Body Keeps Score*, states, 'trauma is not the story of something that happened back then ... it's the current imprint of that pain, horror, and fear living inside people.'[284]

Another trauma inflicted by the Nazis upon Róisín's family was their appropriation of the work of her great-grandfather, Jacob Jacobson. Jacob worked at the *Gesamtarchiv der Deutschen Juden* (Central Archives of the German Jews). When the Nazis came to power, a certificate was required to prove your Aryan status, which in Nazi Germany could ultimately save you from death. Proving racial status was not necessarily a simple process, though, and it was often deeply bureaucratic as there were disputes regarding heritage as many Jews in Germany had assimilated or even converted.

After Hitler was appointed Chancellor, the Nazis' *Reichsstelle für Sippenforschung* (Reich Agency for Genealogical Research), which was devoted to proving ancestry, began to take a strong interest in the archive's documents. Forced by the Nazis to document Germany's Jews, Jacob travelled around the country gathering data on its Jewish communities. Jacob was able to organise visas for his wife, and his son, Marcus, to travel to England, but his own visa was denied, so keen were the Nazis for him to continue this work identifying Jews for them. And worse was to come: once deportations of German Jews began in 1941, Jacob was forced to verify the Jewishness of the deportees. In 1943 Jacob himself was transported to Theresienstadt along with other prominent Jews. Jacob ultimately survived the Shoah and travelled to England after the war. But, understandably, this story is incredibly painful for Róisín's family. Jacob was made to do this work for the Nazis, and the work saved his life. However, he was also forced to take part in the process which resulted in the murder of 165,200 German Jews. Ultimately, we have to recognise this tragic story for what it is – yet another example of Jewish lives being destroyed by the world around them.

The traumas of the Shoah distorted Róisín's relationship with her Jewishness. She was encouraged not to talk about her great-grandfather, Jacob, as her father was ashamed of his actions. She also remembers that her parents were concerned that she would be bullied or rejected by other Jews, especially descendants of survivors, for what Jacob was forced to do. However, in reality, everyone she has spoken to about Jacob has been really kind and recognises how painful and traumatic it must have been for him. As Róisín clearly states, Jacob 'survived against impossible odds and was forced to make impossible decisions.' However, because of the Shoah, during this period, Jewishness represented familial pain and trauma and was devoid of pride or joy. This pain and trauma led Róisín and members of her family to see Jewishness only through the prism of pain. And these ideas of Jewishness were passed on to Róisín and quickly became the basis for her own personal relationship with Jewishness and Judaism.

Like many children of survivors, her father had a very difficult upbringing, partly because of his own father's trauma. When he was 17 (the same age her grandfather was arrested), Róisín's father was taught how to make a Molotov Cocktail by his father 'just in case'. The suffering and anguish his family had experienced was given no opportunity to heal, which is a crucial component of a healthy identity. Róisín describes how her father did try to break this cycle of trauma, but by almost entirely erasing their Jewishness, because this was the only way he knew how. She remembers him telling her: 'The Holocaust is my trauma; I don't want it to be yours.'

The first personal trauma Róisín can remember experiencing was when she was eight years old. She was in religious studies class, and her teacher taught a lesson on the Holocaust. Introducing the Nazis and their crimes to young children without any context resulted in other students making fun of the Holocaust and copying the Nazi salute on a school trip. In response, the teacher (who was well-meaning, but totally unprepared) showed the students documentaries that featured the skeletal bodies of murdered Jews being shovelled into mass graves by bulldozers. Knowing her own family history, Róisín was stunned and asked herself: 'Am I related to them … is that my relative?', while her classmates laughed at her reaction. These experiences of Jewish trauma, both at home and at school, led Róisín to distance herself from her Jewishness, even though there were times when it would emerge in sometimes surprising ways.

As people do in many other cultures around the world, Róisín puts an emphasis on her ancestral connection to her Jewishness. For many years this was all she had. She remembers an almost out-of-body experience she had at Cardiff Castle when she was a child. On a school trip, the tour guide showed them a Hebrew inscription, and asked: 'Does anyone know what language that is?' Much to Róisín's surprise (and that of her mother who was helping with the trip) she blurted out, 'Hebrew!' Hitherto, Róisín's interactions with Hebrew had been limited to a few visits to *Shul* and to *Cheder* (Jewish Sunday School); somehow, though, she remembered.

These small moments of pride managed to break through the dark pain of Róisín's trauma. Like so many other Jews in non-Jewish educational settings, the trauma that Jews carry was not taken into consideration when, aged 12, Róisín studied *The Merchant of Venice*. Indeed, she was made to sit next to one of the very boys who had laughed at the Holocaust and had copied the Hitler salute when she was eight. Every single lesson, this boy would make anti-Jewish remarks about *The Merchant of Venice*, Shylock and Róisín. Róisín remembers there was a deeply racialised image of Shylock on the cover, and her classmate would tell her: 'This is what Jews look like … You are ugly … Your father is ugly.' The racialisation of Jews was also something Róisín grew up experiencing in her own family. Her father has a large nose while Róisín does not (she has her mother's nose), and she remembers always being told 'how lucky I was not to have a "Jewish" nose like my father'. To Róisín, because of the messages she received growing up, to be Jewish was to be ugly. She was not able to see the beauty in Jewish people, nor in our civilisation and culture; instead, it only represented pain, trauma, murder and rejection.

According to Róisín, one of her darkest moments of internalised anti-Jewishness came when she supported Jeremy Corbyn (the former leader of the British Labour Party whose time as leader was a major component in the renormalisation and mainstreaming of Jew-hate we are seeing all over the world). Despite her own pain and trauma, Róisín deems this as the most unhealthy manifestation of her internalised anti-Jewishness. Previously, it was only her personal relationship with her Jewishness that was distorted by the pain of the non-Jewish world's perceptions of Jews and Jewishness, but her support for Corbyn, she says, 'put other Jews in danger'. In our conversation, Róisín tells me that she feels ashamed of backing Corbyn. But I respond by saying that while I understood her feelings I didn't think it was fair. With so much pain, trauma and internalised anti-Jewishness, we feel as if we have failed. These feelings shame us and, while part of our recovery must be to recognise and take responsibility for our actions, we must also understand that, ultimately, there is a much wider context to be aware of here.

Róisín's whole family supported Corbyn. Her father was a doctor, who worked in the incredibly deprived region of South Wales and saw poverty worsen under the Conservative government. I ask how her family responded to the tide of allegations that surrounded Corbyn with regards to his views on Jews. She tells me that they were ignored and minimised. Despite their own experiences, her family didn't see anti-Jewish hate to be 'as bad' as other forms of prejudice, particularly those allegedly propagated by the Conservative Party. And, to many, anti-Jewish hate certainly was not as bad as the poverty that Róisín perceived the Conservative Party to be responsible for.

Róisín also tells me that she believed the anti-Jewish lie that Corbyn was being smeared by the media, which did not want a left-wing leader in power. She says that she 'didn't realise that accusations of Jewish control over the media were themselves examples of conspiracy fantasy'. This is why quality Jewish education is so crucial. How can we expect Jews to identify anti-Jewish tropes if they are not taught to? This kind of knowledge is not inherent.

In December 2019 Corbyn's Labour suffered a massive defeat in the British General Election. Róisín says she was so angry that Corbyn lost and the Conservatives won. She felt that 'supposed prejudice against "white Jews" was less important than real racism against other minorities and poverty, but not according to the biased media'.

Today, Róisín reflects on her former perspective. It was rooted in an almost total rejection of Jewishness and an absorption of non-Jewish ideas about Jewish identity. Róisín's family context meant that she was never given a Jewish anchor. The trauma the Nazis had inflicted upon her family eight decades ago had reverberated down the generations, leaving Róisín with no Jewish foundation to withstand the, often, crushing pressures from a hostile world.

One point which Róisín regrets most is that she allowed herself to be used by left-wing Labour supporters. 'I was their token Jew, telling them that Corbyn was not a racist and that the media was smearing him,' she says. I think Róisín is incredibly brave. Other Jews who supported Corbyn, or who ignored anti-Jewish racism, have not had the courage to face up to their own actions. At this point in our conversation, Róisín and I reflect on the difference between regret and shame. Regret, we decide, can demonstrate introspection and growth, while shame, particularly for things that are not your fault, is rooted in self-blame and judgement. While Róisín regrets her former perspectives and how she allowed herself to be used, she wants to reject the shame. She knows that she was the product of a traumatised Jewish identity which led her to misunderstand Jewish identity.

In the last three years, Róisín has been on a remarkable journey of introspection and growth. Her journey to Jewish Pride began in 2020 and was rooted in responses to the Black Lives Matter movement which she encountered. After graduating from the University of Bristol and studying online in Wales for the end of her degree, Róisín had to return to Bristol in June 2020 to clear out her flat. On her return, she wanted to see where the Edward Colston statue had recently been torn down. (Colston was a British merchant who was involved in the Transatlantic Slave Trade.) When driving through Bristol with her father, they encountered a far-right demonstration protesting against the statue's removal. Even though Róisín's nose was always celebrated for being small, her father remarked: 'I don't think with our big noses we can stay.' Róisín believes that, in this moment, her father racialised himself as a Jew and was really referring to 'big ugly Jewish noses'.

For Róisín, witnessing this demonstration, and her resulting feelings of trauma, were a turning point. She remembers her non-Jewish white friends saying, 'at least the police were there and didn't let it get out of hand', but Róisín was terrified and felt triggered and her other non-Jewish minority friends were also frightened. Although their experience and response differed, this shared fear led Róisín to realise that, while she had always considered herself to be a member of the non-Jewish white majority, she was having a common experience with her other minority friends.

Another experience in the fraught summer of 2020 was also important in Róisín's journey. This occurred when the British rapper Wiley tweeted a series of anti-Jewish statements, such as, 'There are 2 sets of people who nobody has really wanted to challenge #Jewish & #KKK but being in business for 20 years you start to undestand [sic] why … Red Necks Are the KKK and Jewish people are the Law … Work that out.'[285]

For many Jews who were less aware of the renormalisation of Jew-hatred, Wiley's tweets were a wakeup call. It helped them understand just how prevalent Jew-hate is and how even minority groups can perpetuate it. 'Just a few weeks earlier, I felt unsafe as a Jew because of the Right, and with Wiley's racism, I felt unsafe as a Jew because of someone from another traditionally oppressed minority,' Róisín tells me. 'Does everyone just hate us?' In a remarkable moment of introspection, Róisín realised how little she knew about the Jewish experience and began researching. She started reading about anti-Jewish racism and how deeply embedded it was in non-Jewish society. She began the process of freeing herself from non-Jewish perspectives on Jewish identity and she began rejecting the idea that Jews are part of the white majority.

But Róisín also came to realise that solely focusing on Jew-hate was 'really unhealthy'. I am touched when she tells me that reading *Jewish Pride: Rebuilding a People* helped her understand that a strong Jewish identity was not simply rooted in fighting the hate that Jews experience. 'We have to understand our whole experience,' she argues. 'Hatred is tragically part of that, but most importantly, so is joy.' Once again, we see the necessity of those Jewish anchors. They ground us in our Jewishness and help us see it for what it is – rather than what the world around us says it is.

Róisín did not have a Jewish upbringing, but she began to seek out ways she could feel proud of her Jewishness. She began baking challah, making her feel actively Jewish while also feeling connected to Jewish culture and Jewish people all around the world. Recalling her father telling her that Jewish food is disgusting, she now tells him: 'This food is amazing, Dad, what are you talking about?' After tasting her challah, her father responded that it reminded him of Shabbat dinner as a child. That made Róisín feel so proud. In some small way, she says, 'I was helping my dad find his own Jewish Pride.'

Róisín's Jewish journey continued. Through social media, she began connecting with Jews all over the world and she continued learning about what it means to be a Jew. Her journey has, thus far, led to Róisín beginning a Masters in Jewish Studies at UCL in London.

When her course began, she attended the Jewish Society's Sukkot event, which also coincided with the society's president's birthday. In amazement, she saw someone beckon the president over and pull out a chair. With a sigh, the president sat down. Then four other students picked up the chair and began dancing the president around the room. No words were spoken (other than the president's name), but everyone knew instinctively what was about to happen. Seeing this grown man almost fall off a chair made Róisín laugh, and she realised first-hand just how fun, funny and joyous Jewishness and Judaism are. This was not a culture of death and destruction, this was a culture of life, of beauty and of joy.

Though she began engaging with Jewish Pride and joy, a crucial part of Róisín's journey was processing her trauma. Though she had been in therapy for around four years by this point, she made the decision to seek out a Jewish therapist specifically who could understand her experiences. Róisín's therapist talked with her about her growing Jewish Pride: 'Your Jewishness is a mosaic and up until now your mosaic was black and yellow and formed the shape of a yellow star that said "Jude" in the middle, and now you are exploring other pieces and colours that make up the kaleidoscope of Jewish identity.'

Róisín's journey has been epic. She now stands before the world, proud of her Jewishness. Proud to be connected to thousands of years of heritage, ancestry, culture, tradition and thought. She actively celebrates and participates in Jewish life. Recently she ordered new candlesticks for Shabbat and was so excited at their arrival. She also reveals that she is considering making Aliyah (moving to Israel). Róisín is rejecting the shame and trauma imposed on Jews by the non-Jewish world. She is rejecting their racist lies about our people and our experience and now all she wants to do is continue growing, learning and evolving as a proud Jewish woman.

Róisín's journey is an example to each and every one of us.

She did the incredible work to begin her journey of healing; now her strength can inspire all of us to begin ours.

Chapter 6

NICKY RAWLINSON

NICKY RAWLINSON is a 27-year-old British-born American man. He grew up in Highland Park, New Jersey, where there is a sizeable Jewish population. Nicky and I have a lot in common. We both lost our fathers at a relatively young age and we both studied politics (me at Glasgow, him at Cornell) and we are both proud Jews.

But Nicky's journey to Jewish Pride, and his rejection of internalised anti-Jewishness, was complex. Nicky grew up in a conservative (*Masorti*) community. His father, Gordon, was an incredibly proud Jew who instilled a sense of pride and connection in Nicky from a very early age.

Nicky has long been aware of the persecution that Jews faced and that his own family only ended up in the UK and US because of geno-cidal Jew-hate. His maternal grandmother had fled Germany while his paternal grandfather was forced to leave Poland. Nicky tells me that he 'was always aware that persecution had impacted my family growing up'. That sense of his family's history and resilience only added to Nicky's Jewish Pride. His father was British and his mother American, but Nicky did not always feel totally connected to those national identities. Nicky's life has taken him around the world and these travels have allowed him to see and express his Jewishness across borders. He has attended shuls in many different countries. Nicky's primary identity, he says, is that of a Jew, beyond any citizenship he may possess. As we discussed in Chapter 1, this dual connection is not inherently problematic. It is the non-Jewish world who makes it so by accusing Jews of conspiring against non-Jews.

When he was young, Nicky's family life was, he recalls, 'very Jewish'. His home was kosher, which gave him an understanding of the uniqueness of Jewish culture, our food and dietary laws. His earliest memories are of his family gathering together every week to mark Shabbat and spend time together. His father attended synagogue every week and they would sometimes celebrate *Havdalah* (the ceremony to mark the end of Shabbat).

Unlike many Jewish teens, Nicky's involvement with, and engagement in, Jewish life did not diminish following his Bar-Mitzvah. When he was about 13 years old, his older brother joined a youth movement and Nicky followed suit. This took Nicky across the United States doing community service work for Jewish communities. This exposed Nicky to America's many Jewish communities and the educational aspect of the movement brought Nicky more knowledge and understanding of Jewishness and Judaism. 'I loved this experience, which only made me feel more Jewish and deepened my commitment to being a proud Jew,' Nicky remembers.

Nicky went on to join his youth movement on visits to both Israel and Poland. 'Going to Poland was a transformative experience,' Nicky reflects, and he describes how it 'lit a fire inside' him. He embarked on his own educational journey and began reading Holocaust-related literature to understand this experience as much as he could. His trip to Israel also solidified his perspectives and feelings towards Zionism, and he began actively engaging with Israel and Israeli life. He remembers seeing photos of the paratroopers who in 1967 helped liberate the Kotel from the Jordanians who had barred Jews from entering our holy sites after 1948. 'They looked just like me,' he thought. Nicky understood that because he was a Jew, 'this was my story too'. Seeing this expression of Jewish strength and resilience so soon after learning about the incredible trauma of the Shoah felt profound. In 2014, when he was still in his early twenties, Nicky contemplated joining the IDF to support Israel during that summer's war with Hamas. 'Our land was under attack and we had to help,' he felt.

When Nicky's late father fell ill, he began attending shul more regularly. 'My religious observance was totally shaped by my father, both growing up and when he became ill,' he says. *Maariv* (the Jewish evening prayer service) was calming during a chaotic time in his life and with his emotions 'all over the place'. Even after his father's passing, Nicky kept up his religious observance as a way to honour him. That is one of the beautiful things about Jewishness and Judaism. Whether we are willing to acknowledge it or not, the traditions that we practise connect us directly to our ancestors, both those we knew and those unknown. Each of us is part of an unbroken chain of Jewish life and we are inherently connected to one another. For those of us who have sustained loss, this is an incredibly soothing facet of Jewish experience and identity.

The anti-Jewish racism Jews experience has had a big impact on Nicky's Jewishness. Although he understands that Jews are so much more than the persecution we have faced, he also recognises that it has shaped our history. The study of Jewish history – both the positive dimensions and the traumatic aspects – is a crucial component in spreading Jewish Pride, he tells me. 'How can we understand who we are if we don't understand where we came from?' he asks. Jew-hate today has shaken Nicky to his core, particularly as he grew up at the tail end of the period where overt Jew-hate was still taboo. Like those who came before him, the threat facing Jewishness and Judaism has reinvigorated Nicky's commitment to Jewish life. He is now aware that all aspects of his Jewishness, including his religious observance, are acts of resistance in a world where being proudly Jewish is seen as a threat.

Nicky's story is one of such Jewish Pride that you may be wondering how and when he experienced internalised anti-Jewishness. But this is one of the powerful lessons we can learn from Nicky's story.

Even those raised loudly and proudly Jewish, and who develop strong Jewish anchors, can internalise anti-Jewishness. This understanding is crucial when we consider the wide-ranging manifestations of internalised anti-Jewishness. It can harm even the most anchored Jew.

Nicky's first memories of internalised anti-Jewishness are from when he graduated high school and first went to Cornell for college. For the first time in many years, he faced having to build a new life and make new friends. Nicky recalls that, during this period, he would tell people that he was 'half-Jewish', meaning that only one of his parents was Jewish. Although, only having one Jewish parent does not make you any less Jewish, Nicky reflects that he was telling people this 'to seem less different, to be able to integrate more easily'. Like countless Jews before him, Nicky denied his Jewish truth to be able to join non-Jewish society. He reflects that, on some level, he felt that being fully Jewish, from an ancestral perspective, would have inhibited his ability to be accepted and included. He found it easier to connect with friends and with prospective girlfriends by lying about his Jewish heritage. One of the things that shocked Nicky most about this lie was the fact that he 'did it without a second thought'.

Growing up in the United States, Nicky was fully aware of how WASPs (White Anglo-Saxon Protestants, who had historically dominated American society) viewed Jews. This became particularly relevant when Nicky wanted to join a fraternity. The fraternity he ultimately joined, Psi Upsilon, was, he says, 'very "waspy"'. He felt as if its members were the 'American aristocracy and Jews were the foreign other'. He heard a number of anti-Jewish jokes, 'which I participated in because I wanted to be seen as a "good Jew"', he reflects sadly. He has since realised that this was an avoidance tactic. If he diminished and mocked his Jewishness, he could circumvent any potential Jew-hate. Nicky wanted to move through the world with as much ease as possible and wanted to be liked. Anything that could help detract from his difference was positive.

Because of the Racial Libel, which racialises Jews and views Jewish physicality as unattractive, Nicky saw his Jewishness as something that would decrease his attractiveness. Like so many other Jews, Nicky absorbed non-Jewish racist perspectives of the Jewish body. Attributes that were considered attractive, like being a 'jock' are not associated with being Jewish, so he would distance himself from his Jewishness in order not to be associated with such negative and unattractive characteristics. Even though they bore no relevance to his reality. Diminishing his Jewishness meant that it was 'one less thing' that made him different. As Nicky found, because of the dynamics that can exist between Jews and non-Jews in the non-Jewish world, diminished Jewishness is more often than not perceived as being positive. Nicky's story is a warning that even the most committed and engaged Jews are susceptible to internalised anti-Jewishness. And that, even for the proudest of Jews, integrating into non-Jewish societies is difficult.

During Nicky's time at Cornell, he got the opportunity to study at Oxford University. He made a great group of friends but only towards the end of his year did his Jewishness come up. As he had done before, though, he only described himself as half-Jewish. Nicky's friends were upper class and came from old money, and historically, those communities have had very offensive perspectives on Jews. In this subtly anti-Jewish environment, Nicky was trying to 'pass', not necessarily as a non-Jew, but as someone who, at least in some ways, was more like the people by whom he was surrounded. At Oxford, Nicky took some comfort in the fact that his surname, Rawlinson, was not overtly Jewish.

What shocks Nicky today is that his actions and behaviour were completely unconscious. He tells me he 'had no idea any of this was happening until now'. Nicky's experiences also offer us a fascinating insight into internalised anti-Jewishness. He considers himself to be a very introspective, self-aware person, but his personal battle with internalised anti-Jewishness was raging beneath his conscious surface.

He says that one of the worst aspects about this time is that the diminishment of his Jewishness 'was such an instinctive response to being in a non-Jewish setting'.

Nicky's experiences also demonstrate the inherent connection that Jews often have to Jewishness. He wanted to diminish his Jewishness, but he could not deny it outright, so he had to shrink it to become palatable to those around him. One of the tragic elements of this is that Nicky's instinctive response didn't give his non-Jewish friends the opportunity to be accepting. As Róisín described, Jews, so traumatised by hate, move through the world with (even subconscious) suspicion. Although Nicky had experienced anti-Jewishness, and perceived positive feedback from telling people he was half-Jewish, he never gave his friends the chance to accept him.

The reason Nicky agreed to appear in this book was because of a conversation he had with his best friend and his fiancé. They were discussing the frightening rise of Jew-hate and its impact on Jews. It was a moment of reflection and realisation for all of them as they woke up to the fact that each of them had denied or diminished their Jewishness to be accepted at one point in their lives. They looked at each other and thought: 'What the hell?' Nick tells me that this realisation scared him. It was so antithetical to who he thought he was. He tells me he feels ashamed, but we must not entertain those emotions. Nicky and all other Jews who experience internalised anti-Jewishness are responding to deeply embedded hate. The blame for these feelings does not lie with us, it lies with the world around us which tells us that being proudly and distinctly Jewish is a bad thing.

I began Chapter 1 with a quote from Trude Weiss-Rosmarin. It reads, 'To be a Jew in a non-Jewish world has always been and will continue to be a handicap in more ways than one.' Nicky's testimony reflects this. He tells me that he 'didn't want to be held back by his Jewishness.' Part of him was proud when he went on dates with really attractive women because he wasn't being held back by the racial stereotypes of Jewish men. He was proud when he saw an attractive Jewish celebrity, like Mila Kunis or Paul Rudd, who were not being held back by being Jewish and all the baggage that can mean in the non-Jewish world. Nicky was so influenced by the racist perceptions of Jews that he 'got a rush of excitement when I saw an attractive Jewish celebrity who doesn't fit the stereotypes of what Jew is meant to look like.'

Nicky's conversation with his friends was a turning point in his journey to dismantle his internalised anti-Jewishness. It made him conscious, for the first time, of how much we bend to be accepted, of how much of our self-perception is rooted in non-Jewish reflections of our identity. How much we warp and diminish ourselves. How much we shed our Jewish anchors to make the non-Jews around us like us. This often happens on a subconscious level, but now Nicky is very conscious. He tells me he is 'done with it' and now understands that he doesn't 'have anything to prove to anyone about being a Jew'.

Like all my other interviewees, Nicky has had to work hard to understand and confront his internalised anti-Jewishness. He has had to dive into himself to understand the depths of this issue and he has had to face an unsettling and uncomfortable truth: he was not as proud of his Jewishness as he thought he was. Even though Judaism and Jewishness were major parts of his identity he still fell prey to this form of Jew-hate. But Nicky had a strong Jewish anchor. How much deeper would his feelings of internalised anti-Jewishness have gone if he hadn't? This is why developing strong Jewish anchors through Jewish action and education are vital. They can't always prevent internalised anti-Jewishness arising, as Nicky's story tells us. But they can help minimise its impact. 'The more we understand that stereotypes about Jews harm us and we recognise the fallacy then we can reject them,' Nicky rightly argues.

Although complex, Nicky's new-found awareness has been liberating. It has allowed him to begin his journey to authentic Jewish Pride.

'Now I know who I am. Who I really am. And I won't warp or change my Jewishness to be accepted ever again,' he says defiantly.

One of the steps that Nicky took to understand his internalised anti-Jewishness was to have conversations with non-Jews. Instead of being nervous of rejection, he began embracing the fact that he may have been the only Jew in a specific space, and instead of diminishing himself, he celebrated his difference and proudly took up that space as a Jew. He began discussing Jew-hate and Israel, and at Georgetown University, where he is now studying law, he began publicly advocating for Jews. He adopted a leadership role and began writing articles (one of which I helped edit, which is how we first met).

Now he sees no choice in his Jewish Pride. He will not diminish himself or make himself acceptable because now Nicky knows that being a loud, proud Jew is enough. His rejection of internalised anti-Jewishness has brought him even closer to Judaism and Jewishness and even further strengthened his Jewish anchor. Like me, Nicky honours his beloved late father by being actively Jewish and by saying *Kaddish* for him. He believes that Judaism and Jewishness are active and must be rooted in something tangible. He understands that we are caretakers of Jewishness and Judaism and we have to nurture and maintain it for the next generation, and this includes combatting internalised anti-Jewishness.

As we bond over our memories of our fathers, he tells me a story that encapsulates his late father's connection to Jewishness, which he finds so inspiring. While he was in hospital in Switzerland, someone from the Basel Jewish community brought a chanukiah for Chanukah into the hospital. Nicky's father was not in a private room but shared the ward with six others. At first, Nicky didn't want to sing the songs and say the *brachot* (prayers) and thus single the family out as Jewish. He was embarrassed. However, Gordon, his father, insisted they did. So, the family stood together lighting the chanukiah and singing the Chanukah songs like *Ma'oz Tzur*.

Today, Nicky is so motivated by his late father's love of Judaism and Jewishness. And now, he can continue to honour that love, having rejected the internalised anti-Jewishness that was forced on him, ready and able to maintain and defend the Jewish people.

Chapter 7

SHOSHANA BATYA GREENWALD

SHOSHANA BATYA GREENWALD is an American Orthodox Jewish woman. She is an educator and online advocate for Jewish and other marginalised communities. Before Shoshana agreed to be interviewed, I incorrectly believed that, due to the centrality of Judaism and Jewishness to their lives, Orthodox communities do not experience internalised anti-Jewishness. But her story is another reminder that this is a problem that can affect even those Jews with the strongest of Jewish anchors.

Shoshana was born in Santa Clara, California, and her parents were part of the local Yeshiva (a Jewish educational institution that focuses on the study of traditional religious texts). She is the oldest of five children and her father was a rabbi. The family was constantly moving around the country as he was posted to serve various congregations. This exposed Shoshana to a wide variety of Jewish people and gave her a sense of what it meant to be Jewish in different parts of the United States. The family eventually settled in New York after her father was appointed to Lincoln Square synagogue in Manhattan.

Although her family was more 'traditional Orthodox', Shoshana attended a modern-Orthodox Jewish school. The difference in observance led her to feel as if she was always straddling two worlds: the modern and the more traditional. This feeling persists today with her position as a prominent Orthodox Jew on social media.

After high school, Shoshana moved to Israel to study Jewish texts at seminary. She immersed herself in Jewish learning for 18 months and then she met Shlomo and the couple eventually married in 2003. They are the proud parents of four children, Shalom Yishai, Estie, Yakira and Aliza. After living in New York for years, Shoshana and her family moved to New Jersey.

Being a rabbi's daughter 'informed every aspect' of her life, Shoshana recalls. That life was, she adds, 'pretty sheltered' and her entire world was Jewish. She would listen to Jewish music and read Jewish books. She *loved* being Jewish. Shabbat was particularly important for Shoshana and she felt special that Jews were given this day off.

However, the pride that Shoshana felt in her Jewishness and Judaism was complex. She was aware of anti-Jewish accusations of Jewish supremacy and power and she was aware that too much Jewish Pride could have been deemed threatening if it were perceived as confirmation of the idea that Jews think they are better than other people. 'Other minorities are allowed to have pride, they are encouraged to,' she suggests, 'but the fantasy accusations of Jewish power mean that Jewish Pride is seen as equivalent to Jewish supremacy.'

Shoshana was raised with an incredibly thorough Jewish education. And while she was raised with an immense Jewish Pride, she was also always aware of historic Jew-hate. She contrasts her attitude to Jew-hate, especially in America, with that of her grandparents. They were the first generations of their families to be born in the US, and, like many other American Jews, they 'felt as if they had made it'. As Orthodox Jews, they didn't consider America to be 'the new Jerusalem' per se, but they certainly felt as if 'Jew-hate was over'. Shoshana's outlook is vastly different from that of her grandparents. Even before the end of the post-Holocaust Gilded Age of American Jewish life – the period of American Jewish cultural emancipation when overt Jew-hate became, for a brief period, taboo – she often had a sense of 'impending doom'. As someone who had learned about, and understood, the seemingly never-ending pattern of Jew-hate, she did not trust the non-Jewish world as her grandparents had done.

Since the resurgence of overt Jew-hate began, Shoshana says, she has felt scared. 'When you're raised so Jewishly, the concept of Jew-hate is so ingrained. It is impossible to ignore,' she argues. Growing up with this, almost innate, knowledge led Shoshana to suffer trauma. She has lived her adult life knowing that people hate her and, on a wider level, there is almost nothing she can do about it. Her experience of being Orthodox in America, is more akin, she tells me, to being Jewish in Europe. The experience of being visibly Jewish, meant she was always cognisant that the spectre of Jew-hate is always haunting her.

Like many Jews, trauma has been a part of Shoshana's Jewish iden-tity for years. As a child, she feared Hitler would climb through her window at night to kidnap her. The trauma of knowing that within living memory, six million Jews were murdered has a real and last-ing impact on Jewish people. But, as we discussed in Chapter 1, it is not only trauma from the Shoah that scars Jews today. Intergenera-tional trauma from our families' personal experiences, as well as Jews being aware of the reasons we live where we live (such as our families fleeing genocide or ethnic cleansing as refugees) can be scarring as well. The trauma inflicted upon us then creates a situation whereby it becomes a part of, and in some cases, central to our Jewish identity. And although Shoshana was brought up as a proud Orthodox Jewish woman, trauma from Jew-hate was still woven into the tapestries of her identity.

As I've said, I was surprised when Shoshana agreed to take part in this interview. Internalised Jew-hate is often expressed at the expense of the Orthodox community, but I had not yet considered its impact on those very communities. Growing up, the idea of *Kiddush Hashem* (sanctification of God) was drummed into Shoshana. It created a notion that she had to represent the Jewish people. Although she was proud of this role, she also felt being a Jewish ambassador brought with it enormous pressure. But this idea of representing the Jews extended beyond her own behaviour. She tells me that if she was 'with a group of visibly Jewish people I would worry that they will not be on their best behaviour and then they will be hated.' Shoshana feared that if these Jews 'behaved badly' then they would bring Jew-hate on themselves. She tells me that being in large groups of Jews in the non-Jewish world caused her great stress. She wanted to blend in as best she could to avoid Jew-hate.

Shoshana often sees anti-Jewishness aimed at Orthodox Jewry by other Jews. She experienced it a lot during the Covid-19 pandemic. She describes how, throughout the community, the notion of the 'inclusion of Orthodox Jews went out the window'. Orthodox Jews were deemed to be embarrassments to the wider Jewish community. Tragically, she found that people she admired were saying terrible things about the Orthodox community, such as: 'Orthodox Jews who don't wear masks are anti-Black.' This is an offensive and anti-Jewish perspective based on tropes about a Jewish conspiracy to endanger the Black community. The simple fact is that many Black and Orthodox communities are geographically close and many even overlap. There is obviously no Jewish conspiracy to harm Black people. Following the January 2022 hostage situation at Beth Israel, in Texas, Shoshana saw social media posts saying that Orthodox Jews were not recognising the hostages as Jews because they were Reform. This was in spite of the fact that the Rabbinical Council of America wrote a letter of support to Rabbi Cytron-Walker of Beth Israel. Because internalised anti-Jewishness often targets Orthodox Jews, Shoshana finds that she has to deal with other Jews' internalised anti-Jewishness while she is trying to cope with her own.

When she was in graduate school, she went on a trip to London. As an Orthodox Jew she was always openly Jewish, but Shoshana still remembers wanting to be a palatable Orthodox Jew, who 'wasn't too different' from her classmates. Internalised anti-Jewishness is an emotional, not a rational, response, and it therefore does not always follow logic. Shoshana felt it was 'OK' to tell her classmates she was kosher, but she felt very strongly that no one should know she wore a *sheitel* (a wig commonly worn by Orthodox women after marriage because of *tzniut* – modesty standards). While she wore sheitels, it was always important to Shoshana that they looked as 'natural as possible'. During her class trip to London, she felt comfortable sharing with her roommate that she wore a sheitel. The following day, they were on a walking tour of London and Billy, one of the men on the programme, ran up to her and touched her sheitel. Billy, who was Halachically Jewish but he denied his own Jewishness, later confided in a group that included her roommate that 'Shoshana wears a wig'. When she was outed, Shoshana felt great shame. Her difference 'was exposed' and she no longer felt like their 'good palatable Jew'.

Some Hasidic Jewish women wear nude stockings with a seam down the back to demonstrate that they are not bare-legged (this would be seen as immodest). When discussing this one day, Shoshana felt compelled to add, unprompted, 'Oh, I am not one of those Jews.' If we think back to Chapter 2, we discussed the qualifica-tion of Jewishness as a form of subtle internalised anti-Jewishness. Like many other Jews, when Shoshana qualified her Jewishness, she hoped it would prove that she was a 'good Jew'. Shoshana says that 'because of Jew-hate, Jews are scared and this fear can cause us to turn on ourselves'. When someone in the public eye does something wrong, she says, 'Oh, I hope they're not Jewish.' We blame each other, worrying that we bring Jew-hate on ourselves, instead of focusing our attention on the real culprit: the non-Jewish world that shames and traumatises Jewish people.

Despite her experiences of internalised anti-Jewishness, Shoshana is, and has always been, a proud Jew. She has a strong and developed Jewish anchor and talks about her endless Jewish joy and her love of Jewish action, her love of shul, the prayers, songs and traditions. Shoshana's journey from prejudice to pride has not been centred on Jewish action and Jewish joy but on healing. This journey hasn't necessarily been easy and has sometimes involved being confronted with even more Jew-hate. But Shoshana is now coming to terms with the fact that Jew-hate is not our fault.

A product of American society and its struggles with racial binaries, Shoshana found herself wanting to join the fight against other forms of hate. She began using her voice, and her social media platform, to advocate for other communities, even more than she was doing for the Jewish community. Sadly, in her work supporting other minority communities, Shoshana has had terrible experiences with some very large social-justice-oriented Instagram accounts. 'They shamed me and totally disregarded my own experience of Jew-hate and my own trauma,' she says. 'They made me feel as if Jews don't matter at all.' Even though she was working to be a strong and respectful ally, she found herself experiencing anti-Jewish hate in these supposedly anti-racist spaces. Even though she was being a good Jew, Shoshana found that she still wasn't good enough.

While this is an ongoing struggle, she says she is learning never to accept scraps. This doesn't come naturally to Shoshana. She says she 'still cares about *Kiddush Hashem* and being an ambassador for the Jewish people'. She still struggles with the desperate need for Jewish survival and our trauma responses. She still wonders: 'If I am a good Jew will they still hate me? If I am palatable enough, will I be safe?' Although Shoshana knows palatability and safety aren't connected, she still struggles with this idea.

Shoshana is also taking her own practical steps to build a practical bulwark against internalised anti-Jewishness. While she was raised in, and lives, an Orthodox life, she still absorbed specific norms created by the non-Jewish world. She has stopped calling the Torah the 'Old Testament' – its Christian name used to differentiate it from the Christian New Testament. Shoshana has also rejected the idea of Judeo-Christian values. This is a form of propaganda that connects Christianity to Judaism and Jewishness, even though early

Christians actively rejected Judaism to such an extent that they used their 'non-Jewishness' to define their Christian identities. It also erased the millennia of Christian Jew-hate, which bears responsibility for embedding Jew-hate in Western society. Shoshana still cares about other communities and wants to advocate for them, but she is also working hard to reject the notion that this must necessitate the diminishment of her Jewishness or her experience. Previously she has been afraid of using the term 'anti-Jewish racism' because of the specificity of the Black experience. However, she has learned that racism can come in different forms and is working to internalise the fact that it *does* target Jews as much as it targets the Black community. Most of all, Shoshana is working to accept the idea that she cannot define her experience and identity based on the experience of another.

Empathy is a huge part of Shoshana's journey to tackle her internalised anti-Jewishness. This applies to herself, ensuring she is patient and kind to herself on her journey. However, it also applies to other Jews. Instead of condemning Jews who may practise their Judaism differently from her, she seeks to understand them. 'Jews do not bring Jew-hate on themselves and, though we may disagree on fundamental aspects of our identities, we cannot engage in self-blame any longer,' she argues defiantly.

At this point in our conversation, our talk turns to Shoshana's beautiful children. We discuss the difficulty of teaching our children about anti-Jewish racism. Her children know about Jew-hate as it is baked into our history and Shoshana recognises that she has to tell her children about the Holocaust. However, she is determined not to let it consume their perceptions of being Jewish. They know about Jew-hate, because this is a Jewish reality and, as Orthodox Jews, who are disproportionately targeted because they are visible, they have to be especially aware of it. The New York Chanukah Pogrom of December 2019 was particularly frightening for Shoshana and her family. A boy who was as visibly Jewish as her son was beaten up because he was Jewish. She felt as if she was 'yelling and no one cared, even from within our own community'.

Despite the real threats they experience, Shoshana's children under-stand that 'they have done nothing to cause the bad people to want to hurt them.' Their Jewish identity is rooted in Jewish joy and Jewish Pride. In Chapter 1 we discussed internalised anti-Jewishness as an intergenerational problem due to the continuing problem in Jewish education. As Róisín's story taught us, it can also be intergenerational because of trauma. Growing up in the shadow of the Shoah is painful. So much unresolved trauma was imposed on us by the generations that came before us. But Shoshana is determined to break this cycle. Her children must be aware of Jew-hate. It impacts the lives of every single Jew. But they will not be defined by it. Their Jewish identities will be based solely on Jewish joy, Jewish Pride and Jewish action.

And to that I say, Amen.

Chapter 8

AVRAHAM VOFSI

AVRAHAM VOFSI is a 32-year-old portrait artist. He lives in Melbourne, Australia, and his story is one of Jewish self-discovery, self-acceptance and self-love.

Avraham grew up in Melbourne but was the only member of his American family that was born there. Avraham's mother was raised with a 'strong Jewish identity' and worked hard to pass that on to her sons. However, the influence of the non-Jewish society he grew up in proved more powerful in his own battle between universality and specificity.

That said, at different points in his childhood, there were instances of active Jewishness and these are some of Avraham's fondest memories. He remembers his family marking Pesach with a Seder. This was incredibly meaningful to Avraham and he loved it. His family attended Kabbalat Shabbat services and even, for a period, were kosher. These sparked a tiny flame of Jewish Pride and joy in Avraham, one that was not totally extinguished by the internalised anti-Jewishness he later developed.

Because his older brother, Max, had had his Bar-Mitzvah and Avraham looked up to him, this was something he wanted too. This, again, was a period of his early life marked by much Jewish engagement. He attended synagogue and his mother played a game with him rewarding him with M&Ms when he was learning his *Parsha* (Torah portion). But, although he enjoyed the Bar-Mitzvah and the learning process, it was the last time Avraham went to synagogue for years.

Despite his mother's efforts, Avraham's Jewish anchor never fully developed because of the isolation he experienced. Avraham's family lived in the north of the city, while the majority of the Jewish community was centred in the south. This meant he grew up 'physically isolated' from other Jews. He says this isolation, and the fact that he was one of the few Jews at school, contributed to him internalising anti-Jewish hatred.

Indeed, Avraham's schooling was a major component in his development of internalised anti-Jewishness. He tells me the more he thinks about it, the more he realises that 'there were very few Jews and the only Jews who would send their kids there weren't super-interested in being Jewish.' The Jews that were at his school thus shared Avraham's indifference to Jewishness and Judaism. This meant they weren't able to come together and support one another as they navigated school in such a non-Jewish environment. Avraham explains that, while he and his brother were often targeted for being American, he understands that the specific slurs made against them were coded anti-Jewish hate. 'They utilised classic anti-Jewish tropes, it was like the verbal version of the three brackets you see online that are also known as an (((echo)))', Avraham explains. These are often used to signify things, such as power, media and government, that people accuse Jews of controlling. The deep anti-Jewishness which lay in the slurs Avraham and his brother experienced is also evident in the manner in which other American students were not targeted in the same way. From a very young age, Avraham felt that he was singled out for being Jewish. It was not something he saw as a part of himself that he should be proud of. These feelings of shame were compounded by his lack of developed Jewish anchor. Because of this, he tells me, he developed a 'discomfort with being Jewish'.

Fascinatingly, years later, Avraham discovered that one of his really close school friends was also Jewish. When Avraham discovered this, he asked further about his friend's identity, but was told: 'Well, my mum's mum was Jewish, but I am not into religion.' Again, we see the dangers of Jews absorbing non-Jewish definitions of Jewish identity, such as Jewishness being simply a matter of religious identity.

As elsewhere, bullying was a problem at Avraham's school. Looking back nearly twenty years later he recalls that the Jewish students often bullied one another. While these Jewish students might have banded together and bonded over their Jewishness, the anti-Jewish environment at school fostered an ethos of 'divide and conquer'. Jewish students could not be friends with one another and instead they turned upon each other in order to prove themselves to their non-Jewish peers. They wanted to be accepted, so they had to reject their own difference, and torment those that represented that difference.

Avraham's story represents the complexity of identity. On the one hand, he had been brought up with moments of active Jewishness and he himself had chosen to have a Bar-Mitzvah. On the other hand, he wanted to reject his Jewishness as it marked him out as different.

Avraham is a very hairy Jewish man. For Avraham, as he entered puberty, this became the source of painful racialising. Avraham's hairiness (and the hairiness of many other Jewish people) was a physical representation of his indigeneity to the Levant. Although Jewish women are often shamed for their hair, Jewish men can be too, and this was a great source of humiliation for Avraham. He tells me that he hated getting undressed during sports at school. Teenagers often have discomfort with their bodies, but Avraham had the added layer of being marked as different through his hair. This is one of the important things about the racialisation of Jews. It hurts us and makes us feel ashamed and damages our self-esteem. We experience this all the while being gaslighted by members of our own community and the wider world when we are told Jews are not racialised. Avraham was ashamed, but did not understand why, even though he was taught that an element of the physical manifestation of his Jewishness was wrong, and as such he hated it.

When Avraham was 14 years old, he began exploring his creativity. Along with his friend (whose mother is Jewish but who 'isn't interested in religion'), they started making short amateur films. These were written, directed and shot by Avraham, and though he hadn't seen them for years, he rewatched them during lockdown. They revealed something discomforting. The punchline in one of the films he wrote was: 'And you're a Jew!' At a subconscious level, due to his hairiness and his vague understanding of Jewish identity, Avraham was aware 'he was stuck with it', but his coping mechanism was to diminish it and even humiliate it as a way of venting his frustration.

Jewishness was a constant battle for Avraham. There was a brief period at school where he felt able to embrace his difference by wearing a kippah and a Magen David necklace. He tells me that this was an attempt 'to take back control of his Jewishness', but this was not necessarily an attempt to 'reclaim his relationship with his Jewishness. That is different', he says. He reflects, for instance, that he never wanted to engage with Jewishness with other Jews as he wouldn't be in control of those situations. These acts were thus a kind of damage control in order to mitigate his shame. Ultimately, he was not ready to reclaim his Jewishness and when his discomfort became too great, he shed these symbols of Jewishness. His internal battle with his Jewish identity then turned into a desire to 'shame my Jewishness', he reflects sadly. He wanted to turn it into a joke as a way of processing the shame he was experiencing and was unable to overcome. To deal with the shame he felt, Avraham shrank his Jewishness, and it ceased to be an active part of his life.

One of the fascinating parts of these interviews is how little Israel has featured. When I put out a call for Jews who have experienced internalised anti-Jewishness, I expected all of them to be focused on overcoming antizionism. But, in these conversations thus far, Israel has not been at the centre of any of my interviewees' battles with internalised Jew-hate. However, like Róisín, Avraham was a non-Zionist.

Avraham's non-Zionism was an expression of his discomfort with being Jewish. He was not comfortable with anything that marked him as Jewish or different, including the existence of a Jewish state. So, he refused to engage with, or consider, Israel at all. Avraham's journey to Jewish Pride can be seen through the development of his thoughts on Jewish indigeneity, which now form an important part of his Jewish identity. This is a symbol of Avraham's acceptance of his Jewishness as a form of difference, and his great pride in that difference.

After university, Avraham moved to Los Angeles to pursue film-making. This was to become a significant period in both his professional and Jewish lives. For the first time, Avraham found himself surrounded by Jewish people. He found himself being invited to Shabbat dinners and, although many of his friends in LA were not Jewish, his immersion in Jewish life led Avraham to begin the process of reclaiming his Jewish identity. However, even then he witnessed events that shaped how he began to define his Jewishness in the parameters of non-Jewish perspectives of being a 'good Jew'. During his time in LA, Avraham and his friends had a weekly game night for a while. There was one other Jewish person involved sometimes. He was 'super-like "stereotypically Jewish" in a way that's common in America'. Avraham reflects, 'I don't think he was practising, but he was a smart alec, loud, awkward with curly hair. Anyway, he was the butt of every joke, and mercilessly teased.' So, even though he had started dipping his toe into Jewish life, Avraham was always aware of Jewishness being a source of shame and, he suggests that although he 'didn't do much of the teasing, it certainly wasn't something I stopped.'

In his second year in LA, being around Jews reminded Avraham that he loved Seder and he had become comfortable enough with his Jewishness to want to repeat the experiences of childhood. This was a significant step in his journey to Jewish Pride and Avraham felt that these first Seders were him 'dipping a toe into active Jewishness'. While he hosted these dinners, he didn't feel confident to ask any of his guests to do anything specific. Avraham felt that during this period of his life he was exploring 'the parameters of being a "good Jew"'. He was becoming more comfortable with his Jewishness, but within the boundaries of what would be acceptable to his mostly non-Jewish friends. His girlfriend at the time was not fully supportive of his journey, and Avraham's developing Jewish anchor did not yet give him the strength or knowledge to advocate for himself

The lack of support from his girlfriend, and her attitudes towards Jews, explains Avraham's hesitancy and desire to be a 'good Jew'. On their second date, he remembers her telling a story that involved someone 'Jewing out'. He was stunned. However, he found himself gaslit by her, being made to feel like she was just joking around. 'So, what's the big deal?' she asked. Avraham stayed in this relation-ship for two years. Other instances where he was made to feel like Jew-hate was 'just a joke' followed. Although his girlfriend knew he was Jewish, and although Avraham had progressed on his journey to Jewish Pride, he was made to feel as if he couldn't be 'too Jewish'. He had to be her 'good Jew'.

Eventually, Avraham's relationship ended and, after three years in Los Angeles, he moved back to Australia. He brought with him his annual Pesach Seder and his new girlfriend gave him the space and support to slowly explore his Jewishness from a prouder and more authentic place. Together, they began marking Shabbat by having a digital detox and playing board games. It was, he recalls, 'quite a non-Jewish entry to Shabbat. But it was another step on my journey'. Soon after, he began buying *Challot* (Jewish plaited bread tradition-ally eaten on Shabbat) and started saying the *brachot* (prayers). Slowly but surely, Avraham was reclaiming his Jewish birthright and heritage.

Avraham remarks that it is funny that it was his non-Jewish girlfriend who gave him 'permission to be Jewish'. But I think this makes sense and perfectly encapsulates the struggle against internal-ised Jew-hate. In the Diaspora, we are a tiny minority. If we are given the space to explore and define our own identities as Jews, then our Jewish identity can flourish. However, if our identity is shaped by the Broken Mirror and non-Jewish ideas of good or bad Jews, then we can develop internalised anti-Jewishness. This relationship gave Avraham the strength to explore and learn about his Jewishness in a safe space. While beautiful, this is also the crux of the problem. As Avraham suggests: 'We often depend on the non-Jewish world to be proudly Jewish.'

Avraham's creativity moved from film to painting and his healing journey continued with his portraiture. His portraits brought him into contact with a performance group made up of indigenous people from various communities. It was through this community that Avraham really began exploring in a cognitive *and* emotional way what it means to be Jewish. Being around them, and seeing their incredible pride, was infectious and it inspired him to begin to explore his own identity. Although their circumstances were very different, both Avraham and this community of indigenous Australians were considered 'different to the average Australian'. Avraham began to consider who he was and what this difference – his Jewishness – meant to him. He worked with the community for around two years and it changed his life, teaching him that, regardless of how you are treated by the world around you, you have to see your identity as a source of pride, and never shame.

Like many of my other interviewees, his journey to Jewish Pride brought him online where he discovered proud Jewish advocates who inspired him even further. He says a major turning point was the 2021 war between Israel and Hamas which was used to justify a grassroots uprising against Jews all over the world, both on- and offline. This was the moment when many Jews around the world began to reckon with their identities and question what it means to be a Jew as well as our interactions with the non-Jewish world. This led Avraham to consider where he feels at home and who he feels comfortable with. It led him to realise that he had to work hard to pursue the process he had begun in reclaiming his Jewishness.

Avraham's time with indigenous friends also had an important impact as it helped him understand what it means to be indigenous. Although half of the world's Jews live outside our homeland, as a collective, we are still indigenous to that land. This helped him develop his understanding of Jewish identity. It also helped him see his own differences, like his hair, as a source of pride. While he likes being Australian, Avraham is *also* proud to be a Jew, with all that that means.

Being in Australia, a society with a very specific notion of indigeneity, he has been challenged a lot on how he can also be considered indigenous. But Avraham's journey to Jewish Pride, and the development of his Jewish anchor, has led him to knowledge, and, perhaps most importantly, given him the confidence to advocate for his people. He now sees the way Jews are subjected to a 'total double standard'. If he ever feels as if he is doubting his Jewishness and our connection to Israel, he asks himself, 'If the Samoan community was paying for diasporic Samoans to visit Samoa, would anyone have a problem?' In this process, Avraham has had to work hard to overcome the shame that had been imposed on him by the world around him. He takes this work so seriously that he has pursued therapy to help him better understand his feelings towards his Jewish identity.

One of the major ways in which Avraham actively rejected the anti-Jewish rhetoric he had internalised was by adopting his middle name (Avraham) as his primary name. Avraham's first name is actually Leo and, when he was a child, he hated that his middle name was so identifiably Jewish and would never tell it to people. Today, the act of calling himself Avraham publicly is a loud declaration of Jewish Pride. Developing his understanding of Jewish identity from a Jewish perspective (the *only* legitimate perspective) has built his Jewish self-esteem. After reading *Jewish Pride: Rebuilding a People*, Avraham reached out to me and we began discussing ways he could apply his artistic skills to Jewish Pride. In this pursuit, he decided to only paint Jewish people. He reflects on the fact that 'Jews are erased constantly and we are told that we do not matter' and Avraham wants to show Jews that we do matter and that our culture and civilisation are beautiful, special, unique and worth depicting.

At the end of our conversation, Avraham tells me:

'It is time Jews reclaimed our amazing culture. We cannot have our stories told by others. We will not allow them to shame us any longer. This is Jewish Pride and this is how I now see the world.'

I couldn't have put it better myself.

Chapter 9

LYVIA TZAMALI

LYVIA TZAMALI is a 32-year-old woman who grew up between the UK and Greece. She was born to a Jewish British mother and a Welsh non-Jewish father. Her story is an awe-inspiring example of the endless possibilities to heal and pursue Jewish Pride.

Like each of my other interviewees, Jewish trauma informed Lyvia's Jewish experience. Strikingly, as soon as we begin discussing her Jewish roots, she explains that her grandmother found it difficult to talk about her own Ashkenazi background due to the horror that befell her family, and millions of other Ashkenazi Jews, during the Russian Pogroms of 1881.

Although trauma underpinned Lyvia's understanding of her Jewishness, she reflects that Jewish Pride still managed to shine through. She remembers her mother and grandmother 'having a certain amount of pride in their Jewishness' and being Jewish was, to an extent, an active part of Lyvia's life growing up. Jewishness was a topic of conversation and she recalls engaging in Jewish action, like lighting the chanukiah during Chanukah. She remembers too feeling an added layer of connection to her mother and grandmother because of their Jewishness. She was very aware that she was part of 'a trio of three Jewish women' and felt that her mother and grandmother were strong Jewish matriarchs.

But, despite her family's undoubted strength and pride, the almost-constant battle that rages in Jews between Jewish joy and trauma was present in their lives. Lyvia remembers her grandmother being incredibly cautious when telling people that she was Jewish. She didn't want anyone to know where she lived. She didn't want her phone number listed in the phone book. As a young child, in a state of blissful ignorance, none of this made sense to Lyvia. But now she understands.

Although Jewish shame and trauma were present in Lyvia's life growing up, these were not her experiences. Instead, she was observing the experiences of those around her. However, like the vast majority of Jews, there came a time when Lyvia had her own experiences of feeling shame because of her Jewishness. When she was in primary school, Lyvia was very open about being Jewish. She remembers turning in pieces of homework that referenced her Jewish identity. At this stage, she was a Jewish child yet unburdened by the shame imposed on Jews by the non-Jewish world. But from the age of seven, Lyvia was forced to fight her own battle between Jewish shame and pride when her religious studies teacher told her that Jesus was murdered by the Jews. Lyvia recalls that this was 'a great moment of shame'. She had been so open and proud of her Jewishness but was now being told that her people committed the most monstrous of acts. She remembers thinking, 'Oh my god, my people killed Jesus, I wish I hadn't said anything.' At this young age, Lyvia thus learned something incredibly fundamental as to how Jews are perceived by the non-Jewish world. She understood that to Christian Western societies Jesus represented hope and progress; by contrast, the Jews, who were accused of murdering him, were seen as the opposite.

As a response to this painful incident, Lyvia stopped talking about her Jewishness. Her relationship with Jewishness was reframed from something beautiful to be proud of into something incredibly shameful. Over the next five or so years, Lyvia does not remember discussing her Jewishness or engaging with it at all.

However, when she was around twelve years old, Lyvia was invited to a Pesach Seder by her mother's friend. She remembers feeling excited that she was now able to experience the joys of Jewishness and Judaism; she was in a Jewish environment, where non-Jewish ideas about Jewish people or Jewishness did not matter. In this small community, she was protected from the shame that bombards Jews from the non-Jewish world. She felt as if she 'stepped into a whole new world that was exciting and filled with beautiful rituals' she had never experienced before. Prior to this, her idea of the Jewish community was shaped by, and limited to, her family. During this Seder, Lyvia realised that, beyond her family, there was a whole world of Jews engaging with Jewish tradition. Moreover, while she had experienced Pesach before, she had never done so in this way. It lit a fire in her. She understood the significance of the Exodus story and how fundamentally important Pesach is to the formation of Jewish identity. She felt a magnet pull her towards Jewish action and she began to take immense pride in the ancient connection that binds all Jews to our history, our present and our future.

That Pesach dinner opened a door to a period when Lyvia felt able to actively engage with her Jewishness. Her family began hosting Shabbat dinner on Friday nights. She remembers memorising the *brachot* (prayers) and lighting the Shabbat candles. Engaging in their culture in this way again made Lyvia feel proud and excited. Thanks to Lyvia, her mother – who had always prioritised her British identity – began to go to synagogue too. Lyvia thus lit a spark which reignited her mother's own relationship with Jewishness.

Attending synagogue was special for Lyvia. She remembers being invited to the rabbi's house for Shabbat lunch, after *Shacharit* (the morning Shabbat service). Again, in this Jewish environment, Lyvia felt protected from the shame imposed on her by the wider world and was able to feel pride in her Jewishness. She felt that she was discovering a new civilisation and felt deeply connected to it. The rabbi even bestowed on Lyvia a Jewish name, *Chaya* (which means life in Hebrew). Lyvia describes the rabbi's act as 'unlocking another part of my Jewishness'.

However, despite the beauty of these experiences, Lyvia's active Jewishness petered out over the next few years as her attendance at synagogue became more difficult, and she came to feel separated from the support of the community. She recalls that 'if there was a Jewish holiday we would mark it, but only if we happened to remember or were reminded'.

Moreover, she lived part of her teenage years in Greece with her father, which intensified her feelings of being cut off from the Jewish community. Without her own Jewish anchor she 'simply couldn't maintain' her relationship with Jewishness. This could have been a crucial anchor in her life, she now reflects, but it wasn't able to help her feel settled. Instead, the frequent moving around, coupled with never really feeling at home where she lived, fed Lyvia's need for a grounding identity and community.

This yearning was manipulated by several of Lyvia's devout Christian friends. She describes them as 'very proselytising'. They spoke about their Christianity at every available opportunity and encouraged Lyvia to attend church. Although initially uncomfortable, particularly as she could never believe in Jesus as the Messiah, she gave in to their pressure and decided 'to check it out'. Although she was sceptical, she found herself disarmed. 'This was a cool church,' Lyvia explains. 'They had rock music, and so many young people. It was invigorating and exciting to find myself in this amazing vibrant community. This is what drew me in and this is what I focused on. Feeling connected meant it was easy to disregard the parts I couldn't align myself with, like Jesus.'

Lyvia never converted to Christianity and was always open about her Jewishness and why she was there. But when she told people that she was Jewish, she felt as if they viewed her as a 'token Jew'; she was having her first taste of being 'a good Jew'. Lyvia even remembers being pressured into discussing her Jewishness before the whole congregation and feeling as if she was some kind of prize to be won.

Although ultimately wanting her to convert, her Jewishness was met with much excitement. Members of the congregation would tell her: 'We are the same, you understand' in an attempt to demonstrate the relationship between Jews and Christians. Although Lyvia didn't really understand, she was glad to feel part of a community. But, during her year and a half of attending church, she felt more and more pressure to be baptised and accept Jesus. 'Thank goodness I didn't get baptised,' she says now. 'I am really happy that, at that age, I had some level of discernment and Jewish connection even though I felt distanced from it!' Indeed, Lyvia feels that if she had been baptised, 'there would have been no going back'.

During her time attending church Lyvia did alter herself, but physically not spiritually. When she was around 21, she had a nose job. This had been something she had considered for a long time. She had endured being racialised throughout her life. Her father used to 'joke', saying, 'Can you move, please, your nose is blocking out the light.' Nose jobs were so common in her family that she was told there would be money available to cover the operation if she wanted one. The racialisation of her Jewishness continued at church. When she told people there that she was Jewish, they would respond 'I can tell' and look straight at her nose. Not only had she suffered years of racism because of her nose, but she felt that it symbolised her difference and her Jewishness and she did not want to be identified in this way. She states very simply: 'I was racialised my whole life and then I was also tokenised at church. I wanted to erase what made me different. What made me a token.' Although she altered herself permanently to escape her Jewishness, like so many others, this did not ultimately fulfil her. Her nose has been reshaped, but she understands what lengths she went to to distance herself from her Jewishness, and this wounds her.

Lyvia's time attending church came to an end when she was faced with an unspoken ultimatum: accept Jesus or leave. Lyvia chose to leave. Even though her Jewish anchor was not fully formed and was not able to prevent her from attending church, she knew on some level that she could not accept Jesus and that Christianity was not her home.

Lyvia has experienced so many manifestations of internalised anti-Jewishness. From shame and denial to alteration, she has suffered at the hands of the non-Jewish world. One of the most extreme, and dangerous, forms of this phenomenon is Jewish antizionism. Tragically, her lack of Jewish anchor and her desire to be a 'good Jew', left her open to another traumatic experience.

Lyvia says she had 'no tangible perception of Israel growing up'. The Jewish state was simply never discussed, and she felt no connection to it. During her time at church, she actually remembers feeling Israel was more connected with Christianity. She encountered Christians who believed themselves to be the 'New Israelites' and appropriated Israel as a land central to their identity.

She began to feel the rumblings of antizionism during a trip to Berlin in her early twenties. She was staying with a group of young Germans whom she had not told that she was Jewish. Israel came up in conversation and she recalls an ensuing 'barrage of antizionism'. Even though she had no relationship with Israel and, at that point, her Jewish engagement was non-existent, she instinctively understood that the obsessive hatred of Israel she was experiencing was an expression of Jew-hate. She felt uneasy that this should have taken place in Germany. When she suggested that Germany should be particularly sensitive about Jew-hate, she was immediately shut down and told that what was being said was antizionist, not anti-Jewish. During the conversation, she felt shame when she was pointedly asked, 'Don't you know what Israel is doing?' Once again, Lyvia found herself as the only Jew in a room, having her experience defined by others. But while her instincts were right, the shame and isolation led her to think that perhaps these people understood the conflict better than she did, and perhaps they were right that antizionism is different from Jew-hate.

The rise in social media has given a platform for every person to share their opinion as fact. This has had a catastrophic effect on the spread of Jew-hate, especially considering that social media platforms are entirely a numbers game. The more followers you have, the wider your reach. Unsurprisingly, given its prevalence, Lyvia began regularly encountering antizionism on social media. It was always from the same sort of source, she recalls, accounts that preached the left's social justice gospel and focused almost exclusively on the Palestinians. It was, as Lyvia remembers, 'as if the Palestinians were a touch point for people to prove how progressive they were'. Lyvia also found herself becoming friends online with several people from the Middle East who were vocal about their hatred of Israel. 'They always framed Israel as a violent oppressor,' Lyvia recalls. Thus her experiences online meant that Lyvia always saw Israelis as oppressing innocent Palestinians. Although simple, this deluge of propaganda was profound. Just as she had done when she was told, aged seven, that Jews killed Jesus, she asked herself: 'Are we the bad guys?'

As she wrestled with this question, Lyvia began to separate Jews and Israelis. This binary was very simple: the Jews were good, but the Israelis were bad. Here again, we see the impact of the Broken Mirror of Jewish identity. Israel was seen as bad, therefore Lyvia wanted to be good, and she wanted to prove how good she was. Like so many other Jews who felt unable to totally shed their Jewishness, Lyvia felt as if she had to be a palatable Jew. A 'good Jew'. A Jew who hated Israel. Although she never posted online, through her own admission, she began to propagate extreme antizionist discourse in her personal life. Although she would begin the conversations, she soon found that non-Jews around her would seize upon the opportunity to demonise Israel with a Jew, in order to deflect accusations of Jew-hate. She was their token antizionist Jew.

Later, Lyvia had another profound experience of being praised as a good antizionist Jew. At a work meeting, she found herself sitting next to a woman who told her that her partner was 'in Palestine doing relief work'. Most of her colleagues knew she was Jewish, and she worried what they might think of her reaction, so she responded, 'I am Jewish, but I agree with you and your partner is doing great work. There is such an imbalance of power between Israel and the Palestinians.' The reaction that Lyvia experienced, although disconcerting, reinforced her feeling of what it took to be seen as a 'good Jew'. She remembers the woman turning to her, putting her hand on the back of Lyvia's chair, leaning in and saying, 'You're Jewish but you don't agree with Israel? That's fascinating!' Lyvia remembers how this woman's warm body language made her feel. She clearly remembers the visible excitement the woman had in her eyes when she realised that Lyvia was a Jewish antizionist. Over the next few hours, the woman fed Lyvia lines about Israel that she would then repeat. Lyvia looks back with anger. She knows that her Jewishness was used to kosher this woman's Jew-hate. It is why she feels so strongly about the dangers of antizionism. She has experienced first-hand the way token Jews are manipulated to excuse the Jew-hate of others and the feelings Jews experience when they find themselves embraced as a 'good Jew'.

Later, when reflecting on this conversation, something in Lyvia stirred and she said she felt 'icky'. She asked: 'Did I really agree with everything that was said? Why was that woman so fulfilled by hearing me agree with her?' But, at the time, she pushed aside any feelings of doubt, focusing instead on the feelings of being included and accepted. Indeed, Lyvia's antizionism now became more fervent. She would attack anyone who said anything remotely positive about Israel. Ironically, and in a sign of how nefarious these progressive spaces can be for Jews, Lyvia felt accepted as a Jew, but only if she demonised Israel. She was made to feel as if she was unable to celebrate her Jewishness without loudly rejecting Israel.

Lyvia's interest in social justice and her own passionate antizionism led her to support Jeremy Corbyn, the former leader of the British

Labour party. When I asked her how she dealt with accusations that he was racist, she said she 'just rejected them'. 'Corbyn represented hope, progress and equality, so how could he be racist?' she asked. She absorbed and parroted the idea that Corbyn was being smeared (a common accusation to deflect Corbyn's anti-Jewishness) by 'Tory Jews'. As a young left-wing person, she felt passionately that the Conservative party was a danger to Britain.

Lyvia's defence of Corbyn led to feelings similar to those she experienced when she was told that the Jews had killed Jesus. Corbyn represented goodness, hope and progress and Jews, once again, stood counterposed to those ideas. This perception of Jewish identity forced Lyvia – as it has done to other Jews – to feel even more compelled to prove just how palatable they could be. Lyvia thus became a mouthpiece for Corbyn, temporarily damaging her relationship with her grandmother in the process. She used her Jewishness to deflect accusations against Corbyn of Jew-hate and 'reassured people he was just antizionist, but not anti-Jewish'. She told people that Israel was an oppressor and Corbyn was right to hate it.

Although Lyvia found herself deep in the world of antizionism and pro-Corbynism, she experienced a profound challenge to her perspectives in 2019. During this period, she worked with another Jewish woman as well as a Christian man. The man was not proselytising; far from it – he argued with Lyvia, telling her that her perspectives on Israel were anti-Jewish and that Jews should celebrate their connection to their indigenous land. He was one of the first non-Jewish people to give Lyvia space to celebrate her Jewishness without using it to reinforce his own anti-Jewish ideas. This coincided with Lyvia's Jewish colleague reintroducing her to Jewish joy. She felt connected to this woman and saw that she was able to live an active Jewish life, whilst having a strong connection to Israel. And, although she felt able to 'agree to disagree on Israel', these interactions stirred feelings that previously lay dormant. Lyvia's questioning of her perspectives was also intensified by her mother's work at a Jewish cancer charity. She encountered lots of Israelis who contradicted the binary mindset – between Jews and Israelis – that Lyvia had created. She saw that the Israelis were not 'bad', and this started to crack Lyvia's false dichotomy.

Like many progressive Jews, summer 2020 was a significant moment in the development of Lyvia's Jewishness. During the Black Lives Matter protests, she saw that many of the accounts she followed spoke about Israel in an increasingly radicalised way. The situation was no longer referred to as a 'conflict'; instead, accusations of 'apartheid' and 'genocide' perpetrated by Israel became increasingly common. And although Lyvia had been deeply immersed in the culture of antizionist social justice, she still noticed the manner in which the discourse and language around Israel was evolving in a more radical and extreme direction. Nonetheless, as a committed anti-racist, Lyvia put her nascent concerns to one side, feeling she must prioritise the Black community's experience.

However, these trends intensified during the May 2021 war between Israel and Hamas, which, as for many other Jews, became a profound moment of reckoning for Lyvia. The war saw a grass-roots uprising against Jews both on- and offline. Countless social media accounts that presented themselves as anti-racist and pro-human rights participated in the demonisation of Israel. They parroted radicalised rhetoric, and the obscene language used to describe Israel shocked many of us, including Lyvia, who – despite her own antizion-ism – couldn't bring herself to participate in this demonisation of the world's only Jewish state.

And then, quite suddenly, Lyvia recalls, 'the penny dropped'. Despite her efforts to be a 'good Jew', Lyvia realised she was being demonised as a Jew. The hate speech and violence was not just directed at Israel, but was a gleeful attack on all Jews, everywhere. Amid this shocking realisation, the foundations of Lyvia's antizionism began to rapidly crumble. Previously, she had defined Zionists as bad and non-Zionist Jews as good. But now, with the dawning realisation that this dichotomy did not really matter to the non-Jewish world, she could no longer maintain her forced and artificial disconnection from both Israel and most other Jews. She began questioning her beliefs, pulling threads which led the entire edifice of her ideology to unravel. As Lyvia began to seek other perspectives on the war, she started to follow Jewish accounts, like my own.

Lyvia dates her process of deradicalisation back to this moment. For years, she had been conditioned by the non-Jewish world to view her Jewishness through a certain prism. However, Lyvia's journey was now about seeing her Jewishness through her own lens of Jewish Pride. During May 2021, she called her mother to tell her she had been wrong about antizionism and Corbyn. Her mother encouraged her to make *shalom* (peace) with her grandmother, with whom her relationship, though maintained, had become fractured because of Corbynism. Since then, Lyvia has sought to reject non-Jewish definitions of the Jewish experience and identity and embark upon a journey to Jewish Pride.

Lyvia is an astonishing example of Jewish strength. By her own admission she went 'deep down the rabbit hole'. She experienced multiple iterations of Jewish shame and Jewish trauma and she worked incredibly hard to meet the progressive world's definition of a 'good Jew'. But these are categories created by the non-Jewish world that manipulate Jews into thinking that, if we just conform or alter ourselves, we will be accepted. The war in 2021 demonstrated to Lyvia that this was not the case.

Like all of ours, Lyvia's journey continues. She is still working hard to shake off the beliefs which once dominated her thinking and reject non-Jewish ideas about Jewishness. And, in a 180-degree turnaround, Lyvia now sees Jewishness as her primary and grounding identity. She is exploring Jewish history and reading Jewish books to better understand herself and her Jewishness. Although she was unable to develop one as a child, she is now building her own Jewish anchor through Jewish education and Jewish action.

In an act of active Jewishness, Lyvia has started wearing a *Magen David* (Star of David) necklace. She says that this may seem superficial but it is hugely significant. To mark herself as Jewish in a world which sees it as something one should reject is a deeply moving act of resistance.

Lyvia's story is profound, and it offers us all a glimmer of hope. We often think that antizionist Jews are 'too far gone'. They have journeyed too far down the path of prejudice to find their way back, but Lyvia demonstrates that there is always hope. That Jews, no matter how far they stray from the Jewish people and Jewish Pride, can always restart their Jewish journey and heal by working towards Jewish Pride.

Is this necessarily easy? Undoubtedly not. Lyvia has had to do a huge amount of work to overcome her feelings of internalised anti-Jewishness. But she has become a woman anchored by her Jewishness who rejects the non-Jewish perspectives on Jewish identity. Lyvia is a remarkably courageous person, who is a strong and powerful symbol of Jewish Pride.

Chapter 10

FROM PREJUDICE TO PRIDE

'The positive side and worthwhileness of being a Jew will ... have to be stressed and bolstered by props beyond the sullying reach of the Jew hater.'[286]

Trude Weiss-Rosmarin, 1947

Recognising a problem, any problem, is only the first step to overcoming it. The next step is the search for a solution, which, in our case, is the rejection of internalised anti-Jewishness and both the pursuit and utilisation of Jewish Pride. Jewish Pride is a global movement. And it is a goal. But it is not just something we work towards; it is also a tool we can use to lead lives rooted in Jewish self-confidence and self-esteem. It is a flexible framework and a lens that offers us a way to understand ourselves and our history.

In the Introduction, I defined internalised anti-Jewishness as: 'When Jews absorb non-Jewish perceptions of Jews, Jewishness and Judaism and allow the non-Jewish world to define our narrative.' Therefore, our healing journey must be rooted in reclaiming the Jewish story through the framework of Jewish Pride.

For thousands of years many Jews valiantly defended their Jewishness, but, among them, were those not able to withstand the force of Jew-hate that surrounded them. They acquiesced to the demands and pressures of the wider world and allowed our ancient story to be defined by those who do not understand us. These Jews are not bad Jews. They are not even weak Jews. They are Jews who could not come to terms with the fact that being Jewish in the non-Jewish world is a disadvantage and instead seek to make themselves palatable to those around them. Jewishness is as real a disadvantage as any other, and though anti-Jewish racism is not our problem, it has a profound impact on the lives of Jews all over the world.

Recognising these truths about our experience – such as the fact that Jewish integration into diasporic societies is difficult – should not paralyse us with fear or hopelessness. Acknowledging reality can instead be liberating. We know where we stand. We understand the rules of engagement. And we can, fundamentally, stop working so hard to be accepted by those who, as I have argued, often do not really accept us. We should understand that Jews deserve better. We have always deserved better. And though, as if on cue, we are experiencing the latest swelling of Jew-hate, we needn't wait for the world around us to see that. Although its actions continue to have an impact upon us, truly defeating Jew-hate is ultimately their journey. It is their work. And while we should bravely take part in this fight against anti-Jewish racism, we also have our own work to do. Our work is to overcome internalised anti-Jewishness. Our work is to heal. Our work is to reject their narrative and to embrace our own. Our work is to reclaim our story through Pride.

So, as we begin this journey, let us ask:

Do we get to define our own narrative?

Do we get to celebrate and cultivate our cultures?

Do we deserve to feel pride in our identities?

We do.

In fact, we must.

We have not survived for 4,000 years to allow those who hate us to continue to tell our stories. For too long, the wider world has felt able to define who we are, to dictate and then reflect our identities back to us. And to create classifications of good Jew or bad Jew. As a collective, we must say 'no more!'

Jewish Pride is how we rebuild our people.

It is how we reclaim our story.

And it starts now.

As I suggested in the Introduction, we can choose prejudice or we can move towards Jewish Pride. The choice is an obvious one, but it is not an easy one. This journey involves real work, and it can, at times, be painful. It involves introspection and humility. And it also must involve kindness and empathy. We must repeat, almost as a mantra, that these feelings, these perspectives are not our fault. We have experienced a well-documented manifestation of racism and hate. And now we must recognise it and fight against it.

The stories of Róisín, Nick, Shoshanna, Avraham and Lyvia demonstrate, in very real, practical and tangible ways, that it *is* possible to overcome internalised anti-Jewishness and reclaim our relationship with our Jewishness. Individually, they embarked on journeys rooted in introspection, healing and pride and they remind us that, even when this journey seems too difficult or painful, it is always possible.

So, as we begin this final chapter, we will address the main causes of internalised anti-Jewishness and we will explore how we can practically defend ourselves against them. Let this book be our guide, as a Jewish collective and as Jewish individuals, as we journey from prejudice to pride.

JEWISH PRIDE: A FRAMEWORK

In *Jewish Pride: Rebuilding a People*, the manifesto of the modern Jewish Pride movement, I described Jewish Pride as a movement and a goal, something we can build and work towards. However, in the process of writing this book, I have understood that Jewish Pride has another vital component: it is a framework. It is a lens which allows us to see our lives as Jews with pride. It enables us to view our history through our own eyes, not through the perceptions of the world around us. Utilising the framework of Jewish Pride on a day-to-day basis allows Jews to see their Jewishness as a source of pride, and never shame. Despite what the world around us tries to suggest.

In Chapter 1, I discussed the notion of *Wissenschaft des Judentums* (the 'science of Judaism') as an example of self-blame and self-denigration that was rife in 19th-century Germany. As we explored, the Jews who participated in *Wissenschaft* used these modern methods of exploring Jewish history to express their own internalised anti-Jewishness.

Due to its focus on academic study, argues scholar Henry Soussan in *The Gesellschaft zur Forderung der Wissenschaft des Judentums in its Historical Context*, *Wissenschaft* was 'inherently anti-rabbinic'.[287] It was an attempt to recreate Jewishness and Judaism as an academic, scientific study, while disregarding the debates of the great Jewish sages, the Talmud and Jewish superstition and belief. Unsurprisingly, this attempted break with thousands of years of Jewish tradition, provoked opposition from the Orthodox community. However, in an important utilisation of the Jewish Pride framework, Hirsch Hildesheimer, a German historian and author, argued that Modern Orthodox Judaism was indeed compatible with *Wissenschaft des Judentums*. As Soussan notes: 'Hildesheimer took great pride in the academic standards of the *Rabinerseminar* being equal to those of *Jüdisch-Theologisches Seminar* and *Hochschule*.'

Despite its inherent anti-rabbinic nature, Orthodox Jews could interact with *Wissenschaft des Judentums* in a very real and serious way. They were able to utilise modern academic techniques seen through the lens of Jewish Pride. They were not seeking to diminish Jewishness; instead, they were using modern methods of study to demonstrate its worth and to prove their own arguments. *Dorot-Ha-Rishonim*, a six-volume history of Judaism written by the Polish-Jewish historian, Isaak Halevy, for instance, provided a well-respected account of Jewish history. As Soussan argues: 'Halevy displayed immense knowledge of rabbinic literature whilst maintaining the highest scholarly standards.'[288] This was thus a marriage of Jewish spirituality and religious belief with high academic work. Although *Wissenschaft* could have been viewed with suspicion by the wider Orthodox community, Halevy's work was celebrated and several articles in *Israelit*, a 19th-century Orthodox journal, proclaimed: '*Wissenschaft* has returned to Orthodoxy!'[289]

Members of the Orthodox community in Berlin were so enthused with Orthodox *Wissenschaft* that in 1902 they founded the *Jüdisch-Literarischen Gesellschaft* (Jewish Literary Society), a new Orthodox scholarly society rooted in *Wissenschaft des Judentums*. By 1907, it had over 550 members.

It's important to recognise that this fusion of Orthodoxy and *Wissenschaft* was not done in panic as part of an effort to regain lost legitimacy and power. These studies were carried out with confidence and pride. This is how we should utilise the framework of Jewish Pride. It is not just a goal we work towards, nor is it just a movement we are building. It is a tool that enables us to freely interact with the world while remaining rooted in, and proud of, our Jewishness. This example teaches us that *Wissenschaft* in itself was not the problem. The problem was that Jews suffering from internalised anti-Jewishness used it to humiliate and demonise traditional Jews and Judaism. They ranked Jewish culture below German culture and they used *Wissenschaft* to prove this. But the proponents of Orthodox *Wissenschaft* did the opposite. They proudly engaged with this modern academic study, but they refused to diminish their Jewishness.

Other examples of Jewish Pride in action were the experiences of Jewish student organisations that formed during the late 19th century in response to Jew-hatred on campus, such as the Antisemites' Petition of 1881. Launched by leading Jew-haters in Germany, it campaigned for legislative action to deal with the Jewish Question, ultimately aiming to limit or rescind emancipation. In a reference to Jews now being able to enter professions such as teachers and the judiciary, it stated: 'Both were inaccessible to Jews until very recently, and both must again be closed if the concept of authority, the feeling for legality and fatherland, are not to become confused and doubted by the nation.'[290] It was signed by 265,000 people including 4,000 students. A total of 19% of the entire German student body put their names to the petition, and around 41% of students enrolled at the University of Berlin signed it. These numbers reflect a wider anti-Jewish movement: in 1880, militant associations of German students were formed at the university of Berlin, and students at other German universities quickly followed suit and created their own organisations. Their declared central objective was to exclude Jewish students from organised student life.

Although through other means, this attempt to exclude Jews from higher education is being repeated today. In response, as is the case today, some Jews adopted an apologetic stance. This behaviour was rooted in the idea that Jews should just be quiet and get on with things while keeping their heads down. They shouldn't fight back. As we learned in Chapter 2, this is an example of the diminishment of the Jewish self. However, with startling parallels to today, groups of Jewish students began to counter the rising Jew-hate they were facing. They rose up to fight both assimilation and the evolution of Jew-hate following and during emancipation. They saw that, to be accepted, Jews were leaving their Jewishness behind and were shedding their Jewish anchors. These brave German Jewish students rejected this idea. In 1886 in Breslau, *Viadrina*, the Jewish fraternity, was founded; it soon spread across Germany. As the Centre of Jewish History states, *Viadrina*'s 'goal [was] to actively fight anti-Semitism in German academic life as well as [promote] the development of self-assured German Jews, capable of defending their country and of supporting the political and societal equality of Jews in Germany'.[291]

In 1896 *Der Kartell-Convent der Verbindungen deutscher Studenten jüdischen Glaubens* was established. It was like a 19th-century forerunner of the Union of Jewish Students and it created connections between these different organisations. Jewish fraternities were focused on *both* physical fitness and an awareness of Jewish history. On the surface, these aims might not seem to go together, but in reality they are both forms of self-defence and resistance. One is physical and the other is mental. Learning Jewish history, using the framework of pride, builds an armour. It develops anchors – our individual connection to our collective self – and it can act as a bulwark against internalised Jew-hate.

Understanding Jewish history through the lens of Jewish Pride roots Jews into a culture and civilisation that is distinct and something to be proud of. Fighting for our rights as Jews is a basic expression of Jewish Pride, and it is one we continue to see today with Jewish students in Britain, the United States, France and Australia among many other places fighting back against societal and academic Jew-hate with gusto and courage. They, as their predecessors did, have utilised the framework of Jewish Pride to understand their history and their identity so they can advocate for the Jewish people. Seeing the world through the lens of Jewish Pride is crucial. It is not just something we can work towards. It is something we should embody in our day-to-day lives. We must be proud every day. We must celebrate our Jewishness, in whatever way we see fit, every day. And we must honour our specificity and we should know that we deserve better than how we are treated by the wider world every single day.

THE JEWISH MIRROR

The *Endlösung der Judenfrage* (Final Solution to the Jewish Question) was the Nazi response to the century-old Jewish Question that gripped the non-Jewish world. Following the Enlightenment and emancipation, non-Jewish societies grappled with how to define and understand the status and role of Jews in their modern nation-states. These debates about Jews were always rooted in Jew-hate and overcoming the alleged problem caused by Jews' presence. As Holocaust scholar Lucy Dawidowicz argues: 'The histories of … European antisemitism are replete with proffered "solutions to the Jewish question"'.[292] Although the Jewish Question is seen to have emerged as a response to emancipation and negative perceptions of the continuing distinctiveness of the Jew, versions of it had been discussed for millennia, with each iteration of the Jewish Question ultimately being rooted in the notion that Jews are a problem that need to be dealt with.

Discussions of what Jews represented, and what roles we played, had obsessed the non-Jewish world since Paul began the process of forming Christian identity by defining it against Judaism. This cast Judaism as an obsolete ideology but argued that Jews still serve a purpose in the wider world. St Augustine of Hippo suggested that Jews represent the blind man in the mirror. According to St Augustine, their blindness to Jesus would act as a warning of the fate which awaited Christians if they were to stray from Jesus's path. Because he needed us to serve our purpose, we could not be murdered. 'Slay them not, lest my people forget. Scatter them by my might and bring them down,'[293] Augustine argued. But his answer to his Jewish Question was to encourage our persecution and oppression.

Conversations on what should be done with the Jews continued for over a thousand years but began to intensify in the 19th and early 20th centuries when Jews were freed from the ghettos and were finally 'free to join' Western societies. The search for an answer to the Jewish Question was thought to have culminated in the Holocaust and, following the Shoah, there seemed to be a consensus that Jews were to be fully integrated and accepted. For a period, this drove overt-Jew-hatred to the fringes of society, where many thought it would remain. It led to a post-war Gilded Age where Jews were thought to have overcome their previous disadvantages to become fully fledged members of Western societies. However, as we know, Jew-hate never disappeared. Jews in Arab lands and Soviet Jews, among others, were openly persecuted throughout the second half of the 20th century and anti-Jewish racism has once again returned to the very centre of Western social and political life, with iterations of the Jewish Question continuing to be discussed.

Today, as ever, iterations of the Jewish Question continue to be debated. The never-ending debate about the whiteness of Jews is a modern example of this ancient non-Jewish conversation. As we discussed in Chapter 4, this is not a discussion on the literal skin colour of Jewish people. It is a conversation on where Jews are positioned in the hierarchy of power, privilege and oppression, which therefore has an impact upon our role and status in society. These conversations erase Jewish indigeneity, history and identity and the reality of the hate we experience.

The non-Jewish world is obsessed with Jews. It is obsessed with defining our identity, and, tragically, through the Broken Mirror of Jewish identity, these inaccurate definitions are then reflected back to Jews. It is why Jews, even proud Jews like me, Nicky or Shoshana, have qualified our Jewishness to show that we are 'good Jews'. These categorisations of Jewish identity, 'good' or 'bad', do not exist except in the minds of the non-Jewish world. But we absorb them, and we alter our behaviour accordingly. But how can we base our understanding of ourselves on societies that have proven time and time again that they hate us? To heal from internalised anti-Jewishness, we must reject the Broken Mirror of Jewish identity and the non-Jewish world's obsession with and categorisations of our identity.

Dividing Jews into 'good' or 'bad' categories leads us to engage in self-blame and self-denigration. It leads us to cast certain Jewish communities, such as the Orthodox, as 'bad Jews', which then leads us to qualify ourselves against them. In her chapter, Shoshana, a proud Orthodox woman, described wanting the world to know that, while she was Orthodox, she was still palatable. This false dichotomy of 'good' or 'bad' Jews forces us to see ourselves through this lens. To reject non-Jewish reflections of Jewish identity, we must reclaim the Jewish story and feel able to define our own identities. We must not base our understanding of ourselves on whichever non-Jewish society is debating the Jewish Question at that particular moment. We must acknowledge that there are no 'good Jews' or 'bad Jews'. There are just Jews.

In a 2020 article, I identified and named a new subcategory of Jew-hate: 'Erasive Jew-hate'. The erasure of Jewish identity and experience by the non-Jewish world is central to the Broken Mirror of Jewish identity. It is the process by which accurate definitions of Jewish identity and experience are replaced with inaccurate non-Jewish ones rooted in Jew-hate. In March 2021, for instance, the BBC (which is funded by the British taxpayer, which obviously includes Jews) debated on live television whether Jews should count as an ethnic minority. This is despite the fact that Jews are legally an ethnic minority under British law. The BBC's panel, which consisted of five non-Jews and one Jewish person, debated the identity of the most persecuted minority in the history of humankind and erased fundamental truths of Jewish identity. Ultimately, it was nothing more than a non-Jewish debate about where Jews fit into their world and how we should be understood. It was a continuation of the millennia-old discussion of the Jewish Question, aiming to understand how Jews fit into non-Jewish society.

Clearly, the non-Jewish world will continue to endlessly and obsessively discuss the Jewish Question and attempt to erase and define Jewish identity. But we must not let it alter our perceptions of ourselves. Only Jews get to define Jewish identity. Only Jews get to debate Jewish identity. And we must not base these debates on non-Jewish perceptions of our identity. We must base them instead on an understanding of our own history and identity through a framework of Jewish Pride.

Whenever I tell people that I am gay, I am immediately invited to define my own identity. I am asked 'what are your pronouns?', even though my sexual orientation has nothing to do with my gender identity. I am also asked 'what term would you prefer? Gay? Queer? LGBTQ+? Homosexual?' Truly, people fall over themselves to give me space to define what it means for me to be gay. However, I experience the literal opposite when it comes to self-identification as a Jew. When I discuss my Jewish identity and tell people that, while I recognise that one of the advantages I benefit from is being light-skinned, I am not white, I am immediately challenged. I am told 'you can walk around a shop without being followed by the police!' This is true. In the West, no one is targeting me for the colour of my skin, but they can target me for being a Jew (and a gay man). And those experiences matter and are just as valid as any other experience. But just as only gay people get to define gay identity and only Black people get to define Black identity, only Jews get to define Jewish identity and experience.

In the modern world, embracing Jewish definitions of Jewish identity can be complicated because we do not necessarily fit the world's general categorisations of identity (which, of course, continue to influence our own due to our interactions with the non-Jewish world). This complication can lead us to accept non-Jewish defin-itions of our identity. For example, discussions on whether Jews are a race or a religious group are rooted in concepts that postdate the emergence of the Jewish people. We are therefore forced to iden-tify ourselves using concepts that don't quite fit our historical truth. However, we must be able to interact with modern ideas while also interacting with our own story. To do this, to balance this tension, we utilise the lens of Jewish Pride.

Thousands of years ago, early Jews emerged as a distinct ethnic group in the Levant. The first confirmed mention of the word, 'Israel' comes from the Merneptah Stele, an Egyptian stone engraving that references Israel as a people, not a place. The Merneptah Stele is dated from 1208 BCE. That is currently 3,230 years ago, and we can understand that the identity of our ancestors was established enough to warrant a mention in this Stele.

Over the course of thousands of years, the Israelites and their descendants, the Jews, created a civilisation. They ruled independent kingdoms for centuries and developed clear traditions, a distinct culture and one of the world's first monotheistic religions. Despite being colonised by successive foreign empires (the Assyrians, Babylonians, Persians, Greeks and, finally, the Romans) and, ultimately, being ethnically cleansed from our indigenous land in the first centuries of the new millennium, this ancient civilisation continued to evolve. For thousands of years, Jews, the original diasporic people, were forced – often in the face of further genocides and ethnic cleansings – to settle in different countries in different continents. Despite the diasporic nature of our recent history, we clung to our ancient culture. We evolved it, we mixed it with the cultures of our host countries and we developed new cultural practices. When able to, we participated and contributed to our host country's culture and society and we played important roles in the cultural development of many diasporic communities. But each new culture that emerged was an iteration of our original indigenous culture, and, despite settling in new lands, we never stopped yearning and working to return home. We were finally able to do so in 1948 with the rebirth of the State of Israel.

So, what does this mean for Jewish identity today? It means that we were, and are, a Middle Eastern diasporic people. This is our story. We are not, nor have we ever been – as the non-Jewish world likes to imagine – a community bound just by a shared faith. We are, despite the question posed by the BBC, an ethnic group bound by history, tradition, experience, language, land, ancestry and belief. Understanding that we are a Middle Eastern diasporic people that built a civilisation made up of rich and diverse cultures, is to understand Jewish history through the framework of Jewish Pride. This is *our* story. This is who we are. It is a story of strength, resilience and commitment. These are not just fables from the Torah. They are indisputable facts.

The Broken Mirror of Jewish identity harms Jewish people. As we have repeatedly seen – from the Hellenised Jewish men who reversed their circumcisions to Moses Mendelssohn who saw Jewish culture as being less than German culture or to Nicky who would tell people that he was half-Jewish – we have absorbed foreign ideas about Jewishness. To heal, we have to free ourselves from these ideas and from the effort to categorise us as 'good' or 'bad' Jews. We can actively participate in the cultures of our respective diasporic countries just as we are, but we must not base our understanding of ourselves on inaccurate, non-Jewish definitions. As I've said, ultimately, only Jews get to define Jewish identity. And we must understand who and what we are if we are to proceed into the world as proud Jews, without allowing the non-Jewish mirror of Jewish identity to reflect back to us their broken understandings of our identity.

JEWISH HEALING

One of the key factors that define the stories of Róisín, Nick, Shoshanna, Avraham and Lyvia is that their battles with internalised anti-Jewishness were all – in part – responses to Jewish trauma. Trag-ically, intergenerational and epigenetic trauma, as well as our own personal experience of Jew-hate, has a profound impact on our rela-tionship with our Jewishness. In a sense, it steals our Jewishness from us and remakes it into something else, something painful.

When considering how we heal our trauma, we have to recognise that we cannot rewrite history. As Bessel Van Der Kolk, the author of *The Body Keeps Score*, suggests, 'What happened cannot be undone.' We cannot change the past, but we can 'deal with … the imprints of the trauma on the mind, body and soul'.[294] So, although we cannot rewrite our past, we can heal our future. We can reclaim our relationship with Jewishness.

To do this, we must first recognise the source of our pain so that we can truly understand that the hate we have experienced is not our fault. When I was a gay teen, I woke up to the fact that, through societal homophobia, I had been punished for a crime I hadn't committed. I found this realisation to be incredibly freeing. I had done nothing wrong and therefore I didn't deserve to feel shame, embarrassment and pain. Of course, this realisation didn't immediately free me from trauma, but it did set me on a path to healing. Removing these shackles of shame was an integral part of my journey towards LGBTQ+ pride. I was able to free myself from the notion that being gay was wrong or dangerous and I was able to reclaim my sexual orientation and understand the joy and pride in being a gay man. I began to explore LGBTQ+ history and I found figures, such as Harvey Milk (a Jew who was the first openly gay person to be elected to office in the United States), who inspired and empowered me. In short, I realised that being gay was a beautiful thing that could not be defined or diminished by societal hate. In finding LGBTQ+ pride and joy, by fighting against homophobic ideas about LGBTQ+ people, I took control of my own relationship with my sexual orientation, and, over time, these discoveries helped me shake off the shame and trauma I had experienced and developed. And although I still find myself triggered, I now understand why, which itself can be healing.

To heal, we must recognise the trauma we experience. A major factor that led me to build a modern Jewish Pride movement was that there are many aspects of Jewish experience that we fail to address. In many ways, Jews have become a people of denial. To cope with our pain we deny the existence of Jew-hate, we deny our specificity and we deny the clear trauma that has been inflicted upon us by the wider world. To overcome this specific manifestation of internalised anti-Jewishness we have to create an environment where we recognise the reality of our experience.

Jewish trauma exists and it is a response to thousands of years of hate. It has always been there, even in times perceived to have been 'less bad'. As discussed in Chapter 4, the Jewish Cold War was itself, in part, a response to the pain and trauma of Jew-hate, most notably the Shoah. As Susan Glenn argues: 'The tense and excessive language of the Jewish Cold War reveals the deep strains of anxiety that permeated the public culture of post-war American Jews.'[295] And the cultural emancipation that followed the Jewish Cold War created an environment where American Jews were, once again, unable to come to terms with their own experiences.

Of course, denial is easier than facing grim and painful realities. It is easier to pretend we don't experience trauma because, although we can suffer either way, recognising trauma, pain and shame disrupts the status quo and is itself a painful process. Recovery and healing are not easy. Awakening to the pain of our experience can be overwhelming. This is why the Jewish community must create a culture of healing and openness rooted in empathetic discussions of our experiences.

Recognising trauma and the subsequent healing journey forces us to confront our relationships with ourselves and our Jewishness which we then have to work to heal. Regardless of the pain involved in this process, it is necessary work. A journey to Jewish healing must throw open the doors of shame to allow light in. It requires us, both as a collective and as individuals, to have an ongoing dialogue about trauma. We have to spread Jewish joy, allowing all Jews to see their Jewishness as a source of pride, joy and beauty and not something that brings pain or shame. We can acknowledge our experiences and our pain without those becoming the central element of our Jewishness. We can work to prevent trauma in Jewish children by empowering them through the framework of Jewish Pride and we should create a support system so Jewish adults can heal. I believe that we should encourage therapy where necessary. As Róisín and Avraham said in their interviews, therapy has been a way for them to address their Jewish trauma head on and heal. These services should be provided by Jewish community organisations, to ensure the opportunity to overcome trauma is accessible to all Jews, regardless of their socioeconomic background. I have discussed my own history of self-harm and suicide attempts due to the trauma of being a gay teen in a homophobic world. In this way, I, like others, have tried to normalise conversations about mental health. It is not a sign of weakness and discussing trauma does not cast us as victims. Jews are not victims; we are survivors and these important discussions are a symbol of our strength and our resilience. They are a symbol of our survival.

Ultimately, to begin healing, we must understand how and why we experience our Jewishness the way we do. Denying our reality just leads to generations of Jews suffering in silence. As Van Der Kolk argues: 'Trauma is more than a story that happened a long time ago. The emotions and physical sensations that were imprinted during the trauma are experienced not as memories but as disruptive physical reactions in the present.'[296] But, in our case, we are also experiencing trauma because of modern events that have an impact on our lived experiences as Jews. Ultimately, as Róisín bravely described, failing to recognise our trauma leads our relationship with our Jewishness to become defined by the hate and pain we have experienced. By failing to address our experiences, we see our Jewishness as *the* source of trauma and shame; instead, we should identify the *real* source of all of our pain: the non-Jewish world.

Recognising our trauma isn't a failsafe way to healing. Understanding that we have done nothing to deserve the trauma we experience does not immediately have an impact on our emotional response, although it can help. This is an active process we have to participate in regularly and of which we must be mindful. It also enables us as individuals to take control of our emotional relationship with our

Jewishness. Importantly, healing does not mean we do not, or cannot, remember our experiences, or indeed learn from them. Remembrance is key to the continuation of the Jewish people, but in our healing journeys we utilise the framework of pride to understand that these memories do not control us or negatively impact our abilities to live in the world as Jews.

As we have discussed throughout this study, empathy is a vital component in understanding and combatting internalised anti-Jewishness. This empathy helps us understand why Jews react the way we do to the wider world. It helps us engage in these conversations without judgement and shame. And it helps lead us towards a solution; one that enables all Jews to overcome their feelings of internalised anti-Jewishness and the trauma, pain and shame they have been forced to experience. We cannot build an authentic pride movement if we do not address what stands in the way of feeling Jewish Pride. Trauma is a stain on our humanity and our experience. But it is not our fault. And, to reject any notion of internalised anti-Jewishness, we must come together as a collective to enable and empower every Jew to heal.

BLAMING THE REAL CULPRITS

Jew-hate is not a Jewish problem. It is a poison that has long infected the ideologies and societies of the non-Jewish world. Sadly, though, through concepts such as *Viddui* and *Eicha*, as well as our own attempts to come to terms with the long history of Jew-hate, some Jews have developed a predisposition to blame ourselves for our experiences (as we saw, *Viddui* is the prayer of atonement recited on Yom Kippur while the Book of *Eicha* is the biblical retelling of the destruction of the First Temple which is blamed on the sins of the Israelites). As Theodor Lessing suggests, 'The key to the pathology of our national consciousness lies in this acknowledgement of guilt.'[297] The tendency for Jews to blame ourselves for our experience is immensely destructive, as well as ahistorical.

Particularly pernicious is the idea that Jews prior to and during the Holocaust did not do enough to stand up to the Nazis. It has been suggested that Jews walked onto the trains and into the gas chambers willingly, like lambs to the slaughter. Not only is this factually untrue, it also demonstrates the worrying tendency for Jews to argue that 'if we just did more', resisted or 'stood up for ourselves', we could stop Jew-hatred.

In reality, Jews resisted in every way that people could resist during the Shoah. The notion that we could have stopped the Nazis is almost laughable were it not so offensive. Although they fought back with enormous courage, the Jews were powerless in this (and most other historic) context. For two millennia, Jews were without any real power. Our fate rested on the whims of whichever ruler we happened to find ourselves under. Even though we have defended our Jewishness, often to the death, the notion that we can stop Jew-hate fundamentally misunderstands the relationship between Jews and the non-Jewish world.

This is a form of victim-blaming whereby the victims, due to their perceived inaction, are assigned responsibility for their suffering. This perspective lacks both empathy and an understanding of the relationship between Jews and Jew-hate, namely: we have done nothing to deserve our mistreatment at the hands of the non-Jewish world, and we cannot stop them from hating us.

But given that Jew-hate is a non-Jewish problem, where does that leave Jews in the fight against those who wish to destroy us? We, of course, continue to resist, as we have always done. But we must understand why we are resisting. We are not necessarily resisting to destroy Jew-hate. That, tragically, is not something we can achieve. We are resisting to keep the hate we face at bay, and, perhaps most importantly, we resist to reclaim our dignity and humanity. This is why we fight back. Because we deserve better. And although Jew-hate is a non-Jewish problem, Jews continue to engage in self-blame and even self-denigration as a coping mechanism.

Other forms of victim-blaming are rooted in the notion that Jews 'behaving badly' brings Jew-hate on the rest of us. In her interview, Shoshana described feeling uncomfortable in large groups of visibly Jewish Jews in case their actions would provoke Jew-hatred. We should, however, be clear that their actions, whatever they may be, will simply be used by those who already hate Jews to justify their anti-Jewishness. This realisation should free us. We are hated if we conform. We are hated if we are specific. We are hated if we are 'bad Jews'. And we are even eventually hated if we are 'good Jews'. That should lead us to the conclusion that any criticism we make of fellow members of the community should not stem from a belief that Jews 'behaving badly' can bring Jew-hate on themselves, and us. It cannot.

Self-denigration, also a facet of Jewish self-blame, only further harms Jews. We as a community must have the difficult conversations required to come together as one. These conversations should be rooted in love, empathy and a desire to progress. But self-denigration, as we saw with the *Maskilim* towards Eastern European traditional Jews in 19th-century Germany, is not self-criticism. It is anti-Jewish demonisation imposed on Jews by Jews in an attempt to prove our palatability and to distance ourselves from our own Jewish family, in case we are 'tarred with the same brush'. Describing Eastern Jews as 'repulsive'[298] as Jakob Wasserman did in *Mein Weg als Deutscher und Jude* (My Path as a German and a Jew) is an act of Jewish self-denigration, brought on by the desperate desire for German Jews to be seen as German. Statements like Wasserman's were designed to illustrate the difference between the *Maskilim* and the *Ost Juden*. As he suggested, 'If I spoke with a Polish or Galician Jew and tried to understand his way of life and thinking, I could stir myself to feel compassion or sadness, but never a sense of brotherhood.'[299] The *Maskilim* wanted to be German, still Jewish, but German. They wanted to shed their specificity in order to be accepted and they wanted to distance themselves from those who appeared distinctly Jewish, such as the Eastern Jews. This distancing was a way for the Germans to define their own identity. As it is suggested in *East European Jews in the German-Jewish Imagination* exhibition from the Ludwig Rosenberger Library of Judaica: 'The symbol of East European Jewry was an important tool of German-Jewish self-definition'.[300]

We have already discussed the notion that Jews are different and how crucial it is that we accept, and take pride, in this. We should also remember that Jews are a collective. We are a family. Even in our diversity, we are *Am Echad* (one people). This is something Jews must understand. This recognition should not arise from a fear that the perceived bad behaviour of some Jews might be blamed on all of us collectively, but rather to reconcile ourselves with our collective Jewishness. When one kind of Jew is harmed, all Jews are harmed. When an Orthodox Jew is maligned in newspapers or they are beaten in the streets, this is an attack on all Jews. We may wish to align ourselves with the non-Jewish world in order to demonstrate our palatability, but this is ultimately a betrayal of our Jewishness and of Jewish unity.

Of course, Jews are allowed to disagree with one another and even criticise each other; after all, our diversity is a strength. We are one, but we are not a monolith and we are allowed to critique each other and even criticise one another. There are practices, beliefs and traditions in various Jewish communities that I disagree with, but any criticism I make should be rooted in love and in a desire to see my people do better, not in an attempt to demonise them or blame them for how we are treated. Even behaviour we don't agree with is not responsible for Jew-hate. Demonising Jews who do not conform to non-Jewish expectations or denigrating Jews by using non-Jewish ideas of Jewish identity is a tragic and deeply harmful act of self-mutilation. Those who take part in this Jewish denigration are often attempting to prove that they are good Jews, but by denigrating other Jews they contribute to the destruction of Jewish life, and the koshering of Jew-hate. We must, as I stated earlier in this chapter, repeat almost as a mantra that we have done nothing wrong. Jews have not brought Jew-hate on themselves. There is never a justifiable reason to hate Jews, even if we see fault in parts of our community.

Tragically, self-blame and self-denigration, although deeply harmful, are Jewish attempts to understand our experiences. We are looking for answers. And because we are still locked in an abusive and toxic relationship with the non-Jewish world, we blame ourselves instead of blaming them. But we must understand that we are not responsible for our experiences, and we must begin to blame the real culprit: the non-Jewish world.

BELONGING: JEWISH INTEGRATION

Since our emancipation, the non-Jewish world has told Jews they have to choose between specificity and universality. Though directed at Jews as a collective, this has shaped the lives and identities of individual Jews who were told that traditional Jewishness and Judaism are incompatible with membership of the modern nation state. It has told Jews that to be a citizen of these states, we must fundamentally alter our identities. For thousands of years, these non-negotiable terms of our admittance into non-Jewish society were dictated to us. From forced conversion to Christianity to the demand we shed our Jewish specificity in 19th-century Europe, our Jewishness has always been targeted by the majorities that surround us. Following the Enlightenment, because of thousands of years of oppression, we couldn't help but accept. However, the non-Jewish world was wrong. And it is still wrong. Jews are able to be proudly Jewish *and* proudly British, American, French or whatever diasporic identity we have. Israeli Jews are able to be proudly Israeli and be proud members of the global community.

We don't have to choose. We don't have to – as Hellenised Jewish men did – alter ourselves to be accepted. We are able to integrate, where necessary, into the wider world while maintaining our Jewishness.

To successfully integrate into non-Jewish societies, Jews must recognise our reality. We *are* different. We are specific. We are, of course, part of various communities, but we are a distinct people. Growing up in Glasgow, Scotland, I knew that I wasn't the same as everyone else in my mostly non-Jewish secondary school. This was neither inherently good, nor was it necessarily bad. It just was. And although, to an extent, I did feel Scottish and British, I also felt the connection to thousands of years of Jewish civilisation and millions of Jews all around the world. I loved being Jewish. I understood that when my family ate dates and pomegranates on *Rosh Hashanah* (Jewish New Year), we were honouring our connection to our indigenous land. Even as a child, I knew these fruits were not native to Scotland. I learned that they were part of the *Shivat Haminim* (seven species) of Israel (also including wheat, barley, grapes, figs and olives). I knew that Jews belong to a distinct culture and civilisation.

Although it is our very difference and our specificity that so many Jews struggle with, we must have the collective confidence to recognise and embrace our differences. We must reject the forced universalisation or 'Christianisation' of the Jewish people. Remaking Judaism and Jewishness as a symbol of universality is a betrayal of a distinct Jewish identity and experience.

The story of Franz Rosenzweig's close brush with conversion demonstrates the beautiful embrace of Jewish difference. When he was 26 years old, the Jewish philosopher, and author of *The Star of Redemption*, was preparing to convert to Christianity. Like Heinrich Heine and tens of thousands of other German Jews before him, he thought that shedding his Jewishness would enable him to proceed through life with the advantage of being a Christian. But in 1913, because he was going to convert 'as a Jew, not as a "pagan"'[301], he decided to attend *Kol Nidre* services. It is during this service that something transformative took place which ultimately convinced Rosenzweig to abandon his conversion to Christianity. Although we don't necessarily know what exactly convinced him not to go through with his upcoming conversion, his biographer, Nahum N. Glatzer, writes that Rosenzweig's story is 'the story of a rediscovery of Judaism.'[302] This is made even more significant when understanding that Rosenzweig came from an assimilated Jewish family. He was not brought up with a strong Jewish anchor and he hoped to cast it off altogether. But for some reason he could not. And, as Glatzer details, 'This is the voice of a man [born and raised a Jew] who broke with his personal history, and – in an act of conversion – had to become a Jew.' This was an embrace, rather than his planned rejection, of Rosenzweig's Jewish difference.

Every day, I put a kippah on before I leave the house. As a fashion lover, I try to match it to what I am wearing. With this simple act, I am making a huge statement. I am choosing to mark myself as a Jew. Historically, the non-Jewish world marked us as different, but this was a way to segregate and humiliate Jews. Today, when I walk outside my front door, I want the world to know I am Jewish. I am interacting with the wider world, with the society in which I live, but I want to take part in this community while honouring my Jewishness. It goes with me everywhere I go. So no matter what I'm doing, and what other society I am interacting with, I am there as a proud Jew. I can leave my house with a kippah, and I walk around the streets near my flat. I am part of a wider society. I understand it. I relate to it. But I am doing so as a Jew and I do not need to choose.

This is the framework for successful Jewish integration. Every single Jew must be free to chart their own course of how they interact with their respective society. But operating in a framework of pride means we can go out into the world with our heads held high. We can be active citizens of our diasporic societies and we can do so as proud Jews.

Recognising our differences is just the first step to enabling Jews to integrate successfully, while maintaining our identities. Historically, when trying to navigate Jewish differences, there were those of us who warped, subverted or felt shame over our Jewishness because we engaged in a ranking of culture. Moses Mendelssohn, for instance, placed Jewish culture below non-Jewish culture. Despite the rich civilisation from which he emerged, he described his translation of the Torah into German as moving Jews towards culture. He demonised Yiddish and Eastern Jews as they represented more traditional aspects of Jewish culture. But integration was not the problem here. The problem was that Mendelssohn and his supporters believed the non-Jewish world when it demonised Jewish culture. They accepted the version of Jewishness reflected in the Broken Mirror of Jewish identity and they participated in it. They were thus willing to warp their Jewishness to be accepted, because they believed that it was indeed inferior to Germanness.

The only way to navigate our Jewish difference is to take pride in it. Approaching our integration with pride and confidence in our Jewishness keeps the rope in the tug of war between universality vs specificity taut. There will always be tension between these two opposing forces. And that is perfectly fine. We do not need to choose. As discussed in Chapter 1, the canard of dual loyalty is a lie, and this trope is yet another way in which the non-Jewish world attempts to force us to choose. As we discussed, this accusation can force Jews to diminish our Jewishness in order to prove our loyalty to the non-Jewish world. But diasporic Jews can be, say, British and continue to honour our connection to another land, Israel. And there is nothing wrong with doing so. Other diasporic communities maintain their connections to their indigenous lands, and so can we. But, in order to do so, we must have the knowledge and the confidence to understand our connection and to know that it does not represent something nefarious or evil. We have to reject the canard of dual loyalty and honour the truth of our dual connection. We have to define our own story, identity and experience. We must be the ones to say that dual identities are not incompatible and your attempt to make them so is deeply racist. We know we are able to integrate and we will not sever a fundamental aspect of our identity to do so. We state the terms of our own integration. And we do so with pride.

As individuals, by striking this balance we can honour our Jewish culture, civilisation and practice while also carefully selecting which parts of the wider culture we wish to participate in. Of course, we have to live without the mental strain and burden of having to over-think every action in terms of whether it honours our Jewishness or not. We can be actively Jewish and still partake in our various dias-poric societies. I can be British and Jewish and eat both chicken soup and kneidlach and beans on toast without having to worry. Although, as we will explore later, our Jewishness must be an active part of our life (in whatever way is right for each individual Jewish person), there has to be room to manoeuvre and flexibility to simply be. But if the framework of Jewish Pride is utilised, integration into the wider world becomes much easier. And the tension between specificity and our universality can remain balanced.

The Pesach Seder is one of the most observed Jewish holidays. However, as the scholar Siegfried Stein showed in an article in *The Journal of Jewish Studies* in 1957, it drew its inspiration from Hellen-istic symposiums, which were banquets that took place after a meal. In the Biblical period, Seders did not exist.[303] The Torah simply instructed Jews to eat the paschal lamb with *matzot* (unleavened bread) and *marror* (bitter herbs) and that a father should teach his son about the Exodus from Egypt. There is also no record of the Seder from the Second Temple period (516 BCE–70 CE). The first mention of it appears in the *Mishnah* (the first major written collection of the Jewish oral traditions which is known as the Oral Torah) and the *Tosefta* (the compilation of the Jewish oral law from the late 2nd century, the period of the *Mishnah*) which is dated either just before, or after, the destruction of the Second Temple of Jerusalem in 70 CE.

As Stein states, in the time of Homer, the ancient-Greek author, 'men still feasted sitting, but gradually they slid from chairs to couches, taking as their ally relaxation and ease'.[304] Similarly, during the Seder, the *Mishnah* (Pesahim 10:1) states that all Jews must recline on a couch, specifically using one's left arm (Pesahim 108a). During these symposiums, the Greeks and Romans would eat a sandwich of bread and lettuce. Meanwhile, the Haggadah tells us that Hillel the Elder used to eat a 'sandwich' of the paschal lamb, *matzah* and *marror*. It is thus clear that the Jews who created the Seder were inspired by the Greek and Roman symposium. But this example offers us a fantastic opportunity to understand the possibilities of Jewish integration on a deeper level. Jews integrated into non-Jewish culture, but they continued to honour their Jewish. They incorporated traditional elements of how Jews marked the Exodus story, namely the telling of the story while eating *matzot* and *marror*. It was an evolution of culture and a fusion of specific cultural practices.

The rabbis who 'Jewified' the symposium and created the Seder were not assimilating. They were simply interacting with the world around them, just as many of us do. They couldn't avoid the cultural norms and practices of the non-Jewish world and, truthfully, neither can most of us. Dr Joshua Kulp captures this in the *Schechter Haggadah*, where he argues:

> 'With regard to rabbinic "assimilation" of Greco-Roman practice, the rabbis clearly were a group living in the Greco-Roman world, which they could no more avoid than we can avoid living in a world dominated by Western culture. Rather than using the loaded term "assimilation" in describing rabbinic practices parallel to the Greco-Roman symposium, I would say that the rabbis participated in this culture, rejected practices anathematic

to their beliefs and implemented those which they did not find
disturbing.'[305]

The creation of the Seder can be a guide for us today when considering our own integration with non-Jewish culture. We can participate
in the cultures that surround us, disregard practices which do not
align with our own values, experience, culture or identity and participate in those that do, while maintaining a connection to traditional
Jewish traditions through examples of cultural fusion.

Despite what the non-Jewish world argues, and despite the disadvantages imposed upon us, Jews can integrate. We can be active members
of a diasporic society. And we can even take part in the evolution of
culture. Every Jew will engage and interact to a different extent and in
different ways. But the most important factor here is the framework of
Jewish Pride: it guides us as we navigate the non-Jewish world as Jews all
the while keeping the rope in our tug of war between universality and
specificity taut with the tension of balance.

STRONG JEWISH ANCHORS

For thousands of years we have maintained our Jewishness through
strong and stabilising Jewish anchors. These anchors bound us to one
another and to ourselves. They enabled Jews to maintain our specific
culture and civilisation for 2,500 years of exile and displacement. And
they are crucial to the continuity of the Jewish people.

Though Jews became an almost entirely diasporic people after our
expulsion from our spiritual and cultural capital, Jerusalem, in 132 CE,
that was not the first time our people had been forced from our
homeland. In 587 BCE, 718 years earlier, 1,500 Jews were expelled from
the Kingdom of Judah by the Babylonian Empire under the rule of
Nebuchadnezzar II. The war that led to the expulsion also resulted in
the destruction of the first Jewish Temple and the ethnic cleansing of

Jewish elites from Jerusalem. Although these refugee Jews built new lives in Babylon, Psalm 137 tells us of their sorrow and the continuity of the Jewish spirit:

> *How shall we sing the Lord's song in a strange land?*
> *If I forget thee, O Jerusalem, let my right hand forget [her cunning].*
> *If I do not remember thee, let my tongue cleave to the roof of my*
>   *mouth; if I prefer not Jerusalem above my chief joy.*[306]

This ancient version of Zionism powerfully demonstrates the importance of Jewish anchors. These early Jews could have forgotten their homes and settled into their new adopted land. Although they had been forcibly removed from Jerusalem, they were not slaves in Babylon, and were not treated harshly by Nebuchadnezzar. They could take up jobs as merchants or even work in government administration; and were required to help shore up the struggling Babylonian economy. But, while they were treated well and could live freely, these Jewish exiles never forgot their home and many eventually returned to Jerusalem and Judah after the fall of Babylon to the Persians under Cyrus the Great.

It is our Jewish anchors that connect us to our past, but also to our present and, indeed, our future. Our anchors are rooted in memory, action and pride. Whether in Babylon or Britain, Jews never forgot Jerusalem. We remembered our culture and heritage and, most importantly, we continued to participate in it. We allowed our lives to be governed by Jewish law and we continued to evolve our culture. This is truly remarkable. And, as the Dalai Lama understood, after his own expulsion from Tibet by the Chinese, something to be admired and learned from. As Rinchen, a Tibetan participant in a cultural exchange programme coordinated by the Israeli Friends of the Tibetan People in 2000, explained:

'I think the reason we came to Israel is because we have a cultural and traditional affinity. The Jewish past and the present situation we Tibetans are facing in India as exiles are similar. The Jews have been in exile for many years and we are in exile now. Jewish society has been quite inspirational. To know how they were able to have their culture and tradition intact until now, for 2,000 years – this point is crucial for us.'[307]

Rinchen recognised that the only way to maintain an identity through exile and oppression is to anchor yourself to it. To aid the Tibetan people in their exile he looked for inspiration to the Jews to understand how Jewish anchors were passed on through the generations, from parent to child to grandchild.

Intergenerational anchors are developed through an understanding that Jewishness and Judaism do not belong to us. We are simply caretakers of it for future generations of Jews. The example of Mendelssohn is once again instructive. Although, in his own way, he was trying to save Jewishness and Judaism, he did not succeed. He even failed to ensure that his own family maintained their Jewishness, and, as we saw in Chapter 3, only one of his countless grandchildren went to their graves as a Jew. But how could we expect otherwise? We cannot expect children to care about Jewishness if they are never taught why being Jewish is beautiful and special and are not supported in developing their own Jewish anchors. Each Jew is a thread in a much greater tapestry of Jewishness that stretches back thousands of years and will stretch thousands of years into the future. But without proper education and Jewish action, these threads can weaken and ultimately break. As Lyvia demonstrated, to allow each Jew to claim their heritage and play their part in maintaining and cultivating Jewishness they must have a strong Jewish anchor.

Our Jewish anchors are a mindset shored up by knowledge, memory and active practice. We must know who we are. We must, as we have already explored, define our own identity and experience.

And we must live it. This is what defined the experience of Jews in Europe pre-emancipation. They were legally segregated and oppressed and faced multiple ethnic cleansings and genocides, but many maintained their connection to Jewishness through their immovable Jewish anchors. Crypto-Jews in Inquisition-era Spain and Portugal did not give up their Jewish anchors. In public, they shed their Jewish identities and seemingly discarded their anchors, but in private they worked hard – under pain of death – to continue maintaining their Jewishness. This is what our anchors give us: a sense of self, a sense of belonging and a sense of pride in a world that is actively trying to destroy us. Maintaining and developing our anchors must be an active choice. We cannot expect for them to continue rooting us into our Jewishness if we do not actively strengthen them.

While the power of Jewish anchors cannot be understated, they will not erase the pain caused by the cyclical swelling of Jew-hate. Even the proudest of Jews feels the pain caused by historic and current anti-Jewish racism. There is nothing that anyone can say, no inspirational speech that can be made, that will stop Jews feeling the horrors of our experience, but we can, as we discussed, root ourselves in our Jewishness and heal by reclaiming our relationship with it. A Jewish anchor can help us stabilise our own identities against the raging storms of hate. A strong and stable Jewish identity, rooted in memory, action, joy and pride is a key component for combatting internalised anti-Jewishness. It acts as a bulwark against the oppressive pressures from the non-Jewish world, and it helps continue our survival for thousands more years.

DEVELOPING JEWISH ANCHORS – EDUCATION

'We can now see throughout the Jewish world, including Israel, that it takes almost no time for a civilization to be disrupted by lack of proper education of its new generations,'[308] argued Daniel J Elazar, the political scientist.

Education is, and has always been, the lifeblood of the Jewish people. It has been one of the major components of our survival after being ethnically cleansed from our homeland in the first centuries of the new millennium. A strong Jewish education system cultivated and maintained our Jewish anchors and rooted us in our Jewishness for thousands of years.

Quality Jewish education is how we develop Jewish anchors, enable Jews to define their own identities and allow Jews to understand that our Jewishness represents more than murder and tragedy. It is how we enable Jews to defend ourselves against internalised anti-Jewishness. And it is how we teach the framework of Jewish Pride.

Jewish education helps us understand who and what we are, beyond the experiences we have had at the hands of the wider world and perspectives of the wider world. We know that the non-Jewish world loves murdered Jews. They cast us as passive actors in our own stories and frame our history as a never-ending tragedy. As we referenced in Chapter 1, this is also sometimes a feature of Jewish education. To avoid this, to minimise intergenerational trauma, quality Jewish education must utilise the framework of Jewish Pride to teach Jewish history, identity and experience. I have heard Jewish history described as 'one long *Kaddish*'. But this is wrong. Our history is not just one endless mourners' prayer. Jewish history is replete with moments of pride and celebration. But if we fail to utilise the framework of Jewish Pride, we fail to help others see the beauty in our history and we fail to pass it on to future generations.

A book that embodies this notion, and the use of the Jewish Pride framework, is *There Once Was a World: A 900-Year Chronicle of the Shtetl of Eishyshok* by historian Yaffa Eliach.[309] In this immense work, she examines the history of the Lithuanian town of Eishyshok through pride. Eliach demonstrates that Jewish history is filled with joy and amazement and, yes, tears. As this story shows, we are so much more than just what is done to us. Our history is not sad. Our history has sadness, but it is not of and in itself sad. And this is what we must teach as part of quality Jewish education.

Ludwig Philippson, 19th-century German rabbi and follower of Orthodox *Wissenschaft*, understood the primary importance of education. Following in the footsteps of Mendelssohn, but utilising the framework of Jewish Pride, he published a translation of the Torah into German in 1853. However, the marked difference between his translation and Mendelssohn's was that Philippson included the original Hebrew alongside the German. Moreover, to ensure accessibility, Philippson included commentary on the text, not just from a biblical perspective but a cultural one too. This made the Torah accessible to Jewish Germans while helping them understand its continued relevance to their own lives. In another version of Philippson's translation, illustrations by the famed non-Jewish illustrator Gustave Doré were included. It was Philippson's belief that Jews should be literate in their own histories, and thus he created a piece of work that would educate Jewish Germans on what it means to be a Jew. This is fundamentally important.

As discussed in Chapter 4, during the Jewish Cold War, there was also a focus on promoting Jewish education. Kurt Lewin, the chief proponent of Positive Jewishness, argued for an updated curriculum with regards to Jewish education which would inspire and empower young Jews to develop 'stronger Jewish personalities … that can resist infection by the anti-Semitic virus'.[310] And in a mid-20th-century version of Jewish Pride, Israel B. Rappaport, a Jewish educator, in 1946 drafted a policy statement regarding Jewish education for the American Jewish Committee. He wrote that the 'primary task'[311] of Jewish education had to be the prevention of 'unwholesome repressions, evasions and inferiority complexes' and the promotion of 'Jewish self-respect'.

Seventy years on, the centrality of Jewish education to promoting Jewish Pride and combatting internalised anti-Jewishness still cannot be underestimated. It is how we understand the core of what it means to be a Jew. In the absence of such a focus, Jews simply become, as Leon Feldman, a Jewish social worker, put it, an 'absentee owner, a missing heir'.[312] Jews 'may even believe that Judaism is rich and noble,' Feldman suggested, but to them 'being a Jew [implies] no special outlook, acts, or responsibilities ... only a good deal of ill-understood frustrations. To be Jewish is to have responsibility, to maintain, protect and cultivate Jewishness so that we can pass it on to future generations.'

Jewish education, beyond almost anything else, must be the priority of the Jewish people. Quality Jewish education that teaches Jewish history through the framework of Jewish Pride can form a defensive membrane against the hate we experience. But for many Jews, this layer of knowledge is completely missing, or, at the very least, it isn't developed enough to withstand the onslaught of Jew-hate. If we are to survive, if we are to continue to evolve with pride, Jews must recommit to Jewish education. These programmes must be accessible and available for Jews of all ages. While we must be focused on the youth (our future), we must not discount the present. Jews of all ages deserve to understand who they are. Jews of all ages deserve to be literate in Jewish history. And Jews of all ages can contribute to the continuation of the Jewish people.

From a practical perspective, courses on Jewish history and experience must be made available to Jews all over the world, whether online or in person. The internet has offered Jews an opportunity to come together as one, regardless of where they may live. Therefore, geographical location should not be a barrier to a Jew actively learning about their experience or identity. Additionally, programmes must be made available to people of all generations and regardless of how involved in formal Jewish communal structures they are. Education must be rooted in openness and inclusivity, and it is vital that we create learning environments that are empowering and welcoming to all Jews, regardless of their knowledge or experience.

Ultimately, we must also highlight and prioritise the voice of trained educators with expertise, and we must understand that quality and in-depth education cannot take place on social media. Our story is long and complex, and, to do it justice, it needs a more reflective environment than social media can provide.

There will be huge diversity in how Jewish education is delivered, and that diversity (as always) is a strength. But ultimately, it cannot *just* teach Jews biblical stories, nor should it *only* focus on our tragedies; it must enable all Jews to understand Jewishness and Judaism, using the framework of Jewish Pride.

We often talk about important discussions that need to take place in the Jewish community. We want to debate everything from inclusivity to identity. But how can informed discussions take place if those participating are not literate in Jewishness? Before we discuss, debate and engage in dialogue (other key Jewish values) we must first learn. *Daf Yomi* (page of the day) is a beautiful regimen on how to engage with the Talmud. Every scholar studies the Oral Law one page at a time. With their *chevra* (their study partners) they debate the words and thoughts of the great Jewish sages of the past. But to take part in this study, these scholars have learned the basics. And, like them, we cannot discuss key Jewish concepts without first learning the essential components of Jewish history.

Quality Jewish education rooted in Jewish Pride is not only how we combat internalised anti-Jewishness. It is how we survive as a people. This is particularly crucial, when the non-Jewish world continues its endless discussions on the Jewish Question and its continued debate on Jewish identity and experience. We have to know who we are. We have to use the framework of Jewish Pride to understand our history, our story. We have to understand what it means to be a Jew, from the Jewish perspective, so we can move through the world as proud Jews, committed to the continuation of the Jewish people.

DEVELOPING JEWISH ANCHORS - ACTION

For a Jewish anchor to be strong, and for it to be able to withstand the pressures of Jew-hate from the non-Jewish world, it has to be rooted deep in our souls and psyche. Our attachment to Jewishness cannot be weak or loose. It must be strong and profound. Beyond educa-tion, the second fundamental method to ensure strong and powerful Jewish anchors is to root them in Jewish action.

When I light the candles during Chanukah or follow the Seder at Pesach, I remember those same actions from my childhood. I remember standing around with my family singing *Ma'oz Tzur* while we lit the chanukiah. I remember attending Jewish events at Newton Mearns Synagogue in Glasgow organised by the Jewish community. I remember playing a game where I had to eat a sugared doughnut without licking my lips (it is surprisingly hard). I remember the mili-tary operation that was a Shabbat dinner at my house. I remember eating the poppy seed challah my father used to buy from Mark's Deli in Giffnock. Jewishness was an active part of my life. The emotional connection I have to my Jewishness is burrowed deep inside me. I cannot separate it from my childhood. From my family. From my memories. From myself. Nicky also expressed this understanding of his Jewish action. After his late father's passing, he found that religious observance of Judaism connected him to his father. By going to *shul* (synagogue), Nicky had accepted the torch of active Jewishness from his father and by carrying on this tradition he was bound even closer to his father, and also to the whole Jewish people.

Every Shabbat, Jews come together to light our Shabbat candles. We stand as one modern community to observe an ancient Jewish holiday. These actions are what tether us to our history, our present and our futures. The fundamental importance of living active Jewish lives cannot be understated. Of course, it's important to recognise that we do not have to live our Jewish lives exactly the same as one

another. Personally, I see Jewishness as a buffet, filled with an amazing
range of diverse foods. Each Jew will go to the buffet and fill our plates
with different combinations of Jewishness. That is fine, normal and
natural. But the essential thing is that we get up off our seats and we
walk to the buffet to engage with active Jewishness. Within my five
interviewees, there is a huge diversity of Jewish action. But there is, in
each of them, a commitment to living actively Jewish lives. Through
this commitment, they are reaffirming their connection to their families and to our people.

An important part of Jewish action is rooting our modern lives
in our civilisation and its diverse cultures. During the 19th century,
there was a discussion over which language *Wissenschaft der Judentum* should utilise. There were those who preferred German but
there were also those, such as the poet Chaim Nachman Bialik, who
argued that these important works on Jewishness had to be written
in our indigenous language. Out of this discussion a Hebrew strand
of *Wissenschaft* emerged. This was an important and clear example
of Jews embracing Jewish culture and Jewish specificity. Jews do not
need to speak Hebrew to engage in Jewish culture, but I understand
the statement Jews like Bialik were trying to make. It was incredibly
powerful that these Jews were embracing their specificity by telling
our own stories in our language. What a moment of throwing off the
cloak of shame! Ultimately though, whether it is learning Hebrew,
or any of the other Jewish languages (Yiddish, Ladino or the various
Judeo-Arabic languages) or not, Jews must participate in the civilisation they represent.

A way for all Jews to honour Jewish civilisation is to celebrate
our Hebrew birthday (alongside our other birthday). My Western
birthday is the 28 January 1987 and my Hebrew birthday is the
27 Tevet 5747. Knowing this, honouring it, gives me pride. I,
a Jew born in Scotland in the 1980s, am actively taking part in a
culture that began thousands of years ago in the Levant. That is

beautiful. And, importantly, I do not need to stop celebrating my Western birthday. Remember, despite what the non-Jewish world tells us, we do not need to choose. We can integrate. But integration has to be rooted in Jewish Pride. So we should eat Jewish foods, learn Jewish history, engage with Jewish culture, take part in Jewish communal life, celebrate our Jewish birthdays, we should know our Hebrew names (mine is Benyamin Chaim ben Zvi Mordechau vih Sara Leib) and we should honour the Jewish holidays that mark the Jewish calendar.

Active Jewishness is how we revive and maintain our Jewish culture and civilisation. There have been countless moments in history where the non-Jewish world has attempted to destroy the Jewish people. But when faced with genocides like the Holocaust, or efforts to erase our identity or our connection to our indigenous land of Israel, through antizionism, we have fought back. We have revived and resuscitated ourselves for thousands of years. Jewish action is thus an act of resistance. When the world tells us that it is bad to be active Jews, we should reclaim our story and our specificity. We should ignore their hate and commit ourselves to Jewish life.

Ultimately, active Jewishness is how we utilise and spread Jewish Pride. It is one of the ways in which we defend ourselves against internalised anti-Jewishness. We are reclaiming our story. We are healing through taking control of our relationship with our Jewishness. We are engaging in our culture and, through this, we are defining our identity as Jews. So, whether you eat Jewish food, listen to Jewish music, speak Hebrew (or another one of the Jewish languages), read Jewish stories or fight for the Jewish people, you are part of an unbroken chain that stretches back thousands of years, and because of our commitment to active Jewishness, will spread thousands of years into the future.

RECLAIMING OUR STORY:
THE PURSUIT OF JEWISH PRIDE

Jewish Pride is the opposite of internalised anti-Jewishness. It is both a goal and a framework. It is a movement we are building. It is something we can work towards, but it is also, quite crucially, something that we can utilise to heal ourselves. To be Jewish is a wonderful thing. But, because of the treatment we have experienced at the hands of the wider world, many of us have seen our Jewishness as a source of shame. Using Jewish Pride as a lens enables us to clearly see the beauty of our Jewishness; it is how we reject and overcome internalised anti-Jewishness.

Jewish Pride is a modern Jewish liberation movement. It enables us to define our own identities, we understand how to balance our specificity and universality when we integrate into non-Jewish societies and we build and maintain strong and powerful Jewish anchors. We educate ourselves about Jewish experience and history and we live Jewish lives. This is how we use Jewish Pride as a tool to combat internalised anti-Jewishness.

The experiences described in my five interviews, and indeed this entire book, clearly demonstrate that, without this strong framework of Jewish Pride, the power of internalised anti-Jewishness can be too great to resist. Our Jewish anchors are not always strong enough to defend us against the shame, the trauma and the Broken Mirror of Jewish identity. Unless we purposefully decide to utilise the power of Jewish Pride, we are unable to defend ourselves from the pressures of the wider world. But none of this is our fault. We do not look at my interviewees nor the historic Jewish communities, nor the German or American Jews' communities with blame or judgement. We do not condemn them and erase their beauty and richness. We understand their experiences and most importantly *why* they felt and behaved as they did. The pressure from the non-Jewish world can be too great.

Without even realising it, we can absorb its perspectives on Jewishness and Judaism. But now, as we build a modern Jewish Pride movement, we must engage in a wholesale shift of perspective. Using this framework to truly understand ourselves provides us with armour. It gives us an opportunity to go to battle. That battle should not be an internal one, or the sort we have so often engaged in with other Jews. Instead, it must be with the non-Jewish world to reclaim our story, for each other and for ourselves.

We have survived against literally all the odds and, what is more, we have thrived. We have got through everything that has been thrown at us. And we got through it because of our resilience, not because anyone has helped us along the way. We survived because of our commitment to Jewish life. We are a marvel.

We created amazing traditions, through which we can strengthen and sustain ourselves. We created the Talmud. We created the oral history. We built institutions. We built culture. Nay, we built a civilisation. And, through the lens of pride, we can view and understand our story.

As I say to my students when they graduate, 'go into the world and explore', I now say this to you: 'Go into the world, use the framework of Jewish Pride and explore. What wonders can you discover? What joy can you find? What pride can you unearth?'

We will proceed into the world without shame. Without judgement. Without internalising the hate from the world around us.

We will proceed into the world with kindness. With empathy. With joy. And with pride.

So, together we stand as one, and we say proudly to the non-Jewish world that we will not warp, change or bastardise ourselves to be accepted.

We are proud to be Jewish.

We are proud of our history.

And we are proud of our civilisation.

And we reject any attempt to make us feel differently.

Am Yisrael Chai.

The People of Israel Live.

Proudly.

CHAVUROT QUESTIONS

This book is designed to support you, my reader, as you embark on your own journey of Jewish self-discovery as you reject internalised anti-Jewishness by reclaiming our story and pursuing Jewish Pride.

These questions are a supplement to each chapter and will facilitate personal reflection as you move through this book. Please use these questions as you see fit, although they would be most helpful at the end of a chapter. Each question relates to a specific section in each of the chapters.

You are also, of course, free to interact with them either by yourself or with others as you reflect on the journey that each and every one of us must take as we explore internalised Jew-hate and the reject shame imposed on Jews by the non-Jewish world.

Chapter 1 – But Why?

1. How would you define your Jewish identity? Do you think you might utilise non-Jewish frameworks/ideas to define your Jewishness? If so, in what way?
2. Have you ever felt triggered? How did this manifest? How did you respond?
3. As I have, have you ever blamed other Jews for Jew-hate? What was the context?
4. As I did, have you ever denigrated other Jews to demonstrate your own palatability?

5. How do you relate to your diasporic community?

6. I am a British Jew, meaning my primary identity is being Jewish and the additional part is my Britishness. How do you relate to that? Are you, say, a British Jew or a Jewish Brit (or whatever Diasporic identity you may have)?

7. Do you think you feel comfortable being distinctly Jewish in a wider society? Answering either yes or no, how does this manifest itself for you?

8. Were you able to develop a Jewish anchor in childhood? If not, when did you develop it?

9. How do you actively maintain your Jewish anchor today? Do you? What does this look like?

10. Do you relate to this chapter in a personal way? Have you seen any aspect of your experience described in it? How does this make you feel?

Chapter 2 – The Major Manifestations

1. Have you ever diminished your Jewishness?

2. Reflecting on your past, have you ever, as I have, qualified your Jewish identity by using the word 'but' – for example, 'I am Jewish, but …' What were the circumstances in which you said this?

3. Did your family alter their names, as mine did? Do you know what it used to be?

4. Have you ever felt as if you wanted to change an aspect of your appearance? Was it in part, as it was with me, in a bid to look less Jewish? How does that make you feel today?

5. Did you know that Jews experience racism? If you have resisted this idea, why might that be?

6. Do you feel able to confidently stand up for yourself as a Jew? Has this ever not been the case? If so, how does that make you feel? How can we actively fight against the idea that Jews should 'keep their heads down'?

7. Have you ever denied your Jewishness?

8. How did reading about Ella Emhoff make you feel? Why?

9. How can we process Jews like Zemmour, being victims of Jew-hate while still causing harm to our peoplehood? How can we continue to be empathetic while also having strong boundaries?

10. Which of the three major manifestations of internalised anti-Jewishness, if any, do you most relate to?

Chapter 3 – From Pre-Modern to Pre-War

1. What is your response to these historical Jewish experiences? Were you aware that internalised anti-Jewishness has been a part of our experience for so long?

2. Do you feel as if you understand (both emotionally and intellectually) why the individuals featured in this chapter did what they did?

3. Which story stood out to you the most? What surprised you? What did you relate to (if any)?

4. Did any of the historical examples described in this chapter relate to our Jewish world today?

5. There are threads which connect all aspects of our history and experience to one another. Can you identify these threads with regards to internalised anti-Jewishness?

Chapter 4 – From Post-War to Present

1. Were you aware of the American Jewish Cold War? Does this feel familiar today? Does it remind you of other histories from this book?

2. If you are an American Jew, how does this information help you understand your own experience? Did you see your family's experience described in this chapter?

3. How do you think we support American Jews (either as Americans or non-Americans) in reclaiming aspects of Jewishness lost because of the cultural emancipation?

4. If you identify as a cultural Jew, what aspects of Jewish culture is that rooted in? Do you think there's a possibility they may be (even in a small way) based on the Broken Mirror of Jewish identity?

5. Have you been able to reflect on previously loved Jewish characters from a more critical perspective?

6. What other examples of Jewish representation can we critique?

7. Do you understand that the charge of imperialism, genocide, whiteness and apartheid was the result of a purposeful campaign by the Soviet Union and the Arab world?

8. Have you experienced any aspect of The Road from Zionism as I detailed in this chapter?

9. If you define yourself as a progressive, how can you retain your progressive values in the face of progressive Jew-hate?

10. Did you relate to any aspect of this chapter? If so, how?

Interviews – Róisín Jacobson, Nicky Rawlinson, Shoshana Batya Greenwald, Avraham Vofsi and Lyvia Tzamali

1. Are there any aspects of these stories that relate to your own?

2. If so, how does it make you feel seeing your experiences reflected in the experiences of others?

3. Why is empathy such an important part of this exploration?

4. Do these stories help you understand the wide-ranging nature of internalised anti-Jewishness?

5. Have you felt a spark of empowerment by reading these healing stories?

Chapter 10 – From Prejudice to Pride

1. How can you utilise the framework of Jewish Pride in your daily life?

2. Reflect on your Jewish identity now that you understand the Broken Mirror of Jewish identity.

3. Are there moments when trauma you may have has been triggered? How can you process this? What practical steps can you take to reclaim your relationship with Jewishness?

4. How can we shift our focus to Jewish joy?

5. Who is to blame for Jew-hate?

6. How can we critique Jews or Jewish communities without engaging in victim-blaming?

7. Have you ever felt tension in your diasporic identity? How are you able to sit in your Jewishness/your other identity in peace?

8. On a scale of 1–10 how would you rate your Jewish anchor?

9. How can you reinforce it?

10. How can you continue your Jewish learning journey?

11. What practical steps can you take to incorporate Jewish action into your daily life?

12. Using 'I used to think, now I think' technique, reflect on your learning journey thus far. What did you used to think/what do you think now?

13. What does being Jewish mean to you now?

14. What is your favourite thing about being Jewish?

15. Do you feel able to begin the journey to reclaim your Jewish story?

RÓISÍN   NICKY   SHOSHANA

AVRAHAM      LYVIA

THE AUTHOR

NOTES

1   Theodor Lessing, *Jewish Self-Hate*. Translation by Peter Appelbaum (New York: Berghahn Books, 2021) (hereafter Theodor Lessing, *Jewish Self-Hate*)

2   Jacqueline Rose, 'On the Myth of Jewish Self-Hatred', *Verso*, 1 June 2018. Available at: https://www.versobooks.com/blogs/3861-on-the-myth-of-jewish-self-hatred

3   Daniel Levitas, 'Exploring What Is Behind The Rare Phenomenon Of Jewish Anti-Semites', *Southern Poverty Law Center*, 18 December 2002. Available at: https://www.splcenter.org/fighting-hate/intelligence-report/2002/exploring-what-behind-rare-phenomenon-jewish-anti-semites

4   Camara Phyllis Jones, 'Levels of racism: a theoretic framework and a gardener's tale', *American Journal of Public Health*, 1 August 2000. Available at: https://ajph.aphapublications.org/doi/epdf/10.2105/AJPH.90.8.1212

5   James Baldwin, *A Dialogue* (New York: Lippincott, 1973)

6   Theodor Lessing, *Jewish Self-Hate*

7   Hussein Abdilahi Bulhan, *Frantz Fanon and the Psychology of Oppression* (Berlin: Springer, 1985)

8   Susan A. Glenn, 'The Vogue of Jewish Self-Hatred in Post-World War II America', *Jewish Social Studies* (Spring/Summer 2006). Available at: https://history.washington.edu/research/publications/vogue-jewish-self-hatred-post-world-war-ii-america (hereafter Susan A. Glenn, 'The Vogue of Jewish Self-Hatred in Post-World War II America')

9   Frantz Fanon, *Black Skin White Masks*. Translation by Charles Lam Markmann (London: Pluto Press, 1986)

10 Jor-El Caraballo, 'Understanding the minority stress model', Talkspace, 26 December 2019. Available at: https://www.talkspace.com/blog/minority-stress-model/ (hereafter Jor-El Caraballo, 'Understanding the minority stress model')

11 Annette Kämmerer, 'The Scientific Underpinnings and Impacts of Shame', *Scientific American*, 9 August 2019. Available at: https://www.scientificamerican.com/article/the-scientific-underpinnings-and-impacts-of-shame/#:~:text=Guilt%20causes%20us%20to%20focus,low%20self%2Desteem%20and%20depression

12 Jean-Paul Sartre, 'Portrait of the Inauthentic Jew', *Commentary*, May 1948. Available at: https://www.commentary.org/articles/jean-paul-sartre/portrait-of-the-inauthentic-jew/

13 'Self-Hatred', *Psychology Today*. Available at: https://www.psychologytoday.com/us/basics/self-hatred

14 'Internalize', *Cambridge Dictionary*. Available at: https://dictionary.cambridge.org/dictionary/english/internalize

15 Todd M. Endelman, 'Jewish Self-Hatred in Britain and Germany', in *Two Nations: British and German Jews in Comparative Perspective* (Tubingen: JCB Mohr, 1999) (hereafter Todd M. Endelman, 'Jewish Self-Hatred in Britain and Germany')

16 Tia Goldenberg, 'Seth Rogen's Israel comments highlight fraught diaspora ties', CBC, 7 August 2020. Available at: https://www.cbc.ca/news/entertainment/seth-rogen-israel-comments-1.5678114

17 Todd M. Endelman, 'Jewish Self-Hatred in Britain and Germany'

18   'Jewish Historian Salo W. Baron, 94', *Chicago Tribune*, 26 November 1989. Available at: https://www.chicagotribune.com/news/ct-xpm-1989-11-26-8903120935-story.html

19   Salo W. Baron, 'Modern Capitalism and Jewish Fate,' *Menorah Journal* 30, Summer 1942) (hereafter Salo W. Baron, 'Modern Capitalism and Jewish Fate')

20   Kurt Lewin, 'Self-Hatred Among Jews', *Contemporary Jewish Record* 4, June 1941

21   Theodor Lessing, *Jewish Self-Hate*

22   Jewish Agency & World Zionist Organisation, 'The State of Antisemitism in 2021', Department for Combating Antisemitism & Enhancing Resilience, January 2022. Available at: https://www.wzo.org.il/files/2018/2/PDF/antiheb/antisemitism__ENG.pdf

23   Theodor Lessing, *Jewish Self-Hate*

24   Trude Weiss-Rosmarin, 'A Manifesto of Jewish Survivalism', *The Jewish Spectator*, July 1947

25   Sander L. Gilman, *Jewish Self-Hatred: Anti-Semitism and the Hidden Language of the Jews*

26   Speech on Religious Minorities and Questionable Professions, Speech by Clermont-Tonnerre, 23 December 1789. Available at: https://revolution.chnm.org/d/284/

27   'Jewish Emancipation in Western Europe', My Jewish Learning. Available at: https://www.myjewishlearning.com/article/jewish-emancipation-in-western-europe/ (hereafter 'Jewish Emancipation in Western Europe', My Jewish Learning)

28   Sander L. Gilman, *Jewish Self-Hatred: Anti-Semitism and the Hidden Language of the Jews*

29   David Sorkin, 'What was Wissenschaft des Judentums?', Leo Baeck Institute, 25 March 2015. Available at: https://www.lbi.org/de/news/what-was-wissenschaft-des-judentums/

30   Ilana Maymind, 'On the Concept of Self-Hatred: A Misnomer', *Journal of Jewish Identities*, January 2016. Available at: https://muse.jhu.edu/article/614816

31   Ilana Maymind, 'On the Concept of Self-Hatred: A Misnomer', *Journal of Jewish Identities*, January 2016. Available at: https://muse.jhu.edu/article/614816

32   David Friedländer, *Über die Verbesserung der Israeliten im Königreich Pohlen* (London: Forgotten Books, 2019)

33   Heinrich Graetz, *Geschichte der Juden* (Germany, Inktank-Publishing, 2019)

34   Sander L. Gilman, *Jewish Self-Hatred: Anti-Semitism and the Hidden Language of the Jews*

35   Jonathan Sacks, *Future Tense: A Vision for Jews and Judaism in the Global Culture* (London: Hodder & Stoughton, 2010)

36   Björn Krondorfer, 'Unsettling Empathy: Intercultural Dialogue in the Aftermath of Historical and Cultural Trauma.' In *Breaking Intergenerational Cycles of Repetition: A Global Dialogue on Historical Trauma and Memory*, edited by Pumla Gobodo-Madikizela, 2016. Available at: https://www.jstor.org/stable/j.ctvdfo3jc.11

37   Bessel Van Der Kolk, *The Body Keeps the Score: Brain, Mind, and Body in the Healing of Trauma* (New York: Penguin Publishing Group, 2015) (hereafter: Bessel Van Der Kolk, *The Body Keeps the Score: Brain, Mind, and Body in the Healing of Trauma*)

38   Olga Khazan, 'Inherited Trauma Shapes Your Health', *Atlantic*, 16 October 2018. Available at: https://www.theatlantic.com/health/archive/2018/10/trauma-inherited-generations/573055/

39   'Study finds Rwandan genocide chemically modified the DNA of victims and victims' offspring', 10 January 2022. Available at: https://www.usf.edu/news/2022/

study-finds-rwandan-genocides-chemically-modified-the-dna-of-victims-and-victims-offspring.aspx

40   Patricia Dashorst, Trudy M. Mooren, Rolf J. Kleber, Peter J. de Jong & Rafaele C. Huntjens, 'Intergenerational consequences of the Holocaust on offspring mental health: a systematic review of associated factors and mechanisms', *European Journal of Psychotraumatology*, 2019. Available at: https://doi.org/10.1080/20008198.2019.1654065

41   Bessel Van Der Kolk, *The Body Keeps the Score: Brain, Mind, and Body in the Healing of Trauma*

42   Nasrullah Mambrol, 'Trauma Studies', *Literary Theory and Criticism*, 19 December 2018. Available at: https://literariness.org/2018/12/19/trauma-studies/

43   Jeffrey Prager, 'Disrupting the Intergenerational Transmission of Trauma: Recovering Humanity, Repairing Generations' In *Breaking Intergenerational Cycles of Repetition: A Global Dialogue on Historical Trauma and Memory*, edited by Pumla Gobodo-Madikizela, 2016. Available at: https://www.jstor.org/stable/j.ctvdfo3jc.11

44   Jeffrey Prager, 'Disrupting the Intergenerational Transmission of Trauma: Recovering Humanity, Repairing Generations' In *Breaking Intergenerational Cycles of Repetition: A Global Dialogue on Historical Trauma and Memory*, edited by Pumla Gobodo-Madikizela, 2016. Available at: https://www.jstor.org/stable/j.ctvdfo3jc.11

45   Theodor Lessing, *Jewish Self-Hate*

46   'Viduy Confession & Jewish Prayers for the Final Moments of Life', Chabad. Available at: https://www.chabad.org/library/article_cdo/aid/364288/jewish/Viduy-Confession-Jewish-Prayers-for-the-Final-Moments-of-Life.htm#The

47   Theodor Lessing, *Jewish Self-Hate*

48   'A Guide Through Lamentations', Safaria. Available at: https://www.sefaria.org/sheets/16222?lang=bi

49   Theodor Lessing, *Jewish Self-Hate*

50   Donna K. Bivens, 'What is internalized racism?', Racial Equity Tools. Available at: https://www.racialequitytools.org/resourcefiles/What_is_Internalized_Racism.pdf (hereafter Donna K. Bivens, 'What is internalized racism?')

51   Dina Porat, '"Amalek's Accomplices" Blaming Zionism for the Holocaust: Anti-Zionist Ultra-Orthodoxy in Israel during the 1980s', *Journal of Contemporary History*, 1992. Available at: http://www.jstor.org/stable/260949

52   Walter Rathenau, *Die Zukunft*, 1897. Available at: https://lib.uchicago.edu/collex/exhibits/exeej/ghetto-comWalter%20Rathenau,%C2%A0Die%20Zukunft-germany-ostjuden-welfare-cause/

53   Sander L. Gilman, *Jewish Self-Hatred: Anti-Semitism and the Hidden Language of the Jews*

54   Otto Weininger, *Sex and Character* (Indiana: Indiana University Press, 2005)

55   Sander L. Gilman, *Jewish Self-Hatred: Anti-Semitism and the Hidden Language of the Jews*

56   Sander L. Gilman, *Jewish Self-Hatred: Anti-Semitism and the Hidden Language of the Jews*

57   David Nirenberg, *Anti-Judaism: The Western Tradition* (New York: W. W. Norton & Company, 2014) (hereafter David Nirenberg, *Anti-Judaism: The Western Tradition*)

58   David Feldman, 'What we are getting wrong in the fight against antisemitism in Britain', *Guardian*, 18 February 2022. Available at: https://www.theguardian.com/commentisfree/2022/feb/18/antisemitism-britain-anti-jewish-hate-incidents

59   Dara Horn, *People Love Dead Jews: Reports from a Haunted Present* (New York:

W.W. Norton & Company, 2021) (hereafter Dara Horn, *People Love Dead Jews: Reports from a Haunted Present*)

60   David Mamet, *The Wicked Son: Anti-Semitism, Self-hatred, and the Jews* (New York: Schocken, 2009)

61   Theodor Lessing, *Jewish Self-Hate*

62   Michael A Meyer, *Judaism within Modernity: Essays on Jewish History and Religion* (Detroit: Wayne State University Press, 2001) (hereafter Michael A Meyer, *Judaism within Modernity: Essays on Jewish History and Religion*)

63   Richard Alba and Victor Nee, 'Rethinking Assimilation Theory for a New Era of Immigration', *The International Migration Review*, 1997. Available at: https://www.jstor.org/stable/2547416

64   Heinrich Von Treitschke, 'A Word About Our Jewry', 1880. Available at: http://www.berlin.ucla.edu/hypermedia/1871_people/texts/Treitschke.pdf

65   Hannah Arendt, 'The Moral of History', (January 1946) in *The Jew as Pariah: Jewish Identity and Politics in the Modern Age*, ed. and introduction by Ron H. Feldman (New York: Grove Press, 1978)

66   Ilana Maymind, 'On the Concept of Self-Hatred: A Misnomer', *Journal of Jewish Identities*, January 2016. Available at: https://muse.jhu.edu/article/614816

67   Michael A Meyer, *Judaism within Modernity: Essays on Jewish History and Religion*

68   Mordecai M. Kaplan, *Judaism as a Civilization: Toward a Reconstruction of American Jewish Life* (Philadelphia: The Jewish Publication Society, 2010)

69   Sarah E. Rosenblum, 'Positive Jewish Education: A Pathway to Thriving 21st Century Jewish Education', University of Pennsylvania, 2019. Available at: https://repository.upenn.edu/cgi/viewcontent.cgi?article=1198&context=mapp_capstone

70   Rose Clubok, 'Jewish Schools Aren't Making the Grade', JWA, 2 November 2021. Available at: https://jwa.org/blog/failure-jewish-education-0

71   Naomi Miller, 'Jewish Education Fails Students', *Canadian Jewish Chronicle*, 14 March 1969. Available at: https://news.google.com/newspapers?nid=2422&dat=19690314&id=xv9OAAAAIBAJ&sjid=-EsDAAAAIBAJ&pg=1381,5723540

72   George Eliot, *Daniel Deronda* (1876). Available at: http://victorian-studies.net/Eliot-Deronda-6.html

73   Kurt Lewin, 'Self-Hatred Among Jews', *Contemporary Jewish Record 4*, June 1941

74   Hierarchy Of Salience, *Alley Dog*. Available at: https://www.alleydog.com/glossary/definition.php?term=Hierarchy+Of+Salience#:~:text=Hierarchy%20of%20salience%20is%20a,used%20in%20a%20particular%20situation.&text=An%20identity%20high%20in%20the,more%20likely%20to%20be%20used

75   Kylie Ora Lobell, 'Media Continues to Go After Orthodox Jews With New Netflix Show "My Unorthodox Life"', *Jewish Journal*, 12 July 2021. Available at: https://jewishjournal.com/commentary/columnist/338641/media-continues-to-go-after-orthodox-jews-with-new-netflix-show-my-unorthodox-life/

76   Avi Shafran, '"Insular" Orthodox Jews mobilize to save lives, from Haiti to Kabul', *Religion News Service*, 1 September 2021. Available at: https://religionnews.com/2021/09/01/insular-orthodox-jews-mobilize-to-save-lives-from-haiti-to-kabul/

77   Torah Jews, Twitter post, 14 September 2021. Available at: https://twitter.com/TorahJews/status/1437496303089602560

78   Geraldine Heng, 'Defining Race, Periodizing Race' at 'Race and Periodization' symposium. Available at: https://www.folger.edu/institute/scholarly-programs/race-periodization/geraldine-heng

79   Sander Gilman, *The Jew's Body* (Oxfordshire: Routledge, 1992) (hereafter Sander Gilman, *The Jew's Body*)

80   Jakov Lind, *Counting My Steps* (London: Macmillan, 1969)

81   Mary Douglas, *Natural Symbols* (New York: Pantheon Books, 1970)

82   Sander Gilman, *The Jew's Body*

83   Sander Gilman, *The Jew's Body*

84   Sander Gilman, *The Jew's Body*

85   Diana Bletter, 'A Bridge Too Far', *Tablet,* 19 September 2017. Available at: https://www.tabletmag.com/sections/community/articles/a-bridge-too-far

86   Natalie Michie, 'Here's What To Know About the *Cutting Room Floor* Podcast Controversy', *Fashion Magazine,* 21 July 2021. Available at: https://fashionmagazine.com/flare/identity-politics/recho-omond-leandra-medine-podcast/

87   Kirsten Fermaglich, 'What the Jewish Name Changing Narrative Gets Wrong', Zocalo Public Square, 17 September 2020. Available at: https://www.zocalopublicsquare.org/2020/09/17/jewish-name-change-20th-century-new-york-history/ideas/essay/ (hereafter Kirsten Fermaglich, 'What the Jewish Name Changing Narrative Gets Wrong')

88   Kirsten Fermaglich, 'What the Jewish Name Changing Narrative Gets Wrong'

89   David Schneider, Twitter post, 7 November 2019. Available at: https://twitter.com/davidschneider/status/1192402362712969216?lang=en

90   Jonathan D. Sarna, 'Conspiracies about a "catastrophic takeover" by Jews have long been an American problem', *The Conversation,* 19 November 2021. Available at: https://theconversation.com/conspiracies-about-a-catastrophic-takeover-by-jews-have-long-been-an-american-problem-172033

91   Michael Sheetz, 'Gary Cohn says Trump's Charlottesville reaction put "enormous pressure" on him to resign', NBC, 25 August 2021. Available at: https://www.cnbc.com/2017/08/25/gary-cohn-says-trumps-charlottesville-reaction-put-enormous-pressure-on-him-to-resign.html (hereafter Michael Sheetz, 'Gary Cohn says Trump's Charlottesville reaction put "enormous pressure" on him to resign')

92   Michael Sheetz, 'Gary Cohn says Trump's Charlottesville reaction put "enormous pressure" on him to resign'

93   Theodor Lessing, *Jewish Self-Hate*

94   Nathan Stoltzfus, *Resistance of the Heart: Intermarriage and the Rosenstrasse Protest in Nazi Germany* (New Jersey: Rutgers University Press, 2001)

95   Sander L. Gilman, *Jewish Self-Hatred: Anti-Semitism and the Hidden Language of the Jews*

96   Sander L. Gilman, *Jewish Self-Hatred: Anti-Semitism and the Hidden Language of the Jews*

97   Sander L. Gilman, *Jewish Self-Hatred: Anti-Semitism and the Hidden Language of the Jews*

98   Sander L. Gilman, *Jewish Self-Hatred: Anti-Semitism and the Hidden Language of the Jews*

99   Sander L. Gilman, *Jewish Self-Hatred: Anti-Semitism and the Hidden Language of the Jews*

100 Sander L. Gilman, *Jewish Self-Hatred: Anti-Semitism and the Hidden Language of the Jews*

101 Sander L. Gilman, *Jewish Self-Hatred: Anti-Semitism and the Hidden Language of the Jews*

102 Sander L. Gilman, *Jewish Self-Hatred: Anti-Semitism and the Hidden Language of the Jews*

103 Sander L. Gilman, *Jewish Self-Hatred: Anti-Semitism and the Hidden Language of the Jews*

104 Sander L. Gilman, *Jewish Self-Hatred: Anti-Semitism and the Hidden Language of the Jews*

105 Lisa Hendricks, Twitter post, 21 January 2021. Available at: https://twitter.com/MsLisaHendricks/status/1352019056354738176?ref_src=twsrc%5Etfw%7Ctwcamp%5Etweetembed%7Ctwterm%5E1352019056354738176%7Ctwgr%5E%7Ctwcon%5Es1_&ref_url=https%3A%2F%2Fwww.seventeen.com%2Fbeauty%2Fhair%2Fa35278229%2Fella-emhoff-inauguration-curls%2F

106 Jodi Rudoren, 'Ella Emhoff isn't Jewish (and she doesn't want to talk about it)', *Forward*, 22 January 2021. Available at: https://forward.com/opinion/462617/ella-emhoff-isnt-jewish-and-she-doesnt-want-to-talk-about-it/ (hereafter Jodi Rudoren, 'Ella Emhoff isn't Jewish (and she doesn't want to talk about it)')

107 Jodi Rudoren, 'Ella Emhoff isn't Jewish (and she doesn't want to talk about it)'

108 Though the *Halacha* rejects ideas of half-Jewishness, from an ancestral perspective, as her father, Doug, is Jewish, Emhoff is half-Jewish. I personally would describe her as being Jewish and many would describe her as a patrilineal Jew. She may have experienced rejection by the Jewish community because of this, which also may have played a role in her identity forming

109 Molly Tolsky, 'We Were Wrong to Assume Ella Emhoff Is Jewish', *Hey Alma*, 25 January 2021. Available at: https://www.heyalma.com/we-were-wrong-to-assume-ella-emhoff-is-jewish/

110 Jodi Rudoren, 'Ella Emhoff isn't Jewish (and she doesn't want to talk about it)'

111 @jobellerina, Twitter post, 25 January 2021. Available at: https://twitter.com/jobellerina/status/1353453604623933440

112 Nora Levin, *The Jews in the Soviet Union since 1917* (New York: New York University Press, 1988)

113 The Code Noir (The Black Code). Available at: https://revolution.chnm.org/d/335/

114 John Leicester, 'In France, Trump-like TV pundit rocks presidential campaign', *Associated Press*, 26 October 2021. Available at: https://apnews.com/article/immigration-france-paris-europe-migration-a681f51a334fe7e2ccc680d2b52ab4b3

115 Ben Cohen, '"Traitor!": French Pundit Tipped as Far-Right Presidential Candidate in Visceral Attack Against Leading Jewish Intellectual', *Algemeiner*, 15 October 2021. Available at: https://www.algemeiner.com/2021/10/15/traitor-french-pundit-tipped-as-far-right-presidential-candidate-in-visceral-attack-against-leading-jewish-intellectual/

116 Aviya Kushner, 'So, Is "Cosmopolitan" An Anti-Semitic Slur Or Not?', *Forward*, 30 August 2017. Available at: https://forward.com/culture/381388/so-is-cosmopolitan-an-anti-semitic-slur-or-not/

117 Jon Henley, 'Rise of far right puts Dreyfus affair into spotlight in French election race', *Guardian*, 30 October 2021. Available at: https://www.theguardian.com/global/2021/oct/30/rise-of-far-right-puts-dreyfus-affair-into-spotlight-in-french-election-race

118 Shirli Sitbon, 'Zemmour, the "useful Jew" leading far-right push for power in France', *The Jewish Chronicle*, 21 October 2021. Available at: https://www.thejc.com/news/world/zemmour-the-'useful-jew'-leading-far-right-push-for-power-in-france-1.521796

119 Hannah Rose, 'Eric Zemmour: Jewish heritage is a useful tool for the French far right', *The Conversation*, 11 November 2021. Available at: https://theconversation.com/eric-zemmour-jewish-heritage-is-a-useful-tool-for-the-french-far-right-170838 (hereafter Hannah Rose, 'Eric Zemmour: Jewish heritage is a useful tool for the French far right')

120 Hannah Rose, 'Eric Zemmour: Jewish heritage is a useful tool for the French far right'

121 David Haziza, 'The Wicked Son', *Tablet*, 5 January 2022. Available at: https://www.tabletmag.com/sections/news/articles/wicked-son-eric-zemmour (hereafter David Haziza, 'The Wicked Son')

122 David Haziza, 'The Wicked Son'

123 Eric Zemmour, Twitter post, 17 December 2021. Available at: https://twitter.com/ZemmourEric/status/1471585887381250051

124 Hannah Rose, 'Eric Zemmour: Jewish heritage is a useful tool for the French far right'

125 Mitchell Abidor and Miguel Lago, 'Author Eric Zemmour, the French Jewish Trump, Storms to Top of Presidential Polls', *Tablet*, 21 October 2021. Available at: https://www.tabletmag.com/sections/news/articles/eric-zemmour-french-jewish-trump

126 Holly Ann Jordan, 'A History Of Jews In Greek Gymnasia From The Hellenistic Period Through The Late Roman Period', University of Georgia, 2009

127 Jonathan Goldstein, *I Maccabees: A New Translation, with Introduction and Commentary* (New York: Doubleday, 1976)

128 Josh Law, 'Reverse Circumcision in Hellenistic Judaism: The Case for a Gender Critical Readying', The University of Mississippi Undergraduate Research Journal: Vol. 2, Article 1, 2017. Available at: https://egrove.olemiss.edu/umurjournal/vol2/iss1/1

129 Epispasm, *The Circumcision Reference Library.* Available at: http://www.cirp.org/library/restoration/hall1/

130 Jennifer Michael Hecht, *Doubt: A History: The Great Doubters and Their Legacy of Innovation from Socrates and Jesus to Thomas Jefferson and Emily Dickinson* (New York: HarperOne, 2014)

131 Beatrice Brutea (ed.), *Jesus Through Jewish Eyes: Rabbis And Scholars Engage An Ancient Brother In A New Conversation* (New York: Orbis Books, 2001)

132 Thomas of Monmouth, 'The Life and Miracles of St William of Norwich'

133 David B. Green, 'This Day in Jewish History | 1242: France Burns All Known Copies of the Talmud', *Haaretz*, 17 June 2013. Available at: https://www.haaretz.com/jewish/.premium-1242-all-talmuds-in-paris-are-burned-1.5281064

134 Sander L. Gilman, *Jewish Self-Hatred: Anti-Semitism and the Hidden Language of the Jews*

135 'Reform Judaism: The Pittsburgh Platform', Jewish Virtual Library. Available at: https://www.jewishvirtuallibrary.org/the-pittsburgh-platform

136 'Jewish Emancipation in Western Europe', My Jewish Learning

137 Moritz Lazarus, '*Was Heiss National?*' (Berlin: Ferdinand Bummler, 1880)

138 Conrad Alberti, 'Judentum und Antisemitismus: Eine zeitgenössische Studie', *Die Gesellschaft* 4, 1889

139 Sander L. Gilman, *Jewish Self-Hatred: Anti-Semitism and the Hidden Language of the Jews*

140 Sander L. Gilman, *Jewish Self-Hatred: Anti-Semitism and the Hidden Language of the Jews*

141 Matt Plen, 'Moses Mendelssohn', My Jewish Learning. Available at: https://www.myjewishlearning.com/article/moses-mendelssohn/

142 Rachel Seelig, *Strangers in Berlin: Modern Jewish Literature Between East and West, 1919–1933* (Michigan: University of Michigan Press, 2016)

143 Dovid Katz, *Words on Fire: The Unfinished Story of Yiddish* (New York: Basic Books, 2007)

144 Sander L. Gilman, *Jewish Self-Hatred: Anti-Semitism and the Hidden Language of the Jews*

145 Paul Kriwaczek, *Yiddish Civilisation: The Rise and Fall of a Forgotten Nation* (New York: Vintage, 2007)

146 Eli Kavon, 'How Moses Mendelssohn killed Yiddish in Germany', *The Jerusalem Post*, 26 August 2019. Available at: https://www.jpost.com/opinion/how-moses-mendelssohn-killed-yiddish-in-germany-599781(hereafter Eli Kavon, 'How Moses Mendelssohn killed Yiddish in Germany')

147 Eli Kavon, 'How Moses Mendelssohn killed Yiddish in Germany'

148 Moses Mendelssohn, *Jerusalem and Other Jewish Writings* (New York: Schocken Books, 1969)

149 Kaufmann Kohler, 'Personal Reminiscences of My Early Life', in *Studies, Addresses, and Personal Papers by Dr. K. Kohler* (New York: Bloch Publishing, 1931) (hereafter Kaufmann Kohler, 'Personal Reminiscences of My Early Life')

150 Kaufmann Kohler, 'Personal Reminiscences of My Early Life'

151 Emmanuel Levinas, *Difficult Freedom: Essays on Judaism* (Baltimore: The John Hopkins University Press, 1990)

152 Daniel B. Schwartz, *The First Modern Jew: Spinoza and the History of an Image* (Princeton: Princeton University Press, 2012) (hereafter Daniel B. Schwartz, *The First Modern Jew: Spinoza and the History of an Image*

153 Daniel B. Schwartz, *The First Modern Jew: Spinoza and the History of an Image*

154 Paul Mendes-Flohr & Jehuda Reinharz (Eds.), *The Jew in the Modern World: A Documentary History* (Oxford: Oxford University Press, 1995)

155 Chen Malul, 'When Heinrich Heine Revealed His Thoughts on His Conversion to Christianity', The Librarians, 28 October 2019. Available at: https://blog.nli.org.il/en/heinrich-heine/

156 Moses Mendelssohn, *Jerusalem: Or on Religious Power and Judaism* (New Hampshire: Brandeis University Press, 1983)

157 Eli Kavon, 'Heinrich Heine and the disease of Jewish self-hatred', *The Jerusalem Post*, 17 May 2015. Available at: https://www.jpost.com/blogs/past-imperfect-confronting-jewish-history/heinrich-heine-and-the-disease-of-jewish-self-hatred-403322

158 Karl Wilhelm Freidrich Grattenauer, *Uber die physische und moralische Verfassung der heutigen Juden* (Leipzig, 1791)

159 Richard Weikart, *From Darwin to Hitler: Evolutionary Ethics, Eugenics and Racism in Germany* (London: Palgrave Macmillan, 2006)

160 Shulamit Volkov, *Germans, Jews, and Antisemites: Trials in Emancipation* (Cambridge: Cambridge University Press, 2006)

161 Theodor Lessing, *Einmal und nie wieder: Lebenserinnerungen* (Chicago: e-artnow, 2018) (hereafter Theodor Lessing, *Einmal und nie wieder: Lebenserinnerungen*)

162 Paul Reitter, *On the Origins of Jewish Self-hate*, (Princeton: Princeton University Press, 2012)

163 Theodor Lessing, *Jewish Self-Hate*

164 Sander L. Gilman, *Jewish Self-Hatred: Anti-Semitism and the Hidden Language of the Jews*

165 Theodor Lessing, *Einmal und nie wieder: Lebenserinnerungen*

166 Theodor Lessing, *Jewish Self-Hate*

167 Theodor Lessing, *Jewish Self-Hate*

168 Theodor Lessing, *Jewish Self-Hate*

169 Theodor Lessing, *Jewish Self-Hate*

170 Theodor Lessing, *Jewish Self-Hate*

171 Theodor Lessing, *Jewish Self-Hate*

172 Theodor Lessing, *Jewish Self-Hate*

173 Theodor Lessing, *Jewish Self-Hate*

174 'Editorial on the appointment of Adolf Hitler as Reich Chancellor', *Jüdische Rundschau*, 31 January 1933

175 Gerhard Sauder (ed.), *Die Bucherverbrennung: Zum 10. Mai 1933* (Munich: Carl Hanser, 1983)

176 Sander L. Gilman, *Jewish Self-Hatred: Anti-Semitism and the Hidden Language of the Jews*

177 Natan Sharansky & Gil Troy, 'The Un-Jews', *Tablet*, 16 June 2021. Available at: https://www.tabletmag.com/sections/news/articles/the-un-jews-natan-sharansky (hereafter Natan Sharansky & Gil Troy, 'The Un-Jews')

178 Susan A. Glenn, 'The Vogue of Jewish Self-Hatred in Post-World War II America'

179 Susan A. Glenn, 'The Vogue of Jewish Self-Hatred in Post-World War II America'

180 David Riesman, 'Marginality, Conformity, and Insight', *Phylon*, 1953. Available at: http://tucnak.fsv.cuni.cz/~calda/RiesmanConformity.pdf (hereafter David Riesman, 'Marginality, Conformity, and Insight')

181 David Riesman, 'Marginality, Conformity, and Insight'

182 Susan A. Glenn, 'The Vogue of Jewish Self-Hatred in Post-World War II America'

183 David Bernstein, 'Jewish Insecurity and American Realities,' *Commentary*, February 1948

184 Jonathan Sarna, '1950s America: A "Golden Age" for Jews', My Jewish Learning. Available at: https://www.myjewishlearning.com/article/a-golden-age-for-jews/ (hereafter Jonathan Sarna, '1950s America: A "Golden Age" for Jews')

185 Susan A. Glenn, 'The Vogue of Jewish Self-Hatred in Post-World War II America'

186 Abraham H. Miller, 'Is the golden age of American Jewry at an end?', *Baltimore Jewish Times*, 25 July 2021. Available at: https://www.jewishtimes.com/opinion-is-the-golden-age-of-american-jewry-at-an-end/

187 John Steele Gordon, 'The Country Club', *American Heritage*, September/October 1990. Available at: https://www.americanheritage.com/country-club#6

188 'The Jew and the Club', *The Atlantic*, October 1924. Available at: https://www.theatlantic.com/magazine/archive/1924/10/the-jew-and-the-club/306258/

189 Nathan A. Pelcovitz, 'What About Jewish Anti-Semitism: A Prescription to Cure Self-Hatred,' *Commentary*, February 1947). Available via: https://www.proquest.com/openview/9ad4a0a79f214eab7f6114c55ac6e898/1?pq-origsite=gscholar&cbl=1816616 (hereafter Nathan A. Pelcovitz, 'What About Jewish Anti-Semitism: A Prescription to Cure Self-Hatred'

190 Sander L. Gilman, *Jewish Self-Hatred: Anti-Semitism and the Hidden Language of the Jews*

191 Nathan A. Pelcovitz, 'What About Jewish Anti-Semitism: A Prescription to Cure Self-Hatred'

192 David Turner, 'America after the Holocaust: "The Jews", Red Scare and a congressional witch hunt', *The Jerusalem Post*, 27 March 2013. Available at: https://www.jpost.com/blogs/the-jewish-problem---from-anti-judaism-to-anti-semitism/america-after-the-holocaust-the-jews-red-scare-and-a-congressional-witch-hunt-364763 (hereafter David Turner, 'America after the Holocaust: "The Jews", Red Scare and a congressional witch hunt')

193 David Turner, 'America after the Holocaust: "The Jews", Red Scare and a congressional witch hunt'

194 Robert Philpot, 'Was the Rosenberg trial America's Dreyfus affair?', *Times of Israel*, 23 July 2021. Available at: https://www.timesofisrael.com/was-the-rosenberg-trial-americas-dreyfus-affair/

195 Stuart Svonkin, *Jews Against Prejudice: American Jews and the Fight for Civil Liberties* (New York: Columbia University Press, 1997)

196 David Riesman, 'The "Militant" Fight Against Anti-Semitism', *Commentary* 11, 1951

197 David Riesman, 'Some Observations concerning Marginality', *Phylon* (1940–1956) Vol. 12, No. 2 (2nd Qtr., 1951) (hereafter David Riesman, 'Some Observations concerning Marginality')

198 Clement Greenberg, 'Self-Hatred and Jewish Chauvinism'

199 David Riesman, 'Some Observations concerning Marginality'

200 David Riesman, 'The "Militant" Fight Against Anti-Semitism', *Commentary* 11, 1951

201 David Riesman, 'Marginality, Conformity, and Insight'

202 Susan A. Glenn, 'The Vogue of Jewish Self-Hatred in Post-World War II America'

203 Kurt Lewin, 'Self-Hatred Among Jews' *Contemporary Jewish Record* 4, no. 3 (June 1941) (hereafter Kurt Lewin, 'Self-Hatred Among Jews')

204 Kurt Lewin, 'Self-Hatred Among Jews'

205 Milton Steinberg, *A Partisan Guide to the Jewish Problem* (New York: Bobbs-Merrill Company, B'nai B'rith Foundations)

206 Susan A. Glenn, 'The Vogue of Jewish Self-Hatred in Post-World War II America'

207 Julian E. Zelizer, 'Trump Needs to Demilitarize his Rhetoric', *The Atlantic*, 29 October 2018. Available at: https://www.theatlantic.com/ideas/archive/2018/10/americas-long-history-anti-semitism/574234/

208 Jonathan Sarna, '1950s America: A "Golden Age" for Jews'

209 Matt Fieldman, 'White Jews – Wake Up. We're Part of the Problem', *eJewish Philanthropy*, 21 June 2020. Available at: https://ejewishphilanthropy.com/white-jews-wake-up-were-part-of-the-problem/

210 Jonathan D. Sarna, 'Anti-Semitism and America History', *Commentary*, March 1981. Available at: https://www.brandeis.edu/hornstein/sarna/popularandencyclopedia/Archive/Anti-SemitismandAmericanHistory.pdf

211 Earl Raab, 'Anti-Semitism in the 1980s'. Available at: https://jcrc.org/uploads/ANTI-SEMITISM_IN_THE_1980S_FEBRUARY%2C_1983_%281%29.pdf

212 Abraham Miller, 'Campus Intersectionalism Breeds Anti-Semitism Like Chicago "Jewish Privilege" Flyers', *The Federalist*, 28 March 2017. Available at: https://thefederalist.com/2017/03/28/campus-intersectionalism-breeds-anti-semitism-like-chicago-jewish-privilege-flyers/

213 'Race, Ethnicity, Heritage and Immigration Among U.S. Jews', Pew Research Centre, 11 May 2021. Available at: https://www.pewresearch.org/religion/2021/05/11/race-ethnicity-heritage-and-immigration-among-u-s-jews/

214 Henry Bial, *Acting Jewish: Negotiating Ethnicity on the American Stage and Screen* (Michigan: University of Michigan Press, 2005) (hereafter Henry Bial, *Acting Jewish: Negotiating Ethnicity on the American Stage and Screen*)

215 Seth L. Wolitz, 'The Americanization of Tevye or Boarding the Jewish "Mayflower"', *American Quarterly* Vol. 40, No. 4 (December 1988). Available at: https://www.jstor.org/stable/2713000

216 LeAna B. Gloor, 'From the Melting Pot to the Tossed Salad Metaphor: Why Coercive Assimilation Lacks the Flavors Americans Crave', University of Hawaii. Available at: https://hilo.hawaii.edu/campuscenter/hohonu/volumes/documents/Vol04x06FromtheMeltingPot.pdf

217 Bruce Thornton, 'Melting Pots and Salad Bowls', Hoover Institution, 26 October 2012. Available at: https://www.hoover.org/research/melting-pots-and-salad-bowls

218 Malina Saval, 'Too Jewish For Hollywood: As Antisemitism Soars, Hollywood Should Address Its Enduring Hypocrisy In Hyperbolic Caricatures of Jews', *Variety*, 18 June 2021. Available at: https://variety.com/2021/biz/features/jewish-hollywood-antisemitism-hyperbolic-caricatures-casting-jews-hate-crimes-1234997849/

219 Henry Bial, *Acting Jewish: Negotiating Ethnicity on the American Stage and Screen*

220 David Zurawik, *The Jews of Prime Time* (New Hampshire: Brandeis University Press, 2003) (hereafter David Zurawik, *The Jews of Prime Time*)

221 David Zurawik, *The Jews of Prime Time*

222 Paul Brownfield, 'Shtick, stereotypes, and self-parody: How "The Marvelous Mrs. Maisel" gets Jewish culture wrong', *LA Times*, 5 January 2019. Available at: https://www.latimes.com/entertainment/tv/la-et-st-marvelous-maisel-and-judaism-20190105-story.html?fbclid=IwAR0J3I5ZRilVFHSnRMWovHNii5OJNKo5rMr-ZaCcIEnNYSawy7ROEMReH3IU

223 Molly Pascal, 'We need fewer stereotypical Jews on TV – and more Walter Sobchaks', JTA, 25 June 2019. Available at: https://www.jta.org/2019/06/25/opinion/we-need-fewer-stereotypical-jews-on-tv-and-more-walter-sobchaks

224 'Prime-Time Mensch', *Newsweek*, 10 November 1992. Available at: https://www.newsweek.com/prime-time-mensch-199722 (hereafter 'Prime-Time Mensch', *Newsweek*)

225 'Prime-Time Mensch', *Newsweek*

226 Henry Hoffman, 'Revisiting Annie Hall: Exploring Jewish Identity on the Silver Screen', *Kedma: Penn's Journal on Jewish Thought, Jewish Culture, and Israel*, 2020. Available at: https://repository.upenn.edu/cgi/viewcontent.cgi?article=1010&context=kedma

227 Jamie Lauren Keiles, 'Reconsidering the Jewish American Princess', *Vox*, 5 December 2018. Available at: https://www.vox.com/the-goods/2018/12/5/18119890/jewish-american-princess-jap-stereotype

228 Myra Mensh Patner, '"Jap" Jokes Baiting Or Hating? A New Wave Of Anti-Feminist Anti- Semitism Hits The Campus', *Washington Post*. Available at: https://www.washingtonpost.com/archive/opinions/1988/12/04/jap-jokes-baiting-or-hating-a-new-wave-of-anti-feminist-anti-semitism-hits-the-campus/3c3409f2-f961-44c6-b017-439d9ee2fba0/ (hereafter Myra Mensh Patner, '"Jap"Jokes Baiting Or Hating? A New Wave Of Anti-Feminist Anti- Semitism Hits The Campus')

229 Myra Mensh Patner, '"Jap"Jokes Baiting Or Hating? A New Wave Of Anti-Feminist Anti- Semitism Hits The Campus'

230 Myra Mensh Patner, '"Jap"Jokes Baiting Or Hating? A New Wave Of Anti-Feminist Anti- Semitism Hits The Campus'

231 Myra Mensh Patner, '"Jap"Jokes Baiting Or Hating? A New Wave Of Anti-Feminist Anti- Semitism Hits The Campus'

232 'The 15 Most Outrageous Joan Rivers Quotes Ever', *Haaretz*, 4 September 2014. Available at: https://www.haaretz.com/jewish/15-outrageous-joan-rivers-quotes-1.5263345

233 'The Jewish American Princess – Beyond the Stereotype', *The Take*. Available at: https://the-take.com/watch/the-jewish-american-princess-beyond-the-stereotype

234 Amanda Pazornik, 'It's been six years, but they'll always be my Jewish Friends', *Jewish News of North Carolina*, 12 November 2010. Available at: https://jweekly.com/2010/11/12/its-been-six-years-but-theyll-always-be-my-jewish-friends/

235 Samantha Maoz, 'Jews on TV: A Snapshot of Modern Television's Representation of Jewish Characters', *Elon Journal of Undergraduate Research in Communications*, Vol. 9, No. 2, Fall 2018. Available at: https://www.elon.edu/u/academics/communications/journal/wp-content/uploads/sites/153/2018/12/04-Maoz.pdf

236 Dara Horn, *People Love Dead Jews: Reports from a Haunted Present*

237 'Statement by the President on the Passing of Leonard Nimoy', The White House, 27 February 2015. Available at: https://obamawhitehouse.archives.gov/the-press-office/2015/02/27/statement-president-passing-leonard-nimoy

238 Natasha Frost, 'The Forgotten History of New York's Bagel Famines', Atlas Obscura, 9 February 2018. Available at: https://www.atlasobscura.com/articles/bagel-union-strikes-new-york-city

239 Josh Getlin, 'Leaving an Imprint on American Culture', *LA Times*, 23 April 1998. Available at: https://www.latimes.com/archives/la-xpm-1998-apr-23-mn-42233-story.html

240 Jonathan Boyarin (Ed.), Daniel Boyarin (Ed.), *Jews and Other Differences: The New Jewish Cultural Studies* (Minnesota: University Of Minnesota Press, 2008)

241 Will Herberg, *Protestant–Catholic–Jew: An Essay in American Religious Sociology*, (Chicago: University of Chicago Press, 1983)

242 Jonathan Sarna, '1950s America: A "Golden Age" for Jews'

243 Jonathan Sarna, '1950s America: A "Golden Age" for Jews'

244 Will Herberg, 'The Postwar Revival of the Synagogue: Does it Reflect a Religious Reawakening?', *Commentary*, April 1950. Available at: https://www.commentary.org/articles/will-herberg/the-postwar-revival-of-the-synagoguedoes-it-reflect-a-religious-reawakening/

245 Emily Alpert, 'Jewish secularism on rise, Pew survey finds', *LA Times*, 30 September 2013. Available at: https://www.latimes.com/local/la-me-1001-jewish-not-religious-20131001-story.html

246 Leon A Morris, 'Religion Matters: Beware the American "Cultural Jew"', *Haaretz*, 10 April 2018. Available at: https://www.haaretz.com/opinion/.premium-beware-the-u-s-cultural-jew-1.5346987

247 Yehuda Amichai, 'Poem Without an End', Poetry Foundation. Available at: https://www.poetryfoundation.org/poems/56282/poem-without-an-end

248 Dave Rich, *The Left's Jewish Problem: Jeremy Corbyn, Israel and Anti-Semitism* (London: Biteback, 2016) (hereafter Dave Rich, *The Left's Jewish Problem: Jeremy Corbyn, Israel and Anti-Semitism*)

249 Dave Rich, *The Left's Jewish Problem: Jeremy Corbyn, Israel and Anti-Semitism*

250 Dave Rich, *The Left's Jewish Problem: Jeremy Corbyn, Israel and Anti-Semitism*

251 MFA Austria, Twitter post, 4 February 2022. Available at: https://twitter.com/MFA_Austria/status/1489335864496951298

252 Dave Rich, *The Left's Jewish Problem: Jeremy Corbyn, Israel and Anti-Semitism*

253 'A Finding Aid to the American Council for Judaism Records. 1937–1989 (bulk 1957–1968)', American Jewish Archives. Available at: http://collections.americanjewisharchives.org/ms/ms0017/ms0017.html

254 Lawrence Grossman, 'Transformation through crisis: the American Jewish committee and the Six-Day War', *American Jewish History*, Mar 1, 1998. Available at: https://www.thefreelibrary.com/Transformation+through+crisis%3A+the+American+Jewish+committee+and+the...-a020770630 (hereafter Lawrence Grossman, 'Transformation through crisis: the American Jewish committee and the Six-Day War')

255 Lawrence Grossman, 'Transformation through crisis: the American Jewish committee and the Six-Day War'

256 Lawrence Grossman, 'Transformation through crisis: the American Jewish committee and the Six-Day War'

257 Albert Memmi, 'Am I a Traitor?', *Commentary*, October 1962. Available at: https://www.commentary.org/articles/albert-memmi/am-i-a-traitor/

258 Lawrence Grossman, 'Transformation through crisis: the American Jewish committee and the Six-Day War'

259 Lawrence Grossman, 'Transformation through crisis: the American Jewish committee and the Six-Day War'

260 Edward S. Shapiro, *A Time for Healing: American Jewry Since World War II* (Baltimore: John Hopkins University Press, 1992)

261 Frank Newport, 'American Jews, Politics and Israel', Gallup, 27 August 2019. Available at: https://news.gallup.com/opinion/polling-matters/265898/american-jews-politics-israel.aspx

262 'Attitudes of British Jews towards Israel revealed in new study', City University of London, 3 November 2020. Available at: https://www.city.ac.uk/news-and-events/news/2015/11/attitudes-of-british-jews-towards-israel-revealed-in-new-study#:~:text=%E2%80%9COur%20research%20shows%20that%20although,than%20many%20would%20have%20expected

263 Rom Kampeas, 'Poll finds a quarter of US Jews think Israel is "apartheid state"', *The Times of Israel*, 13 July 2021. Available at: https://www.timesofisrael.com/poll-finds-a-quarter-of-us-jews-think-israel-is-apartheid-state/

264 Mike Smith, 'Remembering Durban: Jewish Journalist Looks Back on The Antisemitic Hate Fest', *The Detroit Jewish News*, 13 September 2021. Available at: https://thejewishnews.com/2021/09/13/remembering-durban-jewish-journalist-looks-back-on-the-antisemitic-hate-fest/

265 Jonathan Krasner, 'Justice: The Origins and Evolution of a Jewish Value – Part 3', *A Faith That Does Justice*, 19 January 2021. Available at: https://faith-justice.org/how-tikkun-olam-became-jewish-social-justice-the-origins-and-evolution-of-a-jewish-value-part-3/

266 Pamela Paresky, 'Critical Race Theory and the "Hyper-White" Jew', *Sapir Journal*, Spring 2021. Available at: https://sapirjournal.org/social-justice/2021/05/critical-race-theory-and-the-hyper-white-jew/

267 'The Gaza conflict is stoking an "identity crisis" for some young American Jews', *New York Times*, 20 May 2021. Available at: https://indianexpress.com/article/world/gaza-conflict-identity-crisis-some-young-american-jews-7322558/ (hereafter 'The Gaza conflict is stoking an "identity crisis" for some young American Jews', *New York Times*)

268 Cary Nelson, 'Amnesty International, Israel and Race-Baiting', *Fathom Journal*, March 2022. Available at: https://fathomjournal.org/amnesty-international-israel-and-race-baiting/

269 Oliver Holmes, 'Seth Rogen: "I was fed a huge amount of lies about Israel"', *Guardian*, 29 July 2020. Available at: https://www.theguardian.com/world/2020/jul/29/seth-rogen-israel-palestinians-jewish-actor

270 'The Gaza conflict is stoking an "identity crisis" for some young American Jews', *New York Times*

271 'Young Jewish Europeans: perceptions and experiences of antisemitism', European Union Agency for Fundamental Rights & Institute for Jewish Policy Research. Available at: https://fra.europa.eu/sites/default/files/fra_uploads/fra-2019-young-jewish-europeans_en.pdf

272 'Rabbi Attacks Zionism; Says Jews of Iraq Unanimously Oppose Segregation', *New York Times*, 9 April 1947. Available at: https://www.nytimes.com/1947/04/09/archives/rabbi-attacks-zionism-says-jews-of-iraq-unanimously-oppose.html

273 Paul L. Montgomery, 'Discord Among U.S. Jews Over Israel Seems To Grow', *New York Times*, 15 July 1982. Available at: https://www.nytimes.com/1982/07/15/world/discord-among-us-jews-over-israel-seems-to-grow.html

274 Irving Spiegel, 'Anti-Zionist Jews Report U.S. Gains', *New York Times*, 15 July 1982. Available at: https://www.nytimes.com/1960/05/13/archives/antizionist-jews-report-us-gains-head-of-council-for-judaism-tells.html

275 Laurie Goodstein, 'Feeling Abandoned by Israel, Many American Jews Grow Angry', *New York Times*, 16 November 1997. https://www.nytimes.com/1997/11/16/world/feeling-abandoned-by-israel-many-american-jews-grow-angry.html

276 Lisa W. Foderaro, 'Surge of Violence in Mideast Forces Some Young Jews to Rethink a Rite of Passage', *New York Times*, 23 July 2006. Available at: https://www.nytimes.com/2006/07/23/nyregion/surge-of-violence-in-mideast-forces-some-young-jews-to-rethink-a.html

277 Euan Phillips, Twitter post, 12 July 2019. Available at: https://twitter.com/EuanPhilipps/status/1149375638496829440

278 Jeremy Sharon, 'HRW director accused of justifying antisemitism on Twitter', *The Jerusalem Post*, 19 July 2021. Available at: https://www.jpost.com/diaspora/antisemitism/hrw-director-accused-of-justifying-antisemitism-on-twitter-674346

279 Jarrod Tanny, The Un-Jews Are the Enforcers: A Response to Shaul Magid', *Times of Israel*, 20 July 2021. Available at: https://blogs.timesofisrael.com/the-un-jews-are-the-enforcers-a-response-to-shaul-magid/

280 Maath Musleh, 'Co-Resistance vs. Co-Existence', Ma'an News Agency, 17 July 2011

281 Peter Beinart, Twitter post, 28 October 2021. Available at:https://twitter.com/PeterBeinart/status/1453536241820053506

282 Natan Sharansky & Gil Troy, 'The Un-Jews'

283 Theodor Lessing, *Jewish Self-Hate*

284 Bessel van der Kolk, 'Is Your Client Traumatized? For the Answer, Look to the Body', *Psychotherapy Networker*. Available at: https://www.psychotherapynetworker.org/blog/details/311/video-when-is-it-trauma-bessel-van-der-kolk-explains

285 'UK rapper Wiley goes on hours-long anti-Semitic Twitter rant', *Times of Israel*, 25 July 2020. Available at: https://www.timesofisrael.com/uk-rapper-wiley-goes-on-hours-long-anti-semitic-twitter-rant/

286 Trude Weiss-Rosmarin, 'A Manifesto of Jewish Survivalism', *The Jewish Spectator*, July 1947

287 Henry C. Soussan, *The Gesselscaft zur Forderung der Wissenschaft des Judentums in Its Historical Context* (Tübingen: Mohr Siebeck, 2013) (hereafter Henry C. Soussan, *The Gesselscaft zur Forderung der Wissenschaft des Judentums in Its Historical Context*)

288 Henry C. Soussan, *The Gesellschaft zur Forderung der Wissenschaft des Judentums in Its Historical Context*

289 Henry C. Soussan, *The Gesellschaft zur Forderung der Wissenschaft des Judentums in Its Historical Context*

290 'Antisemites' Petition (1880–1881)', *GHDI*. Available at: https://ghdi.ghi-dc.org/sub_document.cfm?document_id=1801

291 'American Jewish K.C. Fraternity, Inc.', *Snac*. Available at: https://snaccooperative.org/ark:/99166/w6586d45

292 Lucy Dawidowicz, *The War Against the Jews, 1933–1945* (New York: Bantam, 1986)

293 David Nirenberg, *Anti-Judaism: The Western Tradition*

294 Bessel Van Der Kolk, *The Body Keeps the Score: Brain, Mind, and Body in the Healing of Trauma*

295 Susan A. Glenn, *The Jewish Cold War: Anxiety and Identity in the Aftermath of the Holocaust* (Michigan: Jean & Samuel Frankel Center for Judaic Studies, 2014)

296 Bessel Van Der Kolk, *The Body Keeps the Score: Brain, Mind, and Body in the Healing of Trauma*

297 Theodor Lessing, *Jewish Self-Hate*

298 Jakob Wasserman, *Mein Weg als Deutscher und Jude* (Munich: dtv Verlagsgesellschaft mbH & Co, 1994) (hereafter Jakob Wasserman, *Mein Weg als Deutscher und Jude*)

299 Jakob Wasserman, *Mein Weg als Deutscher und Jude*

300 'East European Jews in the German-Jewish Imagination', The Ludwig Rosenberger Library of Judaica, 1 September 2008. Available at: https://www.lib.uchicago.edu/collex/exhibits/exeej/

301 James Winchell, 'A Great Thinker Rediscovers His Judaism on the Day of Atonement', *Tablet*, 10 September 2013. Available at: https://www.tabletmag.com/sections/community/articles/rosenzweig-yom-kippur-conversion

302 Nahum N. Glatzer (ed.), *Franz Rosenzweig: His Life and Thought* (Indianapolis: Hackett Publishing Company, 1998)

303 Siegfried Stein, 'The Influence of Symposia Literature on the Literary Form of the Pesaḥ Haggadah', *Journal of Jewish Studies*, 1957 (hereafter Siegfried Stein, 'The Influence of Symposia Literature on the Literary Form of the Pesaḥ Haggadah')

304 Siegfried Stein, 'The Influence of Symposia Literature on the Literary Form of the Pesaḥ Haggadah'

305 Joshua Kulp, 'The Schechter Haggadah: Art, History and Commentary' (Jerusalem: The Schechter Institute of Jewish Studies, 2015)

306 'Psalm 137', Bible Gateway. Available at: https://www.biblegateway.com/passage/?search=Psalm%20137&version=NIV

307 'Keeping cultures alive in exile: Tibetan children go to Israel', fpmt, September. Available at: https://fpmt.org/mandala/archives/mandala-issues-for-2000/september/keeping-cultures-alive-in-exile-tibetan-children-go-to-israel/

308 Daniel J. Elazar, 'Jewish religious, ethnic, and national identities: Convergences and conflicts', Jerusalem Centre for Public Affairs. Available at: https://www.jcpa.org/dje/articles2/jewreleth.htm

309 Yaffa Eliach, *There Once Was a World: A 900-Year Chronicle of the Shtetl of Eishyshok* (Boston: Little, Brown & Company, 2001)

310 Nathan Hurvitz, 'Understanding the Self-Hate of Young Jewish Adults', *The Reconstructionist*, Nov. 14, 1952

311 Israel B. Rappoport, *Education for Living as American Jews* (New York, 1946)

312 Leon A. Feldman, 'Resources for Jewish Living in American Society', *Jewish Social Service Quarterly 31* (1955)

INDEX

Author photo © Gary Swart

Founder of the modern Jewish Pride movement, a Jewish leader, a Jewish thinker and a Jewish educator, Ben M. Freeman is the author of *Jewish Pride: Rebuilding a People* and *Reclaiming Our Story: The Pursuit of Jewish Pride*. He is an internationally renowned gay Jewish author and educator focusing on Jewish identity and historical and contemporary Jew-hatred. A Holocaust educator and lecturer for over fifteen years, Ben came to prominence during the Corbyn Labour Jew-hate crisis and quickly became one of his generation's leading Jewish thinkers and voices against anti-Jewish racism.